Venture Capital

In the last decade venture capital has been very topical. The image of the venture capitalist as a maverick willing to invest in enterprises considered too risky by more traditional financiers was very much suited to the spirit of the 1980s. However, although much has been written on the subject, the literature has tended to concentrate on the traditional stronghold of North America.

As the title suggests, *Venture Capital: International Comparisons* aims to remedy this situation and open the subject up. This is the first text to offer a geographic and regional study of venture capitalism. Although the importance of this type of capitalism in creating and nurturing small firms has long been recognized, it does not have a uniform global character. In order to illustrate this the book examines the experience of the USA, Canada, UK and for the first time, it includes a discussion of New Zealand and Southeast Asia. *Venture Capital* is also unique in that it looks at national differences as well as international variations, with a chapter comparing practice in different US states. Drawing on previously unused data, Green's book offers a geographic comparison which displays the diverse forms of venture capitalist markets from the well established to the newly emerging and the rapidly disappearing.

The editor, *Milford B. Green*, is Associate Professor in the Department of Geography at the University of Western Ontario. He has long been at the forefront of geographic research on venture capital and has served as a consultant to the industry.

Venture Capital

International comparisons

Edited by Milford B. Green

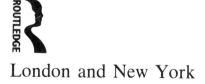

London and New York

First published 1991
by Routledge
11 New Fetter Lane, London EC4P 4EE

Simultaneously published in the USA and Canada
by Routledge
a division of Routledge, Chapman and Hall, Inc.
29 West 35th Street, New York, NY 10001

© 1991 Milford B. Green
hkp

Printed in Great Britain by

Billing & Sons Ltd, Worcester

British Library Cataloguing in Publication Data
Venture capital: international comparisons
    1. Venture capital investment
    I. Green, Milford B.
    332.63
ISBN 0–415–04207–0

Library of Congress Cataloguing in Publication Data
Venture capital: international comparisons/edited by Milford
    B. Green.
        p. cm.
    Includes bibliographical references and index.
    ISBN 0–415–04207–0
    1. Venture capital.   2. Venture capital—United States. .
    I. Green Milford B.
HG4751.V47 1991
332'.0415—dc20   90–47733
                                                            CIP

Contents

Illustrations

Tables

Contributors

Richard Florida is an Assistant Professor of Management and Public Policy, School of Urban and Public Affairs, Carnegie Mellon University, United States

Milford Green is an Associate Professor of Geography, Department of Geography, University of Western Ontario, Canada

Richard Harrison is a Senior Lecturer in the Centre for Executive Development, Ulster Business School, University of Ulster, Northern Ireland

Thomas Leinbach is a Professor of Geography, Department of Geography, University of Kentucky, United States

Rod McNaughton is an Assistant Professor of Geography, Department of Geography, University of Lethbridge, Canada

Colin Mason is a Lecturer in the Department of Geography, University of Southampton, United Kingdom

Martin Perry is a Lecturer in the Department of Geography, National University of Singapore, Singapore

Elizabeth Sechoka is a Graduate Student, School of Urban and Public Affairs, Carnegie Mellon University, United States

Donald Smith is a PhD student at the School of Urban and Public Affairs, Carnegie Mellon University, United States

Chris Thompson is an Assistant Professor of Geography, Department of Geography, University of Wisconsin, United States

Preface

The literature on venture capital has exploded in the last decade, mirroring its growth as an important financial partner in new firm development. The willingness of venture capitalists to undertake investment in enterprises that may be considered too risky by more conventional financial sources has fired the imagination of writers on the subject. Much of the literature is based on anecdotal evidence that portrays venture capitalists as mavericks helping transform economies through investment in high technology. While there is some truth in this characterization, it is only part of the story. A missing component in the literature on the subject is an examination on the broader regional impacts of venture capital investment. Additionally, most studies describe only the US experience. While this is to be expected, given the size and maturity of the US venture capital market, a description of venture capital in other nations could prove instructive. This volume addresses these two components of venture capital research, a concern with regional and national impacts and a description of non-US venture capital investment.

The genesis for this volume came from a meeting held at the Phoenix meetings of the American Association of Geographers in 1988. Many of the contributors to the volume attended this meeting and discussed the emerging geographic literature on venture capital. The level of interest in venture capital by geographers has risen rapidly. The body of literature is expanding rapidly as is the diversification of viewpoints and research approaches on the subject. This volume reflects this diversification of approach both methodologically and regionally. The single unifying theme is a concern with the geography of venture capital. Some may see this as a weakness, but in fact it is a strength. More insight is likely to be gained from a variety of approaches than a single unified approach.

The major geographic contributions to the venture capital literature up to late 1989 are summarized by Rod McNaughton in Chapter One, Venture Capital: The Developing Literature. He divides the literature into a convenient classification of locational studies, market taxonomies, specialization studies, and economic impact studies.

Using these as a classification scheme, Chapter Two, Preferences for US Venture Capital Investment by Milford Green, provides a macro level specialization study of the investment preferences of venture capital firms in the United States for the period since 1972. The assumption explicit in this chapter, that stated preference reflects actual investment, is tested to a degree in Chapters Three and Four. Chapter Three, Venturing on the 'Third Coast': Recipient Firms in the Central States by Chris Thompson, evaluates the investments of 'Third Coast' venture capital firms in a locational context. He finds that the interior portion of the United States exhibits different investment patterns from those found on the East and West Coasts. The majority of venture capital investment is not in high technology but in manufacturing.

Chapter Four, Regional Patterns of Venture Capital Investment by Richard Florida, Donald F. Smith Jr, and Elizabeth Sechoka, provides a detailed description of actual investments for each region of the United States. They argue that the location of venture capital investment closely follows the distribution of high-technology firms. The centers of venture capital finance, such as New York, are not the targets of venture capital investment but are net exporters of capital. There are, then, sources and sinks in the venture capital landscape.

The last chapter on the US venture capital industry is by Chris Thompson. What Do We Know About the Geography of US Venture Capitalists? (Chapter Five) provides an alternative view of venture capital by studying the characteristics of the venture capitalists themselves. This study is the first systematic attempt to study the characteristics of educational and work locations of venture capitalists rather than the investments themselves. The stereotypical venture capitalist is thought to be a middle-aged Harvard MBA. Thompson shows that this is not the case. He also shows that venture capitalists are not diffusing down the urban hierarchy in a systematic way. Different cities of the same size do not exhibit equal numbers of venture capitalists.

Martin Perry, the author of Chapter Six, The Rise and Fall of Venture Capital in New Zealand, provides an interesting case study of the birth and death of a national venture capital industry. His chapter illustrates the fragility of such an industry when subjected to government initiatives and stock market fluctuations. As with the other chapters, Perry finds that a regional bias exists in venture capital placement.

Rod McNaughton provides a description of another small venture capital industry in his description of the Canadian case. Venture Capital in Canada (Chapter Seven) provides a detailed description of the Canadian venture capital industry, its office locations, and investment characteristics. His description of the historical evolution of venture capital in Canada shows a similarity to that experienced in the United States and the United Kingdom.

The actively growing venture capital market in the United Kingdom is chronicled by Colin Mason and Richard Harrison in their chapter, Venture Capital, the Equity Gap and the 'North–South Divide' in the United Kingdom. The impact of governmental involvement in venture capital is ably discussed in this chapter. The problem of regional disparities in venture capital investment seems to be of more concern in the United Kingdom than elsewhere. Many of the initiatives discussed could have lessons for other nations wanting to use venture capital as an engine of growth. In particular the role of Enterprise Boards is most instructive.

The final chapter entitled Asian Venture Capital: Financing Risk Opportunities in the Pacific Rim by Thomas Leinbach provides a fascinating description of the newly emerging venture capital markets of Asia. In contrast with the venture capitalists of other regions, investment is more outward looking. The use of venture capital as a linking mechanism is a different goal than that pursued by venture capitalists in the West.

Having introduced the chapters I now leave the reader to explore venture capital in various countries as described in the rest of this volume.

1 Venture capital: the developing literature

Rod B. McNaughton

Venture capital is unique as it plays an interstitial role between many actors that are individually of interest to researchers in several disciplines. Venture capital is related to such diverse topics as pension fund investment, corporate finance, leveraged buyouts, small business management, entrepreneurship, business incubators, technology transfer, and economic development. The study of the venture capital market itself is largely the domain of business and economic researchers who have shown concern for:

(1) the investment decision-making behavior of venture capitalists,
(2) the performance of venture capital portfolios, and
(3) the availability and cost of venture capital.

The interest of researchers has followed that of the business community as a whole: when levels of investment are high, so is interest in venture capital research. There were many publications in the late 1960s and early 1970s, and a paucity throughout the late 1970s and early 1980s, followed by a recent increase. In part, this is the result of the introspective nature of the industry, which sponsors a significant amount of research in its efforts to lobby governments for legislative changes. The funding of this research is coordinated through national venture capital organizations, such as the Association of Canadian Venture Capital Companies, the National Venture Capital Association, and the National Association of Small Business Investment Companies. A second impetus for venture capital research comes from various government programs concerned with the adequate funding of small business, for example, the Technological Innovation Studies Program (TISP) in Canada, the Experimental Technology Incentive Program (ETIP) in the United States, and several US Senate Select Committees and Congressional Hearings on small business. The TISP, for example, has sponsored

1

more than eighty research projects on entrepreneurship, technology, and small firms.

The latest round of venture capital research is distinct from earlier work in two respects: (1) the topics addressed are more specific and (2) a wider range of perspectives is employed. Of primary importance for economic geographers is the adoption of a spatial component into this research. The distinct regional biases in the venture capital market have not gone unnoticed. Tribus was one of the first to recognize regional variations in venture capital availability:

> . . . supplies of venture capital are adequate, but the total supply is not distributed very evenly geographically. And we find that new entrepreneurs do not have access to all of the sources of capital.
>
> (Tribus 1970: 52)

However, the literature throughout the 1970s was concerned with the geographic pattern of investment in the grossest of terms. Anecdotal descriptions (for example, Dominguez 1974) merely suggested the possibility of economic impacts arising from the concentration and regional parochialism evident in the market. It is only within the last 5 years that economic geographers have shown interest in the market, though a history of interest in capital flows extends back several decades.

This chapter provides a brief overview of recent empirical studies of the venture capital market. Particular attention is paid to the contributions of geographers, though a wider context is set by a discussion of research conducted by business researchers.

SPATIAL PERSPECTIVES

Research which explicitly addresses the spatial behavior of the venture capital market can be grouped into four categories: (1) locational studies of venture capital firms and their investments, (2) taxonomies of regional market structures, (3) market specialization, and (4) economic impact (Table 1.1). Most of this research concerns the large and highly developed American venture capital market, but the Canadian, UK and New Zealand markets are also explored. The literature progressed rather quickly from simple empirical descriptions to more sophisticated considerations of the relationship between location, decision-making, and economic impact.

Table 1.1 Summary of venture capital research

Author(s)	Year	Major finding(s)
Locational studies		
Leinbach and Amrhein	1987	Regional concentration in United States
Mason	1987b	Investment concentrated in southeast United Kingdom
Florida and Kenney	1988a	Criticism of Leinbach and Amrhein 1987
Leinbach and Amrhein	1988	Response to Florida and Kenney 1988a
Florida and Kenney	1988b	Venture capital clusters near established financial and high-tech centers
McNaughton and Green	1987b	Regional concentration in Canada, investment flows are regionally biased
Perry	1988a	Investment concentrated in Auckland, New Zealand
Market taxonomies		
McNaughton and Green	1987a	Markets can be grouped according to interconnections between states
Florida and Kenney	1988c	Three types of venture capital agglomerations: high-tech, financial, and mixed
Specialization		
Green and McNaughton	1988a	Market niches, strong distance-decay for investment
Green	1989	Diffusion of firms, market specialization
McNaughton	1989	Specialization affected by competition in market
Economic impact		
Florida and Kenney	1988d	Venture capital provides institutional setting for innovation
McNaughton	1990	Venture-backed firms have above average financial performance

Locational Studies

Leinbach and Amrhein (1987) were the first to examine the regional availability of venture capital and its implication for small high-technology firms. They made two significant contributions: (1) a time series of the location of venture capital sources and (2) tabulation of regional flows of funds data. Leinbach and Amrhein noted a pronounced concentration of sources, with California, New York, Massachusetts, and Illinois accounting for over 75 per cent of the national total. The destination of funds showed an even more concentrated pattern, with the California/Southwest region receiving 45.7 per cent of the nation's total, followed by New England with 15.3 per cent.

Leinbach and Amrhein also attempted to establish a theoretical justification for the geographic analysis of venture capital, suggesting that it contributes to the growing literature on behavioral approaches to industrial location. In addition, they predicted a role for venture capital research in the development of structural theories of external business environments.

Florida and Kenney (1988a) criticized Leinbach and Amrhein for their lack of attention to the structure of the venture capital industry, and for the use of highly aggregate data that obscured important characteristics of the market. In particular, they felt that Leinbach and Amrhein had overestimated the importance of government licensed Small Business Investment Corporations (SBICs), and had mistakenly portrayed informal investors (angels) as part of the institutional industry. Further, they pointed out that the geographic concentration observed in the market is in part a function of the concentration of potential investments and their technological environment. The aggregate nature of the data used by Leinbach and Amrhein hid the extreme concentration of sources in a few cities, and even in a few zip codes (Florida and Kenney 1988b). Florida and Kenney also felt that Leinbach and Amrhein left the impression that considerable long distance investment takes place, when much of this can be accounted for by deal syndication and branch office locations. Leinbach and Amrhein (1988) replied to these criticisms by agreeing that the use of more disaggregate data would have been desirable if they had been available, and reiterating the introductory and exploratory nature of the work.

McNaughton and Green (1987b, 1989) provided an exploratory examination of the geography of Canadian venture capital investment. Surveys were used of both venture capital investors and their portfolio investments. Venture capital firms were found to be highly concentrated in Toronto, and secondarily in Calgary and Montreal. In terms of investments made, Ontario and Quebec were found to be net exporters, while the Prairies provinces and British Columbia are net importers. Further, Canadian investment patterns showed extreme self-bias in the selection of regional investment location. Significant regional variations were also found in the industrial sector characteristics of portfolio firms.

McNaughton and Green postulated that these spatial characteristics are the result of aggregate-risk averse behavior by venture capitalists. The location of venture capital firms, and the location of investments, are variables that can be manipulated to maximize access to information. Increased access to business information minimizes uncertainty and reduces risk. The need for information accessibility constrains the activity space of venture capital firms and limits the distance over which investment transactions can take place.

A study by Mason (1987b) found that the availability of venture capital is also highly concentrated within the United Kingdom. The primary investment target is the southeast, already the most prosperous region of the United Kingdom. Little investment flows into peripheral regions, especially northern England, which lacks its own development agency (like those of Scotland and Wales) to help fill its equity gap. Mason provides two explanations for this concentration that can be generalized to the venture capital markets in other countries as well: (1) the problem is the lack of entrepreneurial prospects with good growth potential in peripheral regions or (2) the problem is the result of historical legacy, perpetuated by regional prejudice, lack of awareness of local investment opportunities, or the logistical difficulties of adequately monitoring investments in more distant locations.

Perry (1988a) investigated the spatial and sectoral distribution of venture capital in New Zealand using a survey of New Zealand Venture Capital Association (NZVCA) members. He found that the traditional role of venture capital in supporting high-technology firms is not met in New Zealand. Theatrical promotions and primary sector activities are the principal beneficiaries. Further, more than one-quarter of New Zealand venture capital funds are invested outside the country and do not contribute to the support of indigenous enterprise. As in other national settings, the spatial distribution of venture capital investment within New Zealand is highly concentrated: 32.4 per cent is invested in the Auckland economic heartland. Perry noted that the necessity of spatial proximity requires that the office locations of venture capitalists, not simply investment flows, will have to diffuse in order to serve more peripheral locations. He also recognized that improving the quantity of new ventures in these locations requires more than greater availability of capital. The necessary conditions for entrepreneurial take-off also include fundamental shifts in the socio-economic composition of these regions.

Market taxonomies

In an attempt to present a spatially disaggregate evaluation of the organization and functioning of the venture capital market, McNaughton and Green (1987a) and Florida and Kenney (1988c) both presented market taxonomies. McNaughton and Green used a weighted blocking algorithm (WBLOC) to partition inter-state venture capital flows according to their degree of interconnectivity and strength of linkages. Three groupings of states were identified: (1) those with nationally oriented investment patterns (California, New York, and Massachusetts), (2) those with investment patterns that are dominated by their linkages with nationally oriented states (Connecticut, New Jersey, and Texas), and (3) those that invest only in themselves. This research provided clear evidence that the venture capital market is not integrated into a unified national system with equal availability at a spatially invariant price.

Florida and Kenney (1988c) presented their taxonomy based on the reasons for the concentration of venture capital investors. Venture capital complexes were found to exist in three distinct types of area: (1) those with high concentrations of financial resources, (2) those with high concentrations of technology-intensive small businesses, and (3) those with both. New York and Chicago are examples of the first type, San Francisco is an example of the second, and Boston is an example of the third. This research showed that the relationship between technology-oriented and financial-oriented venture capital complexes is symbiotic. While a local venture capital industry is not necessary to facilitate high-technology business formation, the existence of well-developed venture capital networks provides incentives for entrepreneurial start-ups. Venture capitalists were shown to act as both catalyst and capitalist, providing the networks, contacts, linkages, and resources necessary to launch new enterprises.

Market specialization

Green (1989) and Green and McNaughton (1988) investigated interurban differences in the specialization of venture capital investment preferences. Green developed a market specialization model that helps to explain the development and diffusion of the venture capital industry. This model postulates that the industry began with a few firms located in the largest urban centers that acted as training grounds for future venture capitalists. These initial firms had a spatial monopoly, which in turn implied constraints on the firms' operational areas. As associates left and formed their own firms, the erosion of the monopoly market led to a search for distinct market niches. Niches were created by manipulating three major components: (1) firm location, (2) industrial sector specialization, and (3) funding stage specialization.

New venture capital firms found that, at least temporarily, they could gain a spatial monopoly by establishing themselves in second and third order urban centers. Within these centers, specialization became the norm in order to reduce information gathering requirements and because of limited capital pools. Linkages to larger investment pools were maintained through personal contact networks that include the more established firms in first order centers. These established firms were able to expand either by syndicating with the new firms in lower order centers or by opening their own branch offices.

The results of an empirical analysis of interurban variations in venture capital investment characteristics found that most centers display a high degree of regional bias in their investment preferences. New York is an exception in that its investment patterns are nationally oriented. Los Angeles and, to a lesser degree, San Francisco and Boston specialize in seed capital. Most centers specialize in start-up, early growth, and leveraged buyout financing. San Francisco specializes in the computer sector, and Minneapolis in medical related ventures. Houston and Dallas specialize in resource related ventures.

McNaughton (1989) pursued the topic of investment specialization further, investigating differences in levels of specialization between US and Canadian urban markets. He outlined a model which emphasizes the role of differential access to information in developing aggregate patterns of specialization. He hypothesized that the degree of specialization evident in a market is determined by the competition between firms for projects and information. In large markets there is greater information about projects; there is also greater competition for projects. Large markets are less idiosyncratic, and venture capitalists must specialize in order to organize, interpret, and use available information. Specialization results in the creation of a distinct market niche. In small markets there is less information, and fewer projects from which to choose. Small markets must specialize in order to generate enough expertise to make satisfactory decisions. There is little competition in these markets, and firms have a partial spatial monopoly.

Empirical testing of this hypothesis in both US and Canadian urban markets led to the confirmation of Bygrave's (1987, 1988) findings that the relationship between concentration and uncertainty in the US venture capital market follows a U-shaped curve. Generally, in large markets where there are many transactions, venture capitalists must specialize in order to organize, interpret, and use all available information. In small markets, where there are few transactions and little information, venture capitalists must specialize in order to generate expertise. In markets of intermediate size, venture capitalists need not specialize to the same degree in order to use properly available information.

Economic impact

Geographers, and others, have also studied the performance and economic impact of venture capital investments, and of small high-technology firms in general. It is clear from the related literature that the economic value of these firms is multi-faceted and must be measured by several variables. Bollinger *et al.* (1983) isolated the following key variables: revenues, expenditures on taxes, research and development (R&D), exports, and employment generation. McNaughton (1990) designed and administered a survey that collected information on these key variables from Canadian firms that had received venture capital funding between 1980 and 1987. The results showed that venture capitalists invest in the elite of small and medium sized companies. These firms have above average rates of revenue growth, and strong financial positions. They commit large amounts of capital to R&D activity, and are highly export oriented. As a result of their rapid growth, ·they generate many new employment opportunities.

These findings agree with those of earlier surveys of high-technology firms which showed extraordinary growth in terms of revenues and tax expenditures. Morse (1976), in comparing sales data for the period 1969–1974, found that young technology-based businesses had a mean annualized growth rate of 42.5 per cent, compared with 11.4 per cent for the mature firms in his sample. Similarly Zschau (1978) reported on a survey of the members of the American Electronics Association. The youngest firms (those founded between 1971 and 1975) generated a mean of $70,000 in export sales, $15,000 in federal corporate income taxes, $5,000 in state and local taxes, and $33,000 in R&D expenditures for every $100,000 of equity investment. In the Canadian context, Ernst and Whinney (1981) found that, for every $100,000 in equity invested by venture capitalists, portfolio firms generated $348,000 in export sales, $48,000 in corporate and personal taxes, and $8,000 in R&D expenditures.

One of the problems with these studies is that the authors infer that equity investment by venture capitalists is the cause of these large economic multipliers. In fact, the influence of the venture investment is impossible to separate from that of the other sources of equity accessed by these firms. It is clear, however, that venture capitalists are generally involved in firms that have rapid rates of growth, thus maximizing the economic benefits of their investments.

The link between the superior performance of venture-backed firms and changes to existing economic structures is identified by Florida and Kenney (1988d). They suggest that venture capitalists affect economic development by impacting the rate of innovation and the length of technology cycles. The relationship between innovation and economic development is the primary focus of entrepreneurial economics. This perspective is important to those hoping to link venture capital investment with economic growth.

The modern view of entrepreneurship in economic theory can be traced to two sources: (1) the work of those economists who have been influenced by the writings of Joseph Schumpeter and (2) the Austrian School of Economics. Early developments in entrepreneurial theory, including the work of Schumpeter, are reviewed by Marshall (1961), Baumol (1968), and Kilby (1971). Recent contributions include those of Swales (1979), Calvo and Wellisz (1980), Kanbar (1980), Hebert and Link (1982), and Ronen (1983).

The seminal works of Schumpeter (1934, 1939, 1950) are often credited with ascribing the role of innovator to the entrepreneur. His analysis begins with a general equilibrium, in which all markets are perfectly competitive and consumer tastes and production technologies are given. The entrepreneur upsets the equilibrium by carrying out new combinations of the means of production and credit. For a time this act brings proprietary or monopoly profits, but imitators eventually erase these profits and drive the economy back to equilibrium.

The effect of the entrepreneur on the economy is phrased in terms of the creation and destruction of markets:

> It is not price competition which counts but the competition from the new commodity, the new technology, or the new type of organization . . . competition which commands a decisive cost or quality advantage and which strikes not at the margins of the profits and the outputs of the existing firms but at their foundations and their very lives.
>
> (Schumpeter 1950: 84)

In the Schumpeterian view, the venture capitalist–entrepreneur contributes to economic development by fostering the introduction of new goods, services, processes, markets, or industrial organizations, thus shifting existing socio-technical trajectories onto new accelerated development paths. This technological gatekeeping function helps to cause temporary disturbances in the economic cycle, establishing the context for economic restructuring and renewal.

In comparison, the Austrian School of Economics emphasizes the role of information in the entrepreneurial decision-making process, leading to a parallel emphasis on the effects of ignorance and error. Without perfect information, buyers and sellers agree on rational but uneconomic prices (in the sense that they differ from those that would occur under conditions of perfect knowledge) (Menger 1981). The combination of knowledge, ignorance, and error leads to entrepreneurial action. The entrepreneur acts, not on past and present conditions, but on a vision of the future. The successful entrepreneur sees the past and the present as other people do; but he judges the future in a different way (Mises 1966). Because market participants have differing information and perceptions, uneconomic prices prevail. The difference between the successful and the unsuccessful entrepreneur is in the ultimate accuracy of their market expectations.

This perspective leads to the conclusion that the entrepreneur does not upset the equilibrium state instead his actions move the economy toward equilibrium to the extent that future conditions are correctly anticipated. In this view, disequilibrium is a necessary condition for entrepreneurial success, not a consequence of it. These two views are not as diametrically opposed as it would first seem. Each addresses an important component of technological change. Schumpeter's entrepreneur causes disequilibrium in the market by introducing a new innovation. The Austrian's entrepreneur takes advantage of the uneconomic prices that result from this initial monopoly through imitation. The anticipation of future market demand drives prices down, reduces the monopoly of the innovator, and moves the economy toward equilibrium. The key to this process is the identification of those innovations that have the potential for rapid market growth.

The role of innovation and imitation in technological innovation is often discussed within the context of small versus large firms. Large firms and basic research institutions establish the scientific base and technological context necessary for major innovations and act as incubators of technological change (Cooper 1985). These technological opportunities are then exploited and commercialized by small entrepreneurial firms. This interrelationship is helped by the movements of top-level employees and the attendant transfers of technology and managerial capabilities (Roberts and Hauptman 1985), and through the informal exchange of information, research and professional associations, suppliers and vendors (Allen *et al.* 1983). Large firms may eventually recoup their losses by imitating the developments in small firms, applying their economies of scale to production, or by internalizing growth through acquisition.

Pence (1982), and Florida and Kenney (1988d) both provide models of the sequence that relates entrepreneurial activity to new firm formation and growth. Pence's model is the simpler of the two, beginning with two general sources of entrepreneurs: (1) existing corporations or (2) the academic and research communities. Entrepreneurs who come from small established companies bring with them experience in operating new small firms and keeping them moving toward larger market shares. Those from large established firms have proven management ability and a desire to try it out on their own. They may bring with them important product information. Those from academic and research environments have technological abilities, but often need to seek help with managerial aspects of the business. In any case, a prototype is developed, and a new business is formed. Later, high growth should change the size of the firm from small to large and the entrepreneurial process can again recycle.

The Florida and Kenney model considers the role of additional actors in this system, situating venture capitalists as the central players. Investors take on a role that exceeds the mere provision of funds. They command elaborate networks that reach into large corporations, universities, and financial markets. Venture capitalists combine and organize personnel from a variety of these institutions in order to form new firms. They review and screen business proposals, assess market potentials, evaluate technological possibilities, and then mobilize the requisite resources to launch new firms. These new firms affect existing production patterns and market structures and thus have an economic impact determined by the degree of their profits or losses. As the central actors in this system, venture capitalists lend structure and coherence to the dynamic process posited by entrepreneurial economic theory.

The activities of venture capitalists do not always have positive economic effects; sometimes they result in misallocations of resources (Florida and Kenney 1988d). A short-term focus on rapid growth and capital gains may move some firms into the initial public offering market before they have developed a mature organizational structure. In addition, the success of one firm can lead to the support of many similar companies, decreasing the market potential. Sahlman and Stevenson (1985) call this effect venture capital myopia. This myopia appeared in the United States when venture capitalists supported many hard disk drive manufacturers but failed to assist in the development of competitive technologies, such as compact disk read-only memories (CD ROMs).

The competitive entrepreneurial environment created by venture capitalists increases the likelihood of job-hopping, erodes employee commitment and disrupts ongoing research projects. While movement of talented managers and researchers from large corporations and universities to small entrepreneurial firms can aid technology transfer and speed the commercialization of innovations, at the extreme it is self-defeating and disruptive. Venture capitalists that specialize in raiding the talent of large corporations are known as vulture capitalists (Wilson 1985). Finally, in providing equity capital, venture capitalists dilute the ownership share of the entrepreneur. This is of concern to entrepreneurs as (1) returns are diminished and (2) managerial autonomy may be threatened. From the venture capitalist's point of view, some measure of control is necessary to ensure continued managerial competency as the firm makes the transition from a small entrepreneurial enterprise to a large production-oriented company.

the performance of venture capital portfolios, and (3) the
availability and cost of venture capital. The result has been a rather
static interpretation of venture capital, based largely on analogies
with larger financial markets.

The use of a spatial perspective in analyzing venture capital
behavior has led to the development of a new model of venture
capital activity that contrasts sharply with the conventional view of
business and economic researchers. This new model explicitly
recognizes the role of institutional networks in the allocation of
venture capital resources (Florida and Kenney 1988d), spatial
constraints on day-to-day monitoring and investment location
(McNaughton and Green 1989), and the relationship between
information, competition, and market specialization (Green 1989;
McNaughton 1989). Thompson (1989a: 89) summarizes the two
models in the following way.

Conventional model: Simple diffusion with growth in supply,
leading to spatial equilibrium in risk-adjusted rates of return.
Geographical model: Inherently spatially constrained, place-
related behavior, in a disequilibrium situation of constantly
shifting opportunities.

The conventional model predicts that venture capital will eventually
equally available in all regions, while the geographical model
holds that some areas will never be supplied. The implication for
adopting one of these models over the other for use in developing
regional policies is obvious. The first puts the emphasis on
increasing total supply, the second on specific programs in areas
where there are few investment opportunities and even fewer
venture capitalists. Spatial approaches to venture capital research
have not yet approached maturity. Additional research can be
expected in at least two areas: (1) the comparative operation
venture capital markets in different national contexts and (2) t
micro-economic impacts of venture capital investment. An excelle
example of the first area is provided by Clark (1987), who compa
the adoption of the American venture capital model in the Uni
Kingdom and in Japan. Not surprisingly he found that the mar
operates in a similar fashion in the United Kingdom, but i
radically different fashion in Japan.

Two factors work against the adoption of the Amer
investment model in Japan: (1) technological innovations
traditionally commercialized within the existing large corp
structure leaving little room for small new firms and (2) cu

BUSINESS AND ECONOMIC PERSPECTIVES

While geographers have only recently explored the venture capital
market, its distinctive regional biases have long drawn comment
from business researchers. In particular, the concentration of firms
and their investments is noted in surveys of investment activity (for
example, Crane 1972; Knight 1973; Mao 1974), and in industry
sponsored reviews of the industry (for example, Ernst and Whinney
1979–86). Much of the existing literature arises from business
concerns for the general availability of venture capital funds
(Grieve, 1972; Batler 1973; Fells 1974, 1975). Knight is particularly
prolific in the field, having investigated the criteria used by venture
capitalists in selecting their portfolio firms (Knight 1986), the
performance of firms rejected by venture capitalists (Knight 1985),
and the success of government sponsored programs (Knight and
Ferguson 1984).

The business literature about the American venture capital
market is substantial. Libecap (1986), for example, provides a
bibliography of 140 references about the economics of technical
change, 45 about finance and venture capital, 327 about entrepreneurship and intrapreneurship, and 64 about small business.
Three salient research streams have developed (Timmons and
Bygrave 1986). The first approach addresses concern for the
investment decision-making behavior of venture capitalists, the
second focuses on the evaluation of the performance of venture
capital portfolios, and the third focuses on the availability and cost
of venture capital. In addition, researchers have studied such
diverse topics as the strategic role of the venture capital director,
syndicated investment relationships, criteria used to evaluate new
venture proposals, the investment patterns of informal risk capital
investors, the performance of firms rejected by venture capitalists,
and several others. Churchill and Hornaday (1987) provide a useful
bibliography of this research.

Many of the studies on decision-making and characteristics of
successful investments are unpublished dissertations (Tyebjee and
Bruno 1981, 1984). Further, they tend to point out the difficulties
and uncertainties of this type of research. Wells (1974) was one of
the first to address the decision-making behavior of venture
capitalists. In a descriptive study of seven venture capital firms, he
attempted to analyze perceived risk–return tradeoffs in terms of
three variables: operating risk, man-time risk and stock market risk.
A major problem arose in attempting to establish a common

definition of risk that would universally characterize all portfolio investments. Wells concluded that venture capitalists are risk-averse, given that their expectations of return can be equated with actual returns.

Later, Hoban (1976) in his dissertation began by identifying a universal set of venture characteristics that could be operationalized into a set of predictive variables. These variables were used in an attempt to determine the ultimate success or failure of individual portfolio investments. Hoban found, however, that all risk factors could not be reduced to a single scale. The individuality and uniqueness of each investment prevented the creation of a constant set of predictive variables. Intervening factors such as general economic conditions, market forces, and entrepreneurial ability were found to be impossible to model. At approximately the same time Poindexter (1976) attempted to measure the amount of risk venture capitalists accept as a first step in determining the efficiency of the market, as represented by the Capital Asset Pricing Model. Poindexter showed that this model inadequately predicts risk differentials in the venture capital market. Again, the primary problem was found to be the lack of a common definition of market risk.

Pence (1982) attempted to control for the large number of potentially relevant variables that may comprise a definition of market risk by limiting the universe of investments to those involving early stage start-up companies displaying a high degree of technological innovation. She concluded that venture capitalists' investment behavior is based on the same fundamentals as are most financial decisions – those of risk, return, and liquidity. A set of predictive variables still did not emerge. Pence suggested that a further restriction of the study universe is needed, particularly by geographic location. According to her 'it would be interesting to conduct a more intensive study using similar techniques in one geographic location'. This because 'the entrepreneur should first consider investors who are located close to a new enterprise . . . if they want both to benefit from the financier's expertise and to improve their chances of finding adequate financing quickly' (Pence 1982: 53).

Several studies on performance that were conducted throughout the early 1970s showed that new ventures supported by venture capital companies had a significantly lower failure rate (20–30 per cent) compared with the failure rate of companies in the economy at large (80–90 per cent) (Taylor 1969; Roberts 1970; Faucett 1971).

Huntsman and Hoban (1980) studied 110 investment institutions prominent in the funding of new annualized rate of return generated by the compo 18.9 per cent was found over the 15-year period fro More important, the study illustrated that abc investments failed and that relatively few investm ordinarily high rates of return. This observation w DeHudy *et al.* (1981) who analyzed the portfolios o venture capital firms (218 investments). They report of 14.7 per cent and an average annual return of 1 the three leading venture capital firms.

Bean *et al.* (1975) concluded that little is kn potential market imperfections involving venture cap Charles River Associates (1976) concluded that sr based companies paid higher interest rates and yiel of return than did other small ventures. This study no significant imperfections existed in the venture Thus, they could not support the argument that ve make inordinately high average returns. As a resul became accepted that public policy should be des would not interfere with the efficient operation of

SUMMARY

A resurgence of interest in the venture capital ind few years has resulted in an increased numb publications. This research explores a wider range the past, and is conducted in part by research traditional fields of business and economics. The economic geographers is particularly conspicuous Over the past 5 years geographers have added empi anecdotal observations of market concentration parochialism. They have also extended interest into as the specialization and spatial extent of ma consequent implications for economic development

Thompson (1989a), after reviewing the venture criticized the conventional working model of distribution for being overly dependent on no equilibrium, and for neglecting venture capital's unevenness. This criticism is largely warranted. Bus have traditionally focused on (1) concerns for decision-making behavior of venture capitalists, (.

considerations such as lifetime employment, aversion to contractual dealings with strangers and the lifetime commitment of equity ownership do not readily foster entrepreneurialism. Despite these impediments, a venture capital system has emerged. This system is funded in part by government sources, but primarily from subsidiaries of the large sogo shosha (trading houses). As small firms tend to grow slowly and initial public offerings are uncommon, emphasis is placed on the subordinate debt financing of older firms that need additional funds for expansion. This system seems to foster innovation spawned within existing large corporate structures and operationalized by associated firms, subsidiaries, and joint ventures. In the United States this approach is called intrapreneurial as opposed to entrepreneurial behavior. Continued research along these lines could be very helpful in clarifying the relationships between the socio-economic setting, cultural values, and the enabling mechanism of capital in fostering economic benefits from innovation.

A second area that needs additional attention is the micro-economic impacts of venture capital investment. While McNaughton (1990) and others have shown that venture-backed firms generally have above average rates of growth, innovation, and employment generation, it is assumed that this has a beneficial impact on local economies. Substantiation of this link will require additional research at finer geographic and economic scales. Future research should find out whether venture-backed firms contribute to local development through the enhancement of multiplier effects, local ownership, local reinvestment of profits, local control over investment and location of physical capital, enhancement of employee welfare, and employment skill and pay levels, to name a few examples. The challenge of meeting these demands for more research, and the importance of gaining information on the role of capital availability in economic development, offers an exceptional motivation for continued geographic research into venture capital markets.

2 Preferences for US venture capital investment 1970-1988

Milford B. Green

INTRODUCTION

The increasing pressure being exerted upon the American economy by foreign competition and innovation has led to a concern with economic redevelopment and renewal of the economy. An important vehicle for such redevelopment lies with the small firm. Small firm formation is dependent upon the availability of speculative capital partially provided by the organized venture capital industry (Davis 1986). As Leinbach and Amrhein (1987) persuasively argue venture capital can help in small firm formation with the attendant benefits (Storey 1980) of job creation and the spawning of innovation. Florida and Kenney (1988b) maintain that venture capital is an important element in high-technology entrepreneurship.

VENTURE CAPITAL

Liles (1974) states in his definition of venture capital that it is characterized by the following.

(1) Investment in any high risk financial venture.
(2) Investment in unproven ideas, products, or start-up situations. This is seed capital.
(3) Investment in going concerns that are unable to raise funds from conventional public or commercial sources.
(4) Investment in large publicly traded companies and possibly obtaining controlling interest in such companies where uncertainty is significant.

Venture capital is also associated with equity financing. 'It is thought of as a type of direct investment in the securities of new speculative firms or technologically oriented enterprises undergoing internal expansion . . . It is also characterized as a high-risk investment with large returns expected in dividends and capital gains' (Dominguez 1974: 1).

Venture capital is further distinguished from traditional investment forms by its concurrent provision of business and managerial advice to the borrower. High levels of risk are present in venture capital investment. It is the commercialization of high risk, promising products or services, with the expectation of large returns.

A basic division of venture capital firms is private firms and quasi-public firms (Dominguez 1974). Private firms are often associated with family fortunes or are subsidiaries of large corporations (Liles 1974). Quasi-public or government sponsored firms are federally funded and licensed under the Small Business Investment Company (SBIC) and the Minority Enterprise Small Business Investment Company (MESBIC) programs (Dominguez 1974).

Private firms in this chapter refer to either publicly or privately held companies or subsidiaries of companies that do not receive government loans or assistance. Government sponsored firms are defined to be licensees of either the SBIC or MESBIC programs. The locations and specializations of these public firms are more probably linked to the licensing and leveraging practices of the Small Business Administration (SBA) than free market forces.

In terms of funds available, Pratt (1983) estimates that between 1969 and 1977 total commitment to the venture capital pool was roughly $2.5 billion to $3 billion. In 1978 a dramatic expansion of the market began, such that by 1988 the pool totalled some $20 billion (Florida and Kenney 1988c). The data used in this chapter, however, suggest that the total capital pool is over $33.5 billion.

Discussion of venture capital issues was until recently largely confined to trade journals and popular business magazines. Academic consideration has come from business concerns with the investment decision-making process (Wells 1974; Hoban 1976; Poindexter 1976; Pence 1982), economic concerns with the functioning of financial markets (Kryanowski and Giraldeau 1977; Huntsman and Hoban 1980), and regional development concerns for the structure of the venture capital market (Charles River Associates 1976).

Nongeographers have recognized regional variations in the venture capital market. As Tribus (1970: 52) states: 'supplies of venture capital are adequate, but the total supply is not distributed very evenly geographically . . . And we find that new entrepreneurs do not have access to all of the sources of venture capital.' Most studies of the industry have been at highly aggregate levels, however, and few have considered the geographic pattern of venture capital investment except in the grossest of terms.

Anecdotal descriptions, based on informal observation, have suggested two characteristics of venture capital investment patterns: (1) concentration and (2) regional parochialism. Tribus (1970), Dominguez (1974), Pratt (1983), Oakey (1984), and Hooper and Walker (1983) have all noted regional variations in the importance and availability of venture capital financing. Pence (1982), Wetzel and Seymour (1981), and Silver (1985) have each noted that geographic proximity is the first step in adding value and efficient monitoring to an investment and that, as a result, venture capital firms have a strong tendency to invest in their own regions.

Silver (1985) further suggests that there are two market types: (1) localized regional markets and (2) nationally oriented markets. Localized regional markets experience enhanced performance because they are the first funds in their areas and receive the benefits afforded to monopolists. Nationally oriented markets both attract and invest capital in all regions. They are more typical of the price-taking, integrated markets described by neoclassical theory.

Geographic work has only recently commenced with work by Leinbach and Amrhein (1987), McNaughton and Green (1987a, b, 1989), Florida and Kenney (1988a, b, c, d) and Thompson (1989a) who all substantiate much of the previous discussion.

Leinbach and Amrhein (1987) provide a description of venture capital investment by state and region for 1982. New York, California, and Massachusetts are the dominant locations for venture capital firms. They also find a regional propensity for self-investment. McNaughton and Green (1987a) present evidence that a three level hierarchical structure characterizes the venture capital market.

Florida and Kenney (1988b) show that venture capital flows mainly to established high-technology centers such as Boston or Silicon Valley. They classify venture capital locations into complexes. Venture capital complexes can be characterized as technology-oriented complexes, finance-oriented complexes and hybrid complexes. Technology complexes invest locally and attract extraregional capital, finance complexes export capital and hybrid complexes exhibit characteristics of both technology and finance complexes. Florida and Kenney also emphasize the importance of personal contacts within the venture capital industry.

Thompson (1989a) in his recent review of the literature on venture capital provides a geographic model of investment. He argues that inclusion of institutional networks, spatial constraints and personal contact networks are necessary to understand better the role of venture capital in regional development.

THE GEOGRAPHY OF VENTURE CAPITAL

To understand the spatial aspects of the American venture capital industry the following theoretical description of the spatial expansion of private firms is provided. As noted previously, quasi-public firms do not operate in free market conditions. SBIC or MESBIC licensees have experienced an accelerated version of the model described below. A desire by the SBA to encourage equality in regional representation of quasi-public firms led to the introduction of quasi-public venture capital firms at smaller order urban places than would a free market. Much of this description is based on anecdotal evidence provided by venture capitalists themselves (Silver 1985; Wilson 1985). The following discussion only addresses the supply side of the industry. The assumption is that entrepreneurial talent is ubiquitous in space.

After the Second World War the number of technologically innovative business opportunities increased. This, coupled with the ever increasing speed of technological change, created a capital vacuum for entrepreneurs with high-risk and high-return product ideas. The infant venture capital market rose to meet this demand.

As Leinbach and Amrhein (1987) and Florida and Kenney (1988b) point out, the initial firms in the venture capital industry were privately owned and were usually associated with a wealthy family or individual. These initial firms served as role models for later firms and provided training for new venture capitalists (Figure 2.1). The firms were located in large urban centers with a history of high-risk investment.

These initial venture capital companies had a spatial monopoly since entrepreneurs normally prefer to start their firms locally. Maintenance of this monopoly also implies the creation of spatial constraints on the firm's activities. As the number of potential investments grew, the number of venture capital firms that a large centre could support also grew. However, the spatial proximity of the firms leads to an erosion of their monopoly market. This erosion forces firms to search for distinct market niches.

These market niches are created through the manipulation of three major components: the location of the firm, the industrial specialization of investment, and the stage of financing. All these

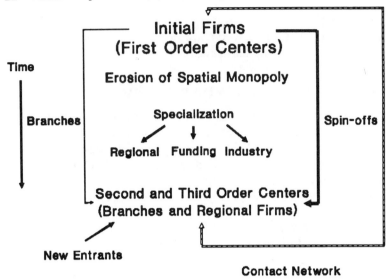

Figure 2.1 Venture capital diffusion

components are interrelated. The choice of a particular city or region constrains the types of proposals submitted to the firm. If the venture capital firm wishes to specialize in a particular industry, the number of potential locations is constrained. Concurrently, the choice of either industry or location constrains the decision on the stage of funding. As opportunities and their complexity increase, specialization also becomes necessary for information management. Only through increased specialization can the growing market be efficiently monitored.

An individual capitalist's typical route of entry into the industry is as a salaried associate within an established firm (Silver 1985; Florida and Kenney 1987). As the individual gains enough experience he/she leaves to start his/her own firm. This decision, to start one's own firm, leads to a decision regarding the creation of a market niche. Some elect to remain in the same general location, but others, because of their experiences and contacts, start up at a different location. This new location provides a degree of spatial monopoly concerning received proposals. Such decisions are more likely in periods of competition for proposals and economically buoyant periods than in recessionary periods.

As the larger centers become more saturated, the smaller centers become targets for locations. A hierarchical diffusion effect can therefore be expected. Specialization of firms within centers becomes the norm. Such specialization reduces information gathering requirements and information overload. Specialization is further mandated by limited capital pools. Linkages are maintained between centers through personal contacts. Venture capitalists are often highly dependent upon their contact networks. Such a high dependence leads to a restriction of the activity space of the firm and poor integration of the market.

As the successful firms in the initial centers become larger, they require more proposals from farther regions. These successful firms can proceed along two paths. One is the establishment of branch offices both on a national and international level, which has occurred in recent years. The other involves the use of smaller more regionally based firms. These more recently established smaller firms need access to larger amounts of capital then they themselves can raise. In addition, jointly funded proposals allow for diversification of risk. The mutual need for additional proposals and additional capital leads to a hierarchical system of firms. Such a system is characterized at the top level by national scope firms fed by a system of regionally focused smaller firms. As this process continues, a third level of local small firms develops. This is similar to the historical development of the American banking industry (Sylla 1980).

This geography of venture capital is important because of its implications for risk and information access. To minimize uncertainty and risk, access to information flows must be maximized. This constrains the activity space of the firm, and limits the distance over which transactions take place. Such distance limitations allow the creation of the spatial monopoly of a firm.

Several conditions affect the transmission of information. For the venture capital firm one important aspect is the extent of the personal contacts and business acquaintances possessed by the firm's management team. Personal referrals are often a major consideration in the investment decision. Further, venture capitalists invest primarily in small firms, and such firms cannot afford the high cost of informing investors nationwide about the characteristics and soundness of small, unknown investments.

The provision of effective assistance requires frequent face to face interchanges. Since distance represents cost in terms of time and money, investment proximity lowers overheads and helps to insure the success of a venture (Florida and Kenney 1988b).

Pred (1977) and others have shown that the effect of distance on the transmission of information becomes less over time. The early dominance of the Middle Atlantic region (and specifically of New York City) has afforded it a more pervasive contact network, and better access to informational resources. Further, as already noted, urban size may also be an important consideration. This leads to less uncertainty when transacting at a distance, and less restrictive spatial bounds. The locations of branch offices and the syndication of deals are also used to expand the informational network.

Within the spatial bounds set by the processes outlined above, risk aversion is further shown by specialization in certain industries and stages of the funding cycle. The Office of Technology Assessment (OTA 1984) provides a review of sectoral disbursements. Venture capital firms prefer to invest in 'high-tech' sectors such as computers, electronics, communications, medicine, and genetic engineering. The concern is for products that can be easily commercialized and have large market growth potential.

The market characteristics of concentration and regional parochialism are a function not only of spatial constraints but of the need to maintain highly specialized contact networks and a distinctive market niche. The general effect is to create a poorly integrated investment market, where discrepancies may occur between profitability and the existence of barriers in obtaining long-term debt and equity (Kieschnick and Daniels 1978). Such discrepancies imply imperfections and inefficiencies in the market. These imperfections are compounded when the regional biases arising from differential rates of capital accumulation, job creation (Kieschnick 1979), and industrial diversification (Peterson 1977) are considered.

The model of development proposed here leads to several hypotheses regarding the spatial structure of venture capital in the United States. These are as follows.

(1) Venture capital firms are highly concentrated in a few cities, including New York, San Francisco, and Boston. These centers represent the areas with initial advantages.
(2) The concentration of venture capital firms is lessening over time. Diffusion to smaller order centers is accompanying the maturation of the venture capital market.
(3) Each of these centers has differing preferences among industries and funding stages, implying specialization.
(4) Specialization is related to the type of venture capital firm, either quasi-public or private.

(5) The investment of funds can be described by strong self-bias by firms for their own city.

DATA

The ensuing analysis employs directories of venture capital firms compiled by Rubel (1970b, 1972, 1974), Pratt (1977, 1981, 1983), and Morris (1986, 1988) and cross checked with other directories (Sinclair 1971; Dominguez 1974; Johnson 1976; *Venture* magazine 1985; Dow Jones and Irwin, 1986, 1988). These directories have been published periodically since 1970. More recent versions provide information on geographical investment preferences. Additional information is also available on office location, preferred investment size and type, and several other characteristics from a survey of venture capital firms.

Use of the Morris, Pratt, and Rubel directories presents a problem since it is unknown whether the preferences coded in the survey show actual investment characteristics. Actual investment characteristics are influenced by the availability of sound business proposals that have an acceptable risk–return mix. A limited test of the concordance between stated investment preferences for regions and actual regional investment patterns can be conducted for SBICs. The SBA maintains a listing of all SBIC investments by zip code by individual firm by year. Such data for 1983 were merged with the Pratt directory for the same year. There are 189 SBICs listed in the Pratt directory, of which 106 actively made investments in 1983. These firms made 646 investments, in 419 of which the actual location matched the preferred location. This concordance is significantly different from that expected under the assumption of randomness at the 0.01 probability level on the binomial distribution. Thus, actual investment locations are equivalent to stated regional preferences. There is then limited empirical support for the assumption that the stated preferences mirror actual investments.

The postal addresses of the firms listed in the directories were used to assign a firm to a city. For those firms with branch offices, it is assumed that the head office makes the final investment decisions, and therefore branch offices are not included in the analysis. The cities having more than 1 per cent of the total number of venture capital firms since 1970 were then determined. In recognition of the ease of communication within urban areas and local personal contact networks, these cities were then further aggregated into their respective Consolidated Metropolitan Statistical Areas

(CMSAs). This reduced the number of cities to fifteen.

As with many commercial directories, systematic coverage of the industry is sometimes suspect. This is particularly true of the early directories. However, cross checking with SBA reports and other directories minimizes this problem. Bias is likely to exist, however, concerning the smaller firms, where coverage is sporadic.

ANALYSES

Investment levels

The venture capital firms are divided into two groups for the purposes of this analysis: government sponsored firms (SBICs and MESBICs) and private firms (both publicly traded and privately owned). As discussed previously, these two types of firms have different characteristics. This is illustrated and substantiated by the data presented in Table 2.1. This table presents the median values of the minimum required investment, the preferred investment

Table 2.1 Medians of private, SBIC, and MESBIC firms; medians of minimum and preferred investment

Levels by firm type (US$'00,000)	Minimum investment			Preferred investment		
	Private	SBIC	MESBIC	Private	SBIC	MESBIC
1970	100	na	na	500	250	100
1972	100	na	na	1000	250	100
1974	200	200	100	450	200	100
1977	300	100	100	450	200	100
1981	300	300	100	600	300	300
1983	300	300	100	600	300	300
1985	250	100	100	750	250	250
1988	250	100	100	750	375	250

Medians of capital under management by firm type (US$ million)

	Private	SBIC	MESBIC
1977	9	na	na
1981	10	3	2
1983	16	4	2
1985	22	3	2
1988	34	11	6

Notes: Categories significantly different at $p = 0.000$.
  na, not available.

levels, and the capital under management for both quasi-public and private firms. The median is used to guard against the influence of extreme values. The medians for the minimum and preferred investment preferences represent a reported range of values. The directories report the data as within such a range, for example, $250,000–$500,000.

In all three investment variables and for all three types of firms the values increase over time. This is partially due to inflation, but it also represents the maturing of the venture capital industry and the increasing size of firms. A median test shows that private, SBIC, and MESBIC firms are statistically different in their median values. The private firms are the largest followed by SBICs and then MESBICs.

While the minimum and preferred investment levels have experienced moderate increases, the median capital under management has increased almost fourfold since 1977. The differences between the types of firms are quite dramatic by 1988 for capital under investment.

Diffusion

Maps 2.1–2.16 provide a visual record of the spatial diffusion of venture capital firms for the period 1970–1988. The locations and numbers of public type venture capital firms for the years 1970–1988 are shown in Maps 2.1–2.8 (see map portfolio at the end of this chapter).

Table 2.2, a detailed account of quasi-public firms for the most important venture capital centers, reveals that there has been a gradual increase in the number of medium and small centers. The number of firms found within the large metropolitan areas has also increased, although the dominance of New York City has been constant since 1970.

The locations and numbers of private venture capital firms are depicted in Maps 2.9–2.16 (see pp. 47–54) and Table 2.3. It is immediately obvious that the spatial distribution of private firms is much more circumscribed. Private firms are more likely in the larger urban centers. Spatial diffusion has been much less dramatic than that of their publicly regulated counterparts. New York City has been steadily losing its share of private venture capital firms since 1970, largely because of increases in the other major urban centers. This might well be expected to continue as the venture capital market continues to mature. Increasing national integration and the

Table 2.2 The number of government sponsored venture capital firms in selected Consolidated Statistical Areas, 1970–88

	1970	1972	1974	1977	1981	1983	1985	1988	Total
Atlanta	3	8	5	5	3	2	5	2	33
	2.2	2.3	1.9	1.5	1.2	0.8	1.0	0.6	1.4
Boston	8	19	10	17	12	10	13	9	98
	5.9	5.4	3.8	5.2	4.7	3.9	2.7	2.5	4.0
Chicago	7	17	13	14	15	12	19	14	111
	5.2	4.9	4.9	4.3	5.9	4.7	4.0	3.9	4.6
Cleveland	2	3	3	6	5	5	7	5	36
	1.5	0.9	1.1	1.8	2.0	2.0	1.5	1.4	1.5
Dallas	4	12	10	10	9	9	14	11	79
	3.0	3.4	3.8	3.1	3.6	3.5	2.9	3.1	3.3
Denver	1	2	2	2	1	2	4	3	17
	0.7	0.6	0.8	0.6	0.4	0.	0.8	0.8	0.7
Detroit		4	4	5	2	5	10	3	33
		1.1	1.5	1.5	0.8	2.	2.1	0.8	1.4
Houston	4	6	5	7	7	12	22	17	80
	3.0	1.7	1.9	2.1	2.8	4.7	4.6	4.7	3.3
Los Angeles	7	19	12	18	13	14	34	25	142
	5.2	5.4	4.5	5.5	5.1	5.5	7.1	7.0	5.9
Miami		5	6	6	7	8	14	9	55
		1.4	2.3	1.8	2.8	3.1	2.9	2.5	2.3
Minneapolis	3	4	5	6	8	9	10	7	52
	2.2	1.1	1.9	1.8	3.2	3.5	2.1	2.0	2.1
New York	22	63	39	44	39	38	79	52	376
	16.3	18.1	14.8	13.5	15.4	14.8	16.4	14.5	15.5
Philadelphia	4	11	8	9	7	4	5	4	52
	3.0	3.2	3.0	2.8	2.8	1.6	1.0	1.1	2.1
San Francisco	14	18	11	15	15	18	21	18	130
	10.4	5.2	4.2	4.6	5.9	7.0	4.4	5.0	5.4
Washington DC	3	9	9	12	8	7	18	14	80
	2.2	2.6	3.4	3.7	3.2	2.7	3.7	3.9	3.3
Others	53	149	122	150	102	101	206	165	1048
	39.3	42.7	46.2	46.0	40.3	39.5	42.8	46.1	43.3
otals	135	349	264	326	253	256	481	358	2422
	5.6	1.4	10.9	13.5	10.4	10.6	19.9	14.8	100.0

downward diffusion of private firms makes location within New York less of a locational imperative.

The dominance of large urban centers in the location of venture capital firms can be verified if the row totals in Tables 2.2 and 2.3 are examined for the fifteen largest centers versus all other locations. In 1988, 54 per cent of the government sponsored firms and 75 per cent of the private firms are within these CMSAs. It is also clear that population size alone is insufficient to guarantee a substantial presence of venture capital firms. Cities such as Baltimore, Pittsburgh, Cincinnati, and Indianapolis are not promin-

Table 2.3 The number of private venture capital firms in selected Consolidated Statistical Areas, 1970–88

	1970	1972	1974	1977	1981	1983	1985	1988	Total
Atlanta	1	2	3	2	2	4	10	8	32
	0.2	0.4	0.8	0.6	0.7	1.2	1.6	1.3	32
Boston	38	47	41	38	37	45	63	61	370
	9.3	9.9	10.4	11.2	13.2	13.8	9.8	10.0	10.7
Chicago	21	25	19	16	15	19	23	25	163
	5.2	5.2	4.8	4.7	5.3	5.8	3.6	4.1	4.7
Cleveland	4	5	8	5	7	8	8	6	51
	1.0	1.0	2.0	1.5	2.5	2.5	1.2	1.0	1.5
Dallas	9	10	8	8	5	6	23	14	83
	2.2	2.1	2.0	2.4	1.8	1.8	3.6	2.3	2.4
Denver	5	6	4	4	4	7	20	12	62
	1.2	1.3	1.0	1.2	1.4	2.1	3.1	2.0	1.8
Detroit	2	4	8	7	3	3	3	5	35
	0.5	0.8	2.0	2.1	1.1	0.9	0.5	0.8	1.0
Houston	5	6	7	6	5	3	15	32	199
	1.2	1.3	1.8	1.8	1.8	0.9	2.3	2.0	1.7
Los Angeles	30	38	20	18	17	17	27	32	199
	7.4	8.0	5.1	5.3	6.0	5.2	4.2	5.3	5.7
Miami		1				0.3	0.2	0	3
		0.2				0.3	0.2	0	0.1
Minneapolis	10	9	6	5	5	4	12	7	58
	2.5	1.9	1.5	1.5	1.8	1.2	1.9	1.2	1.7
New York	154	169	124	85	69	69	109	88	867
	37.8	35.4	31.6	25.0	24.6	21.2	17.0	14.5	25.0
Philadelphia	12	13	10	8	5	8	17	15	88
	2.9	2.7	2.5	2.4	1.8	2.5	2.6	2.5	2.5
San Francisco	37	42	46	47	35	43	102	110	462
	9.1	8.8	11.7	13.8	12.5	13.2	15.9	18.1	13.3
Washington, DC	6	10	7	5	4	10	17	13	72
	1.5	2.1	1.8	1.5	1.4	3.1	2.6	2.1	2.1
Others	73	90	82	86	68	79	192	200	870
	17.9	18.9	20.9	25.3	24.2	24.2	29.9	32.9	25.0
Total	407	477	393	340	281	326	642	608	3474
	11.7	13.7	11.3	9.8	8.1	9.4	18.5	17.5	100.0

ent locations. Access to venture capital is therefore spatially biased. The reasons for the location of venture capital in certain cities are a function of historical experience with risky investments and a desire for specialization by venture capitalists.

This concentration of venture capital is illustrated by figures 2.2 and 2.3 for quasi-public firms, and figures 2.4 and 2.5 for private firms. The cumulative percentage of the number of firms both weighted (by capital under management) and unweighted versus the number of cities in rank order of importance is shown in all four figures. The graphs for the years 1981, the first year for which

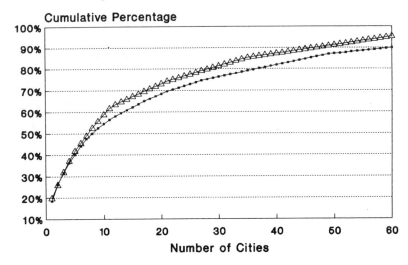

Figure 2.2 Unweighted comparisons for government sponsored firms: ——■—, government unweighted, 1988; —△—, government unweighted, 1981

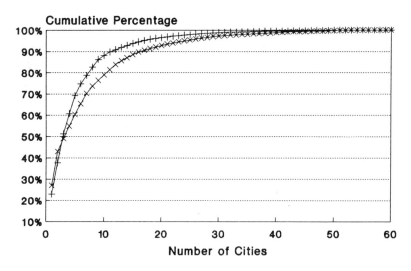

Figure 2.3 Weighted comparisons for government sponsored firms: —+—, government weighted, 1988; —×—, government weighted, 1981

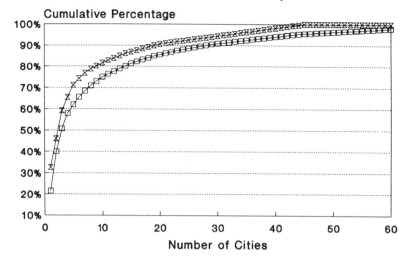

Figure 2.4 Unweighted comparisons for private firms: —□—, private unweighted, 1988; —✕—, private unweighted, 1981

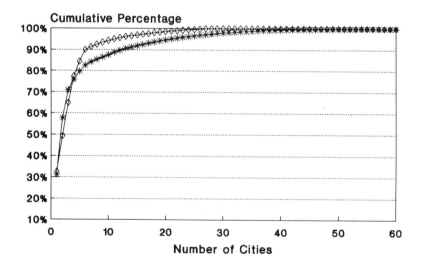

Figure 2.5 Weighted comparisons for private firms: —✳—, private weighted, 1988; —◇—, private weighted, 1981

reliable capital figures are available, and 1988 show a decreasing concentration of capital in both kinds of firms.

Two of the largest centers, New York and San Francisco, account for 37 per cent of the private firms and almost 21 per cent of the public firms. Recent literature attributes the dominance of these two centers to early involvement in venture financing and proximity to a few large research centers (Leinbach and Amrhein 1987).

Hambrecht (1984) cites the Radiation Laboratories at MIT and the Radio Research Laboratories at Harvard as nodes of innovation attracting entrepreneurs and venture capital investment to the Boston–New York City corridor. In California, Cal Tech and Stanford are seen as important sponsors of innovation and entrepreneurial activity.

Specialization

An appendix at the end of this chapter presents the results of a three way full effects median polish model fitted to measures of investment preference data for the top fifteen venture capital centers for both public and private firms. This appendix reports results for twenty-five variables collected into three dimensions: (1) preferred census region for investment, (2) preferred funding stage, and (3) preferred industry.

The region variables are the nine major census regions with the addition of a category for firms preferring investment anywhere in the United States. The regional categories and the US category are not mutually exclusive. A firm that expressed a preference for all regions was coded as preferring all the United States and each individual region. Firms that only expressed a preference for the whole United States were also included in the final category. These regions are mandated by the level of regional preference data collected in the directories.

The funding stage variables are defined by Pratt (1983) into seven classes. These are seed financing (to prove an idea), start-up (product development), first stage (to initiate commercial sales), second stage (working capital), mezzanine stage (major expansion funding), fourth stage (to go public), acquisition financing and leveraged buyouts financing.

The industry classes are also defined by Pratt (1983) as computer related, distribution, manufacturing, medical, natural resources, real estate, retail, and services. The reader should note that investment in the real estate sector is restricted for SBICs and

MESBICs because of misuse of investment funds for speculation in the beginnings of the programs. The degree of preference of a city for a particular region, stage of investment, or industry is based on the number of times the variable was listed as a preference by a firm located in that city divided by the total number of firms located there. This in effect standardizes the preference variables for each of the major venture capital centers.

The variables are collapsed across the time period 1970–1988. This aggregation is justified from the results of a multiple preference matrix individual scaling (INDSCAL) procedure applied to the temporally disaggregate data. The initial assumption was that there was temporal variation, hence the INDSCAL procedure. However, the analysis revealed no significant differences between exhibited preference patterns across time. This lack of temporal variability is further substantiated by a series of Wilcoxon matched pair ranked sign tests that also revealed no systematic differences between years.

The principle of scientific parsimony was then invoked, that is, the simplest model or description of the observed data was used. Since there was no significant temporal variation, little is lost by collapsing across time to make the analysis simpler. This is further justified since such an approach is similar to use of pooled variances in inferential statistics. Such an approach provides more robust estimates.

This aggregation procedure in effect weights firms by their longevity of representation in the directories. This is justified upon two grounds. First, the longer a firm has been operating the more likely it is to be a role model in the industry. Longevity does confer some credibility. Second, investments are not made one year and pulled out the next. A weighting of the firms gives some consideration to the carry-over of investment across time. Not to include all occurrences of a firm seriously biases the results toward firms of more recent origin and disregards investment preferences maintained over time

To provide estimates of the city versus investment preference variables, matrices are analyzed by three way full effects median polishing (Cook 1985; Tukey 1977). Median polish is less complex than other contingency table techniques such as log-linear analysis or information statistics based approaches, and still provides estimates of row, column, and layer effects. The full effects median polish procedure fits an additive effects model of the following form to the matrices of investment preferences of the fifteen most active venture capital centers:

$$Y_{ijk} = t + r_i + c_j + l_k + r_i{}^*c_j + r_i{}^*l_k + c_j{}^*l_k + z_{ijk} \qquad (1)$$

where

> Y_{ijk} is data array element in row i, column j, and layer k
> t is a typical value
> r_i is a row effect of row i
> c_j is a column effect of column j
> l_k is a layer effect of layer k
> z_{ijk} is the residual effect of element ijk

The procedure begins by finding the median of each column in the data matrix and subtracting it from all elements in the column. This operation 'sweeps' a contribution from the column into the fit. This produces a row of column medians and a new table from which a partial effect has been removed. This process is repeated for all rows, including the newly created one of the partial column effects. The procedure is done again using the layers that comprise both the column and row partial effects.

Two-dimensional cross sections of the data matrix are treated in a similar fashion, generating median estimates of the interaction effects of the rows, columns, and layers. This sweeping of the data continues in an iterative fashion until the change in the sum of the magnitudes of the residuals reaches a specified amount or the estimates converge. In the model used in this chapter convergence was achieved. This procedure results in estimates of medians for the main effects of the three variables and the medians of all the interaction effects. The algorithm for the solution is described more fully by Cook (1985).

The values for the row, column, and layer effects measure the relative importance of the row or column or layer once the effects of other terms have been removed. Similarly, the interaction effects measure the importance of interplay between two variables with the effect of all other terms removed. Therefore, results may sometimes be counterintuitive if examined in isolation from one another. This is because intuition is based on the total expected result and not on a recognition of the individual effects. As equation (1) states, the value of a cell within a contingency table is the additive effect of the overall median, the row, column, and layer medians, and the interaction medians.

It should be clear that the median polish is like both a three way analysis of variance (ANOVA) and the additive form of the log-linear model. The primary difference is that the three way ANOVA uses the row, column, and layer means to find a solution. The median is a preferable measure of central tendency because of its insensitivity to a few extreme values (Tukey 1977).

Such insensitivity is particularly useful and desirable for non-normally distributed data, such as the data analyzed here. Like other contingency table methods, there are no significance measures for individual terms.

Estimated effects

Matrix 1 in the appendix presents the median polish parameter estimates for city effects for the analyses of the regional, funding, and industry data. The city effects measure the spatial variation in the expressed preferences of firms by city. The variation between city effects is a measure of spatial nonhomogeneity of the venture capital market. The city effects are small compared with other parameters of the model. This suggests little variation between cities when all other effects have been removed. The larger the parameter value the more specific are the preferences by firms located in that city.

Other things being equal, Washington, DC, firms with a value of 11 for the regional model and 8.5 for the industry model reveal more definite investment preferences. The overall regional median of 0.0 shows that strong preferences are the rule for all firms in all cities for regions of investment.

This is because for the median to be 0.0 many of the cells of the regional data matrix must also be 0.0. Large numbers of zeros can only occur if many categories are not preferred. The larger overall medians for the funding and industry models coupled with the moderate city effects show a more even spread of preference across the funding and industry choices.

The differences between the quasi-public and private firms are summarized in matrix 2. Private firms are slightly less parochial in their choice of regions (value −0.5), substantially less particular in choice of funding stage (value −10.0), and somewhat less particular in the choice of industry than their quasi-public counterparts. Private firms are more wide ranging in their investment preferences than are government sponsored firms.

The interaction effects between city location of firms and the type of firm are listed in matrix 3. The values, as in the case of the straight city effects, are moderate except for Atlanta in the funding model and Minneapolis in the industry model. In the Atlanta case private firms show less definite choices compared with their quasi-public counterparts. Minneapolis firms show a reversed situation in industry choice.

The most interesting portion of the results from a geographic perspective is matrix 4 in the appendix. The large positive parameter values for firms with their own census region (marked in bold) and adjacent census regions show a strong parochial nature to venture capital investment. Only Atlanta and Washington, DC, do not have as their highest effects those associated with their home region. In both cases, however, adjacent regions are the preferred choice. New York appears to be the least affected center by this distance decay effect. While New York City firms preferred their home region of the Middle Atlantic, the effect is much weaker than in other centers. The effect values are more even across the ten regions of choice.

The interaction between city location of the venture capital firms and the stage of preferred funding is displayed in matrix 5. The table shows that San Francisco based firms have the highest preference for seed, start-up, and first stage opportunities, while Miami has the lowest for seed and Philadelphia has the lowest for start-ups and stage one. Cleveland firms are interested in start-up situations and first stage fundings. Miami firms prefer fourth stage funding (taking a firm public) while Houston and Philadelphia firms are most interested in acquisition and buyout opportunities. San Francisco appears to be an incubating center while the eastern cities are more interested in more mature firms. New York, the dominant capital center occupies a neutral position with regard to the effects. This is not inconsistent with the conclusion of Florida and Kenney (1988c) that New York serves as a financial complex distributing funds to other centers.

Industry and city interaction results are exhibited in matrix 6 of the appendix. The 'high-tech' computer and medical industries are preferred by firms in Boston, Denver, and San Francisco, while manufacturing is the choice in Denver and Detroit. Not surprisingly, natural resources are the choice of Houston and Dallas firms. The firms of the southern cities of Atlanta and Miami specialize in real estate, while Denver and Minneapolis firms shy away from such investments.

Matrix 7 details the main effects values for the regional variable and its interaction with the firm type variable. The most notable regional effect is the large value (21.5) for the category 'all of the United States'. This shows that it is the most popular target for venture capital firms. The interaction values are small with again the exception of 'all of the United States'. Private firms are more likely to have a national orientation than quasi-public firms.

Matrix 8 provides the parameter estimates for the funding variable's main effects and its interaction with firm type. Seed capital is the least likely choice (value −24.0) followed by mezzanine (value −21.5) and fourth stage (value −12) fundings. The most popular funding stages are second stage (working capital) with a value of 21.5 and acquisition/buyout financing with 8.5.

The estimates of the interaction effects between firm type and funding stage show that private firms are more likely to prefer seed and start-up situations. This is a reflection of the greater risk taking ability of private firms because of their larger capital pools (Table 2.1). Quasi-public firms, on the other hand, need a debt-like structure to pay off their leveraged funds, making them more risk averse.

The final matrix (matrix 9) shows the industry preference parameters and the interaction effects between industry and firm type. Manufacturing is the most preferred sector (value 33.5) belying the popular conception that venture capital is all 'high-tech' investment. Computer and medical investments are the next most preferred sectors. Real estate (value −15.5) and retailing (value −7.5) are the most unpopular investment sectors.

Private firms prefer the 'high-tech' computer and medical sectors, while the government sponsored firms prefer the less risky and mundane manufacturing, real estate, retail, and service sectors.

CONCLUSIONS

In this chapter interurban variations in venture capital investment characteristics, for the fifteen most active venture capital centers have been described. A three way full effects median polish of regional, industry, and funding preferences gave the following results.

(1) Most centers' firms display a high degree of regional parochialism in their investment preference.
(2) San Francisco firms and to a lesser degree Boston firms, specialize in seed and start-up capital. Most centers specialize in later stage financing.
(3) Miami and Atlanta firms were most likely to prefer investment in the real estate sector.
(4) San Francisco, Boston, Denver, and Minneapolis firms specialize in computer and medical related ventures.
(5) Private venture capital firms are less risk averse and are more likely to prefer high-technology investments.

(6) Diffusion of venture capital firms has occurred since 1970 but not in a systematic way. Public firms diffused much more widely than did their private counterparts. The existence of government funding tied to geographic regions is the likely explanation.

These results support the model of spatial development presented earlier. Geographic space helps in the creation of market niches for firms. Space impedes venture capitalists' access to perfect information regarding investment opportunities outside its home region, but it also confers protection from competitors. In attempting to control for this uncertainty, and manage their risk factors, venture capitalists place spatial constraints on their investment activity. Within these spatial bounds, access to information is increased by specializing in the funding of certain industries or stages of the funding cycle.

The implications for small firm development are clear. Since access to capital is a major problem facing small firms, differential spatial availability of that capital may lead to spatial variations in success and growth of small firms. While entrepreneurial talent may exist everywhere, it cannot make an economic contribution if the enabling mechanism of capital is not available. In any case, those entrepreneurs with the greatest desire to succeed may be drawn to those cities with a financial community willing to undertake the risk of venture capital. If this is the case, economic growth and job creation might concentrate in these cities.

Local economic development is therefore dependent upon a recognition that venture capital and its attendant managerial advice and help is a major component in small firm growth. While the organized venture capital industry is not the only or even major form of small firm financing, it shows the attitudes regarding, and the availability of, funds for small business. It is also clear that capital of this type is not equally available everywhere.

NOTE

This chapter is a revision of 'Patterns of Preference for Venture Capital Investment in the United States 1970–1985', *Environment and Planning C*, vol. 7, 205–22.

Map Portfolio

The following pages of Maps 2.1–2.16 show the spatial spread and growth of both quasi-public government sponsored firms and privately held venture capital firms for the period 1970–1988.

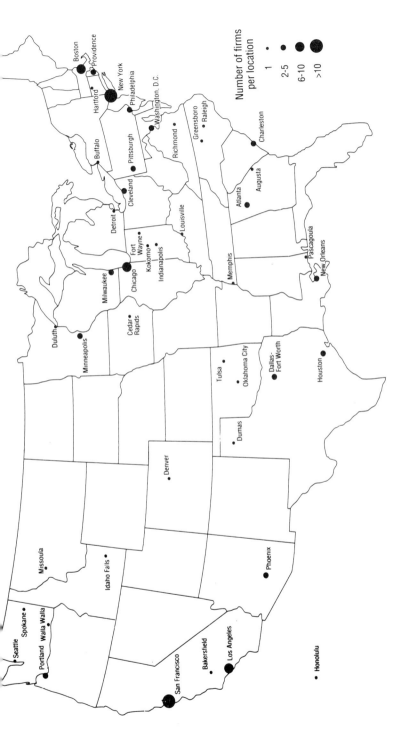

Map 2.1 Locations of SBIC and MESBIC firms, 1970

Number of firms
per location

· 1
• 2-5
● 6-10
⬤ >10

Seattle
Spokane
Portland Walla Walla
Missoula
Idaho Falls
San Francisco
Bakersfield
Los Angeles
Phoenix
Denver
Honolulu
Dumas
Tulsa
Oklahoma City
Dallas-Fort Worth
Houston
Duluth
Minneapolis
Cedar Rapids
Milwaukee
Chicago
Fort Wayne
Kokomo
Indianapolis
Detroit
Cleveland
Louisville
Memphis
Pascagoula
New Orleans
Atlanta
Augusta
Charleston
Richmond
Greensboro
Raleigh
Washington. D. C.
Pittsburgh
Buffalo
Hartford
New York
Philadelphia
Boston
Providence

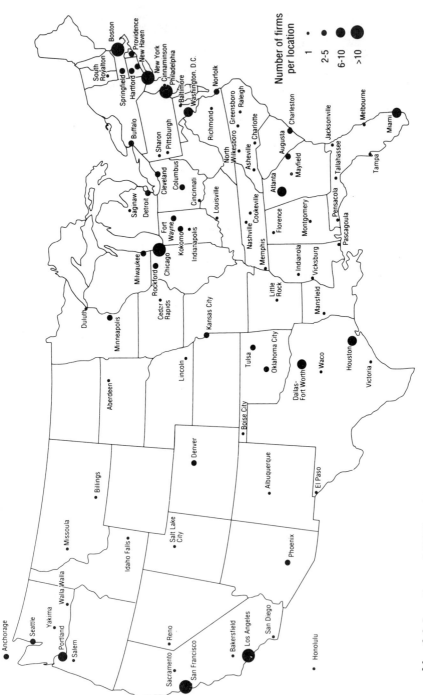

Map 2.2 Locations of SBIC and MESBIC firms, 1972

Number of firms
per location

·   1

●   2-5

⬤   6-10

⬤   >10

Map 2.3 Locations of SBIC and MESBIC firms, 1974

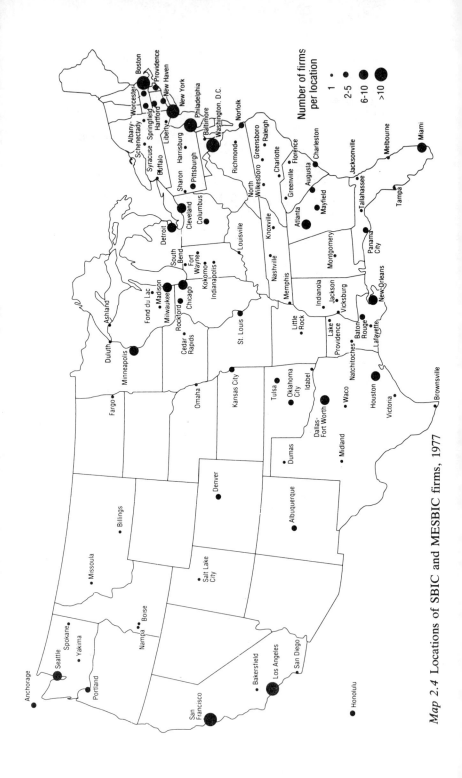

Map 2.4 Locations of SBIC and MESBIC firms, 1977

Number of firms
per location

· 1
● 2-5
● 6-10
● >10

Anchorage

Seattle
Spokane
Yakima
Portland
Nampa Boise
Missoula
Billings
Salt Lake City
San Francisco
Bakersfield
Los Angeles
San Diego
Honolulu

Denver
Albuquerque
Fargo
Minneapolis
Duluth
Ashland
Fond du Lac
Madison
Milwaukee
Cedar Rapids
Rockford
Chicago
South Bend
Fort Wayne
Kokomo
Indianapolis
Omaha
Kansas City
St. Louis
Tulsa
Oklahoma City
Idabel
Dumas
Dallas-Fort Worth
Midland
Waco
Victoria
Brownsville
Houston
Natchitoches
Lafayette
Baton Rouge
Lake Providence
New Orleans
Little Rock
Vicksburg
Jackson
Indianola
Memphis
Nashville
Montgomery
Louisville
Knoxville
Detroit
Cleveland
Columbus
Pittsburgh
Sharon
Buffalo
Harrisburg
Syracuse
Albany-Schenectady
Springfield
Hartford
Worcester
Boston
Providence
New Haven
New York
Liberty
Philadelphia
Baltimore
Washington, D.C.
Norfolk
Richmond
Greensboro
Raleigh
North Wilkesboro
Charlotte
Greenville
Florence
Charleston
Augusta
Atlanta
Mayfield
Jacksonville
Melbourne
Miami
Tallahassee
Tampa
Panama City
Panama City

Map 2.5 Locations of SBIC and MESBIC firms, 1981

Number of firms
per location

·   1

●   2-5

●   6-10

●   >10

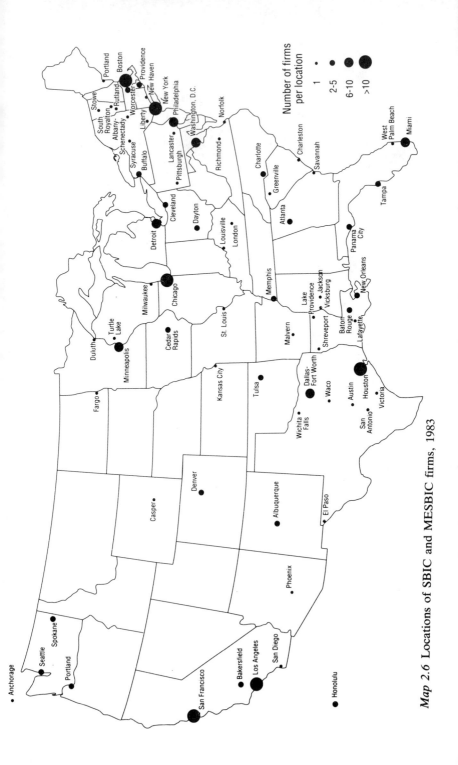

Map 2.6 Locations of SBIC and MESBIC firms, 1983

Number of firms
per location

· 1
● 2-5
● 6-10
⬤ >10

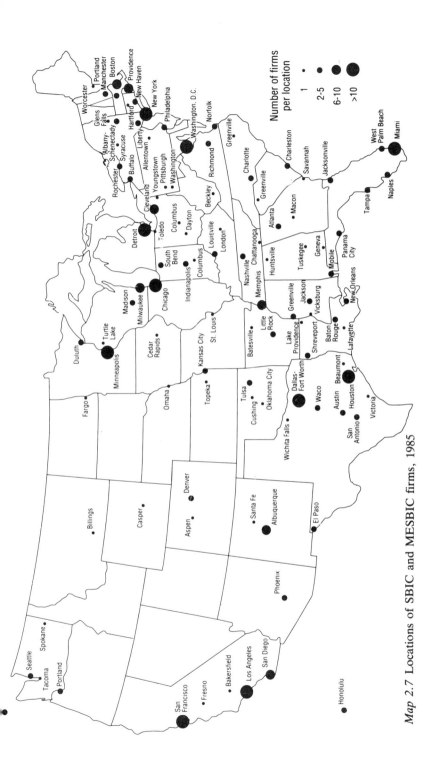

Number of firms per location

- · 1
- • 2-5
- ● 6-10
- ⬤ >10

Map 2.7 Locations of SBIC and MESBIC firms, 1985

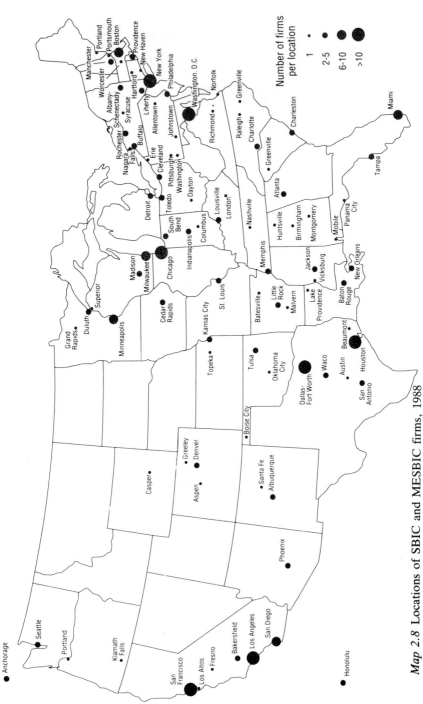

Number of firms per location

- · 1
- • 2-5
- ● 6-10
- ⬤ >10

Map 2.8 Locations of SBIC and MESBIC firms, 1988

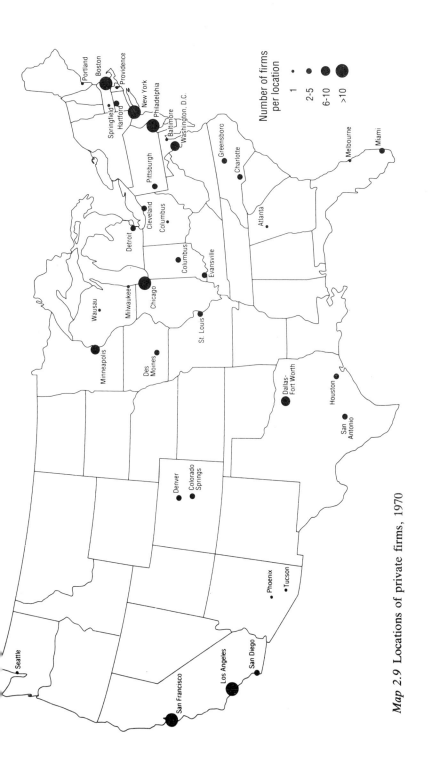

Number of firms
per location

· 1
● 2-5
● 6-10
● >10

Portland
Boston
Providence
New York
Springfield
Hartford
Philadelphia
Baltimore
Washington, D.C.
Pittsburgh
Greensboro
Charlotte
Melbourne
Miami
Cleveland
Columbus
Detroit
Columbus
Evansville
Atlanta
Wausau
Milwaukee
Chicago
Minneapolis
Des Moines
St. Louis
Dallas-Fort Worth
Houston
San Antonio
Denver
Colorado Springs
Phoenix
Tucson
Seattle
San Francisco
Los Angeles
San Diego

Map 2.9 Locations of private firms, 1970

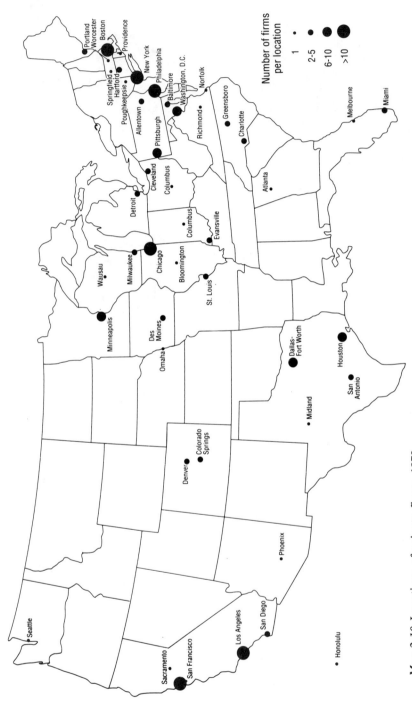

Number of firms
per location

1   2-5   6-10   >10

Portland
Worcester
Boston
Providence

Springfield
Hartford
Poughkeepsie
Allentown
Pittsburgh

New York
Philadelphia
Baltimore
Washington, D.C.
Norfolk
Richmond
Greensboro
Charlotte

Melbourne   Miami

Cleveland
Columbus
Detroit

Columbus
Evansville

Atlanta

Wausau
Milwaukee   Chicago
Bloomington
St. Louis

Minneapolis
Des Moines
Omaha

Dallas-
Fort Worth
Houston
San Antonio

Midland

Denver   Colorado
Springs

Phoenix

Seattle

Sacramento   San Francisco
Los Angeles   San Diego

Honolulu

Map 2.10 Locations of private firms, 1972

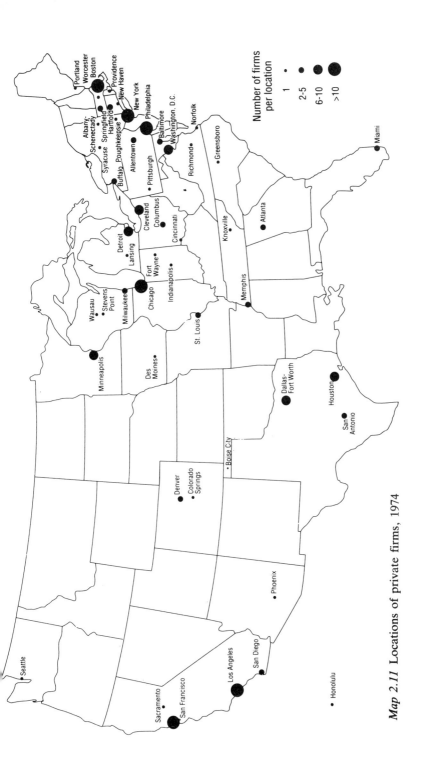

Map 2.11 Locations of private firms, 1974

Number of firms
per location

·   1
●   2-5
●   6-10
●   >10

Portland
Worcester
Boston
Providence
New Haven
New York
Philadelphia
Baltimore
Washington, D.C.
Norfolk
Albany
Schenectady
Springfield
Hartford
Poughkeepsie
Syracuse
Buffalo
Allentown
Pittsburgh
Richmond
Greensboro
Miami

Cleveland
Columbus
Cincinnati
Knoxville
Atlanta

Detroit
Lansing
Fort Wayne
Indianapolis
Memphis

Wausau
Stevens Point
Milwaukee
Chicago
St. Louis

Minneapolis
Des Moines
Dallas-Fort Worth
Houston
San Antonio

Boise City

Denver
Colorado Springs

Phoenix

Seattle

Sacramento
San Francisco
Los Angeles
San Diego

Honolulu

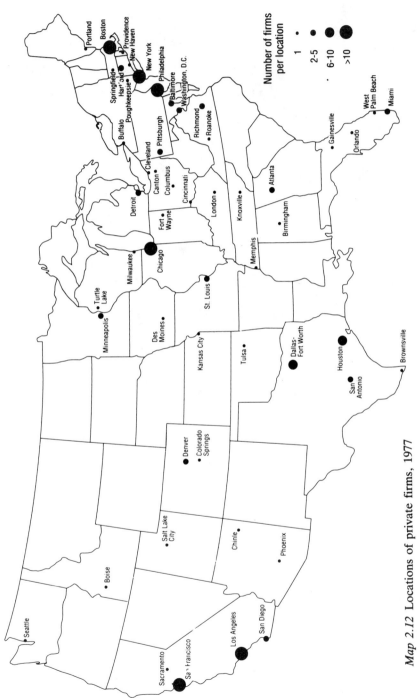

Number of firms
per location

· 1
• 2-5
● 6-10
● >10

Portland
Boston
Providence
New Haven
Springfield
Har'ord
Poughkeepsie
New York
Philadelphia
Baltimore
Washington, D.C.
Buffalo
Richmond
Roanoke
Pittsburgh
Cleveland
Canton
Columbus
Cincinnati
Detroit
Fort Wayne
London
Knoxville
Atlanta
Gainesville
Orlando
West Palm Beach
Miami
Milwaukee
Chicago
Birmingham
Turtle Lake
Minneapolis
Des Moines
Kansas City
St. Louis
Memphis
Tulsa
Dallas-Fort Worth
Houston
Brownsville
San Antonio
Denver
Colorado Springs
Salt Lake City
Chi≡le
Phoenix
Boise
Seattle
Sacramento
San Francisco
Los Angeles
San Diego

Map 2.12 Locations of private firms, 1977

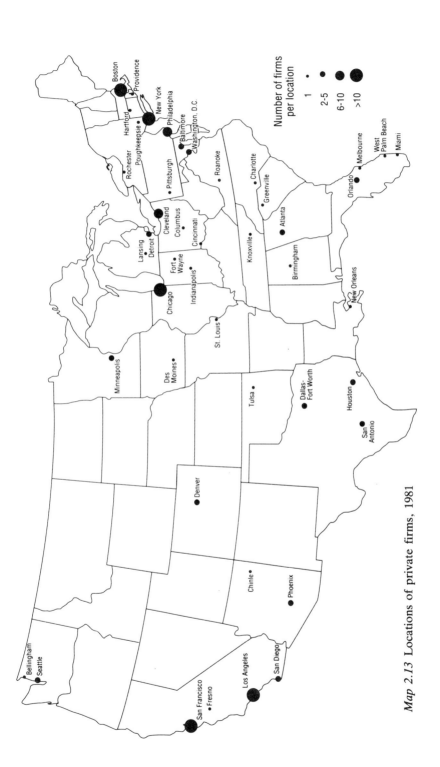

Map 2.13 Locations of private firms, 1981

Number of firms
per location

·   1
•   2-5
●   6-10
⬤   >10

Bellingham
Seattle
San Francisco
Fresno
Los Angeles
San Diego
Chinle
Phoenix
Denver
Minneapolis
Des
Moines
Tulsa
Dallas-
Fort Worth
Houston
San
Antonio
St. Louis
Chicago
Indianapolis
Fort
Wayne
Lansing
Detroit
Cleveland
Columbus
Cincinnati
New Orleans
Birmingham
Knoxville
Atlanta
Greenville
Charlotte
Roanoke
Pittsburgh
Rochester
Poughkeepsie
Hartford
Boston
Providence
New York
Philadelphia
Baltimore
Washington, D.C.
Orlando
Melbourne
West
Palm Beach
Miami

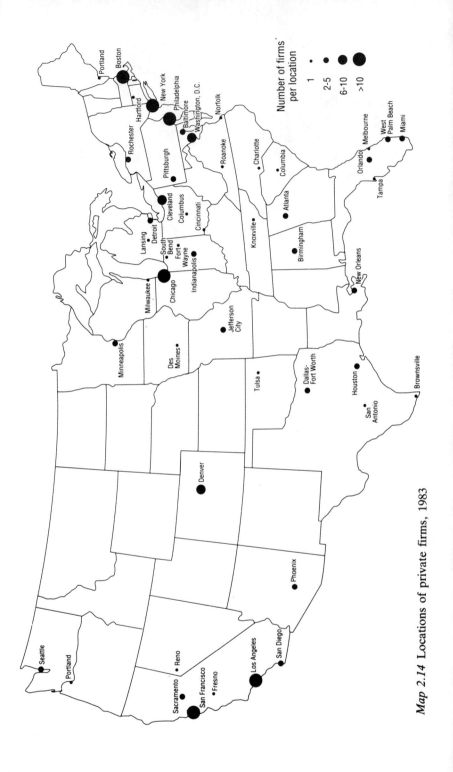

Map 2.14 Locations of private firms, 1983

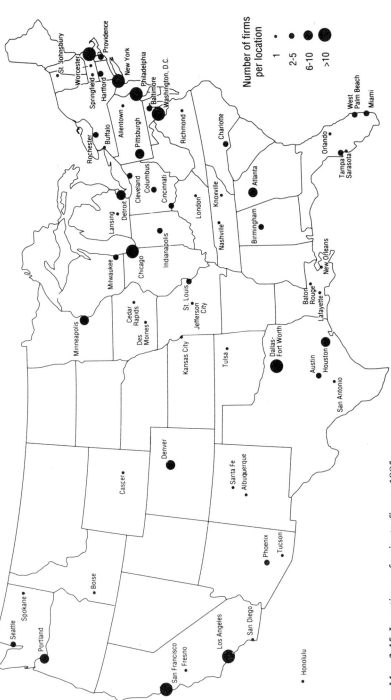

Map 2.15 Locations of private firms, 1985

Number of firms
per location

·   1
●   2-5
⬤   6-10
⬤   >10

St. Johnsbury
Worcester
Springfield
Hartford
Providence
New York
Philadelphia
Washington, D.C.
Baltimore
Allentown
Pittsburgh
Rochester
Buffalo
Richmond
Charlotte
Cleveland
Columbus
Cincinnati
Detroit
Lansing
London
Knoxville
Nashville
Atlanta
Birmingham
Milwaukee
Chicago
Indianapolis
Minneapolis
Cedar Rapids
Des Moines
St. Louis
Jefferson City
Kansas City
Tulsa
Baton Rouge
Lafayette
New Orleans
Dallas-Fort Worth
Austin
Houston
San Antonio
Denver
Casper
Santa Fe
Albuquerque
Phoenix
Tucson
Boise
Seattle
Spokane
Portland
San Francisco
Fresno
Los Angeles
San Diego
Honolulu
Orlando
Tampa
Sarasota
West Palm Beach
Miami

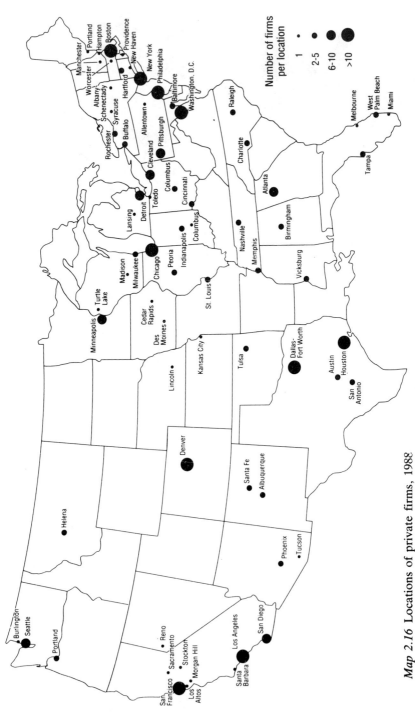

Legend:

Number of firms per location

· 1
● 2-5
● 6-10
● >10

Map 2.16 Locations of private firms, 1988

APPENDIX: MODEL PARAMETERS

Overall medians: region, 0.0; funding 35.5; industry 29.0

Matrix 1
City Effects

	Regional	Funding	Industry
Atlanta	−1.5	−4.0	−5.0
Boston	−1.5	−3.5	−4.0
Chicago	−1.0	−1.5	−3.5
Cleveland	−0.5	−1.0	−3.0
Dallas	−0.5	−1.0	−3.0
Denver	0.0	−0.5	−2.0
Detroit	0.0	−0.5	−1.5
Houston	0.0	0.0	0.0
Los Angeles	0.0	0.0	1.0
Miami	0.5	0.0	1.0
Minneapolis	0.5	0.0	2.5
New York	3.0	1.0	4.0
Philadelphia	4.0	2.0	4.5
San Francisco	4.5	3.0	5.5
Washington, DC	11.0	4.0	8.5

Matrix 2
Firm type effects

	Regional	Funding	Industry
Private (P)	−0.5	−10.0	−3.5
Government (G)	0.0	10.0	4.0

Matrix 3
City and firm type

	Regional		Funding		Industry	
	P	G	P	G	P	G
Atlanta	0.0	0.0	15.0	−15.0	1.0	−1.5
Boston	0.0	0.0	4.0	−4.0	0.5	−0.5
Chicago	−0.5	0.5	−0.5	0.5	−4.5	4.5
Cleveland	−2.0	2.0	−2.0	2.0	3.5	−4.0
Dallas	2.0	−2.0	−0.5	0.5	0.5	0.0
Denver	0.0	0.0	−1.0	1.0	−0.5	1.0
Detroit	0.0	0.0	−4.0	4.0	1.0	−1.0
Houston	0.0	0.0	1.5	−1.5	−3.0	2.5
Los Angeles	0.0	0.0	0.0	0.0	−1.5	1.0
Miami	4.0	−4.5	1.5	−1.5	5.0	−5.0
Minneapolis	−1.0	1.5	−3.0	3.0	−10.0	10.0
New York	−0.5	0.5	0.5	−0.5	0.0	−0.5
Philadelphia	−1.0	1.0	0.0	0.0	−2.0	2.0
San Francisco	0.0	0.0	2.5	−2.5	−1.5	1.0
Washington, DC	−2.5	3.0	−3.0	3.0	0.5	0.0

Matrix 4
City and census regions

	NE	MA	WNC	MTN	PAC	WSC	ESC	SA	ENC	US
Atlanta	8.0	49.0	**47.5**	0.0	-10.5	8.0	49.0	**47.5**	0.0	-10.5
Boston	0.5	-0.5	-0.5	-1.0	8.0	0.5	-0.5	-0.5	-1.0	8.0
Chicago	0.0	-1.0	-1.0	**25.0**	14.0	0.0	-1.0	-1.0	**25.0**	14.0
Cleveland	-4.5	-3.0	-4.5	**21.0**	13.5	-4.5	-3.0	-4.5	**21.0**	13.5
Dallas	**35.0**	0.0	0.5	0.0	-5.0	**35.0**	0.0	0.5	0.0	-5.0
Denver	6.5	-0.5	-0.5	1.5	-6.0	6.5	-0.5	-0.5	1.5	6.0
Detroit	0.0	0.0	-1.0	**37.5**	-1.5	0.0	0.0	-1.0	**37.5**	-1.5
Houston	**41.5**	8.5	9.5	-2.0	-3.0	**41.5**	8.5	9.5	-2.0	-3.0
Los Angeles	4.0	0.0	0.0	1.5	1.0	4.0	0.0	0.0	-1.5	1.0
Miami	0.0	29.0	**32.5**	1.0	-1.0	0.0	29.0	**32.5**	1.0	-1.0
Minneapolis	0.0	-1.0	-1.5	26.0	0.0	0.0	-1.0	-1.5	26.0	0.0
New York	-0.5	0.0	0.0	-2.5	13.5	-0.5	0.0	0.0	-2.5	13.5
Philadelphia	-0.5	1.5	1.5	-1.0	-5.0	-0.5	1.5	1.5	-1.0	-5.0
San Francisco	2.0	-1.5	-1.5	-2.0	0.5	2.0	-1.5	-1.5	-2.0	0.5
Washington, DC	-3.0	6.0	**15.5**	-2.0	2.0	-3.0	6.0	**15.5**	-2.0	2.0

Bold type, investment in the census region of the city; NE, New England; MA, Middle Atlantic;; WNC, West North Central; MTN, Mountain; PAC, Pacific; WSC, West South Central; ESC, East South Central; SA, South Atlantic; ENC, East North Central; US, all of the United States.

Matrix 5
City and funding stages

	Seed	Start-up	1st	2nd	Mezzanine	4th	Buyout
Atlanta	0.0	−5.5	−4.5	4.5	5.5	4.5	4.0
Boston	0.5	5.0	2.5	−1.0	−1.5	0.5	−0.5
Chicago	−2.5	−3.5	3.5	1.0	0.5	0.0	5.0
Cleveland	−1.0	10.0	8.0	3.0	−2.5	−2.5	4.5
Dallas	4.5	−5.5	−4.5	−7.5	3.5	3.0	0.0
Denver	2.0	1.0	−1.5	0.0	−0.5	−1.0	1.0
Detroit	3.0	5.0	6.5	−6.5	−0.5	−1.0	−6.0
Houston	−2.0	−9.0	−3.0	−1.5	3.0	2.5	9.0
Los Angeles	1.0	0.0	5.5	−2.0	0.0	−1.0	−4.0
Miami	−10.0	4.5	4.0	8.0	−1.5	12.0	−3.5
Minneapolis	−4.0	−4.0	0.0	2.0	2.0	−2.0	−5.5
New York	0.0	0.0	−7.5	−3.0	−1.0	0.5	1.5
Philadelphia	−2.0	−10.0	−9.0	3.0	3.5	−0.5	9.5
San Francisco	11.0	18.0	11.5	0.0	−1.5	−0.5	−5.0
Washington, DC	−4.0	−4.0	2.5	−2.5	0.5	1.5	0.0

Matrix 6
City by industry effects

	Comp	Dist	Mfg	Med	NR	RE	Retail	Serv
Atlanta	−0.5	3.0	−5.0	−9.5	−0.5	18.0	4.0	2.5
Boston	3.5	−2.0	−1.5	4.5	2.0	−3.5	−2.5	4.0
Chicago	−1.0	2.0	2.0	−1.0	−2.0	−5.0	1.0	6.5
Cleveland	−2.0	−1.0	1.0	5.5	6.0	0.0	−3.5	0.5
Dallas	−1.0	4.0	−4.0	−3.5	4.5	4.5	−1.5	−4.5
Denver	14.0	3.5	17.0	7.0	0.0	−11.5	−10.5	−3.0
Detroit	0.0	−1.0	11.5	5.5	−2.0	−4.0	0.0	−1.5
Houston	−7.0	0.0	−3.0	−1.0	19.5	2.0	5.5	−1.0
Los Angeles	0.5	2.0	3.0	0.0	−4.5	−2.5	1.0	−1.0
Miami	2.5	−1.5	0.0	0.0	−12.5	8.5	5.0	5.5
Minneapolis	2.5	−4.0	2.0	4.5	−7.5	−12.0	2.5	3.0
New York	−2.5	0.0	−1.0	−5.5	0.0	3.5	1.0	5.0
Philadelphia	−1.0	7.5	0.0	1.5	0.5	0.5	−4.5	−3.0
San Francisco	20.5	−0.5	5.0	15.0	1.0	−4.5	−6.5	−4.0
Washington, DC	5.0	−1.0	−1.0	−11.0	−0.5	1.5	−1.5	0.0

Note: Comp, computer; Dist, distribution; Mfg, manufacturing; Med, medical; NR, natural resources; RE, real estate; Retail, retailing; Serv, services.

Matrix 7

Region	Main Effects	Firm type Effects P	G
New England	0.0	−0.5	0.5
Middle Atlantic	0.0	−0.5	0.5
West North Central	−1.0	0.5	−0.5
Mountain	0.0	0.0	0.0
Pacific	−1.5	0.0	0.0
West South Central	−2.0	0.5	−1.0
East South Central	−1.0	−0.5	0.5
South Atlantic	−1.0	0.0	0.0
East North Central	0.5	0.0	0.0
All of USA	21.5	7.5	−7.5

Note: P, private; G, government sponsored.

Matrix 8

Funding	Main Effects	Firm type Effects P	G
Seed	−24.0	0.0	0.0
Startup	0.5	8.5	−8.5
First Stage	3.0	4.5	−4.5
Second Stage	21.5	−1.5	1.5
Mezzanine	−22.5	−3.0	3.0
Fourth	−12.0	−4.5	4.5
Acquisition/Buyout	8.5	0.5	−0.5

Note: P, private; G, government sponsored.

Matrix 9

Industry	Main Effects	Firm type Effects P	G
Computer	6.5	6.0	−6.0
Distribution	−0.5	1.0	−1.0
Manufacturing	33.5	−1.0	0.5
Medical	15.5	4.0	−4.0
Natural Resources	−3.0	3.0	−2.5
Real Estate	−15.5	−2.5	3.0
Retail	−7.5	−2.5	2.5
Services	1.5	−1.0	1.0

Note: P, private; G, government sponsored.

3 Venturing on the 'Third Coast': recipient firms in the Central States

Chris Thompson

To avoid confusion in this chapter, the capitalized form of 'Fund' and 'Funds' will be used when referring to venture capital institutions, while the lower case form of 'funds' will be used when referring to dollar amounts. Venture capital recipient firms will be abbreviated to VCRFs.

Venture capital has attracted much interest in recent years because of the rapidly expanding pool of venture dollars, the spectacularly high returns on some venture investments, and venture capital's potential for encouraging new industrial development (JEC 1982, 1984; Timmons *et al.* 1984; Hisrich 1986; OECD 1986; Fried and Hisrich 1988; Henderson 1989a; Thompson 1989a). However, most previous academic studies have focused on, and developed theoretical models from, venturing phenomena observed in the traditional hotbeds of such activity: Massachusetts and California. It is to these geographical areas, as much as to venture capital's distinctive financial attributes, that we owe our stereotypical image of venture capital as being primarily involved with the funding of new, small, high-technology, start-up companies (Hoban 1981; Timmons *et al.* 1983; Henderson 1989b), which may in turn be the source of 'a disproportionately large share of employment growth' (Timmons *et al.* 1983: 317; Timmons and Bygrave 1986:162).

This 'Coastal' emphasis is understandable for several general reasons: the conspicuous success of the Silicon Valley (Franson 1979; Dolan 1983) and 'Massachusetts Miracle' (Lampe 1988) areas as the high-tech growth poles of the new so-called 'Bi-Coastal Economy' (JEC 1986); the recent academic interest in new flexible forms of industrial and urban agglomerations and 'technopoles' being spawned in these areas (Scott 1988, 1989); and the renewed debate about general regional divergence during the Reagan era

59

(Browne 1989; Thompson 1989b). The emphasis is also understandable with regard to early venture capital in particular, because of the high degree of spatial concentration of venture activities found there: for example, the legendary '3000 Sand Hill Rd' address was at one time home to as many as 23 venture capital Funds (Levine 1983), and fully 40 per cent of all venture financings in the United States in 1983 were believed to be for companies in Santa Clara County, California, alone (Hambrecht 1984; Hatras 1984; Rees 1986: 57).

The stereotypical image of venture capital as financing the next industrial revolution has been drawn out of this setting. It is an image which has been often invoked during, for example, the hearings and studies on venture capital for the congressional Joint Economic Committee (JEC 1984; Lungren, 1984), and during debates on capital gains taxation, pension funds, and Securities and Exchange Commission regulations (for example, Jepsen 1984: iii). It is also an image that some venture capitalists themselves are keen to portray: for example Norman Fast, the Managing Director of Venture Economics, asserts that the main reason why the economic impact of the venture capital industry is 'substantial' is that 'venture capital is focused selectively within the small business sector on those companies that are not going to remain small for very long'. As a consequence, he argues, the venture capitalist plays 'a critical and unique role in the commercialization of new technologies' and 'venture capital investment activity can serve as a leading indicator and driving force in the development of new emerging industries' (Fast 1982: 1).

However, in many areas of decision-making, imagery can be as important as substance, and may sometimes even cloud our chances of a deeper understanding of the phenomenon it purports to represent. Enough research and anecdotal evidence on venture capital exists to confirm that the stereotype is a possible outcome and one which has been the case in certain spectacular instances: the successes of Apple Computers, Federal Express, and Digital Equipment Corporation, for example, are well known. What is rarely questioned, though, is whether such examples are necessary outcomes to venture activity, whether the new activity that venture capital does generate is significant in aggregate compared with the total, and whether the individual professional venture capitalists, venture institutions, and pools of dollars under management, all which are well established at high absolute numbers on both Coasts, contain most of the story of venturing. These are the entities which have been traditionally monitored by academic researchers, but tying the paper financial assets of venture Funds solely to their central business district addresses probably makes only as much sense as, for example, allocating all Ford's sales to Detroit. It is only when venture dollars have actually been invested in tangible projects and when recipient firms become actors in their host systems that venture capital makes an impact on the economic landscape. Thus, there is merit to studying the characteristics of investees, and not just the already more thoroughly observed investors.

Most important of all, there is the question of the extent to which the abstract stereotype is context specific and, if it is, which features in the context condition venture possibilities, and how they do so. For example, one statistical study found, contrary to the predictions of the stereotype, that the 'number of accessible venture capital Funds' was not selected as a significant variable in a stepwise discriminant analysis aiming to explain the difference between high-tech and non-high tech counties, throughout the United States, in terms of their antecedent conditions (Thompson 1988a). Another study found that fewer than 5 per cent of 464 venture Funds accounted for nearly 25 per cent of all the investments in techno-logical ventures (Timmons and Bygrave 1986: 162). What difference would it make to the stereotype model (aside from changes in scale and levels of activity), therefore, if venture capital phenomena were to be observed in different geographical settings? Would it then be possible to understand something of the particular conditions which can cause different forms of venture activity and types of outcomes? Would it, in turn, be possible to arrive at a more 'realistic' picture of what venturing has to offer? It is the major starting assumption of this study that the time is now appropriate for closer systematic examination of venturing in other geographical areas, because to continue the Coastal emphasis would be to neglect several important factors to do with the changing economic landscape of the United States and with the recent evolution of venturing in particular.

First, while San Francisco, Boston, and New York are the places usually cited as the main centers of US venture capital, it is not often acknowledged that Chicago too has a nationally important presence: LaSalle Street is home to a dozen venture Funds, and if First National Plaza, Michigan Avenue, Wacker Drive, and Clark Street are also included, then roughly an eight block downtown area is home to thirty-one Funds (seven of them with over $100 million).

The 114 individual venture capitalists working in this cluster in 1989 manage a total of $2,528 million venture dollars (Morris and Isenstein 1989). At the city scale, Chicago even ranks ahead of San Francisco and Los Angeles in terms of the absolute number of individual professional venture capitalists present (Thompson, Chapter Five of this volume; Silver 1984).

Second, there has been some geographical diffusion of venturing away from the early coastal cores during the 1980s (Haslett 1984; JEC 1984). Minneapolis–St Paul, Dallas–Houston, and Cleveland–Columbus are also now important secondary centers. In fact, the list of the top ten Metropolitan Statistical Area (MSAs) for the number of working venture capitalists per million of their population in 1984 (Thompson, Chapter Five of this volume) includes six located in the Central states region: Minneapolis–St Paul (MN), Milwaukee–Racine (WI), Chicago–Gary–Lake (IL–IN), and Columbus (OH), are ranked fourth through seventh, respectively, while Denver–Boulder (CO) is ninth, and Houston–Galveston–Brazoria (TX) tenth.

In addition, the rapid growth in the size of the total venture capital pool after 1979, which contributed to the rise of these second order centers, is unlikely to have meant only spatial diffusion, filtering down the hierarchy, and passive increases in activity levels. There are indications that growth in supply has also been accompanied by qualitative changes in the venturing processes and preferences, and by the emergence of a new industry structure (Timmons and Bygrave 1986; *et al.* 1987). Detailed changes in processes and preferences include increased specialization and diversity of Fund objectives, activities, strategies, and resources; an escalation in the size of minimum investments; the initiation of foreign ventures (Marton 1986; *Fortune* 1987; Flanigan 1988); an increasing legal component, to go with the rising incidence of litigation and the creation of specific rights beyond traditional equity ownership; and, in mature Funds, an increasing preoccupation of venture capitalists' time with fire-fighting the problems in existing portfolio companies, 'romancing investors with "dog-and-pony shows"' to get new funds (Rundle 1989), and hunting for repurchase bargains in a devalued initial public offering market, rather than participating in new deals and building companies. Detailed changes to industry structure include the creation of 'megafunds' with over $100 million (and, more recently, with over $1 billion); the launching of new specialized seed and first stage Funds; and the development of 'feeder Funds' and a possible 'department store/ boutique' Fund dualism (Bygrave 1987: 140). All these changes could in time have implications for a drift of real venture activity away from that presumed by the stereotypical model, and also away from that observable during the 1967–82 period examined by Timmons and Bygrave (1986).

Third, not every region may be destined to enjoy (or suffer) the Califuture: different circumstances, heritages, and industrial structures may predispose different forms or levels of venturing activity in different places, each of which deserves to be understood in its own right. The interaction between diffused venture capital and the economic characteristics of 'interior' states may be the more 'normal' future scenario for mature venturing in the United States than the heady 'gold rush' atmosphere of early venturing in Boston and San Francisco (Janeway 1986: 440; Rind and Delong 1986).

There is a general feeling now among some venture capitalists that the high tide of rapid product innovation associated with the current long wave is subsiding, while biotechnology, as the heir apparent to the computer industry, is approaching its rapid product innovation and commercialization stage much more slowly than was originally hoped. As a result, profit opportunities have to be sought through improvements to product quality, reductions in costs, and the optimization of resources used to produce the product (Lardner 1986: 2). This subtle change in emphasis may then, in turn, transfer geographical advantage away from the high-technology research and development (R&D) seedbed areas like Boston and San Francisco and back to more traditional industrial areas. Interestingly, this could be happening at the same time as a silent but strong bounce back of basic manufacturing and agriculture in many Central states, which has been particularly noticeable since late 1986 when a fall in the dollar began to stimulate demand for durable goods. Meanwhile, modest industry-specific slowdowns are also occurring as a result of several factors such as defense cutbacks, the 'Wall Street recession', and declining yuppie consumer spending, all of which had been most frenzied on both coasts. As a result, the Federal Reserve's May 1989 'Tan Book' survey of business conditions around the country notes that 'economic expansion has been stronger lately in the South and Midwest than elsewhere in the country'. Some business forecasters are no longer commenting on the demise of the 'Rust Belt', but instead are referring to it as an area of 'unlimited opportunities' (Lardner 1986), while others even speculate about a possible 'Bi-Coastal Recession' (Yardeni 1989).

The heart of the heartland may thus yet have a more desirable long-term economic development situation than the more spectacular, but less stable, 'hot tech' Coasts with their increasing traffic congestion, sky-rocketing house prices (Saxenian 1985), white-collar lay-offs (*Time* 1984; ITT 1986), unsightly sprawling 'tilt-up' developments, exploitation of undocumented workers, and vulnerability of overly-specialized communities to the downturns resulting from rapid high-tech product shifts (Harrison 1982; Hogue 1983; Kuhn 1983; Burgan 1985; Thompson 1988b; *New York Times* 1989). With the recent highly publicized exodus from Los Angeles (*Wisconsin State Journal* 1989a), popular surveys of perceived 'ideal' living places and quality of life characteristics are beginning to generate desired landscapes which more closely resemble semi-rural 'circle city' areas like Dane County, Wisconsin, than they do exurban ones like San Jose, California, or urban ones like Los Angeles. Cyra McFadden's 'Marinspeak', Armistead Maupin's 'Tales of the City', and New York's 'Village Voice' may thus have had their day as signposts to breaking social trends. Instead, Garrison Keillor's 'Prairie Home Companion' and 'talking Minnesotan' are 'in', and the Midwest is the new chic (*Wisconsin State Journal* 1989b).

All these reasons suggest that non-Coastal venturing may present other situations and ultimately lead to models different from the stereotype. In this chapter we seek to remedy the previous imbalances and to extend existing knowledge and documentation of venturing geographically. We do this by tracking systematically the outcomes of venture investment in terms of the characteristics and locations of firms which have received venture dollars in the seventeen Central Region states – the USA's so-called 'Third Coast'.

Throughout this chapter, the term 'Central Region' refers to the seventeen member states of the US Central States Conference of Bankers Associations (CSCBA) (that is, Arkansas, Colorado, Illinois, Indiana, Iowa, Kansas, Kentucky, Michigan, Minnesota, Missouri, Nebraska, North Dakota, Ohio, Oklahoma, South Dakota, Wisconsin, and Texas). The recent addition of Texas to this group means that this Central region now extends from the nation's northern border to its southern border, allowing for a clear threefold division of the country when tabulating and contrasting results: thus, the term Eastern Region will be used throughout to refer to the twenty-two states (including Washington, DC) to the east of the Central Region, and the term 'Western region' will refer to the 12 states (including Alaska and Hawaii) to the west of the Central Region. The 'USA total' is thus fifty states plus Washington, DC. These regions are shown for reference in Map 3.1.

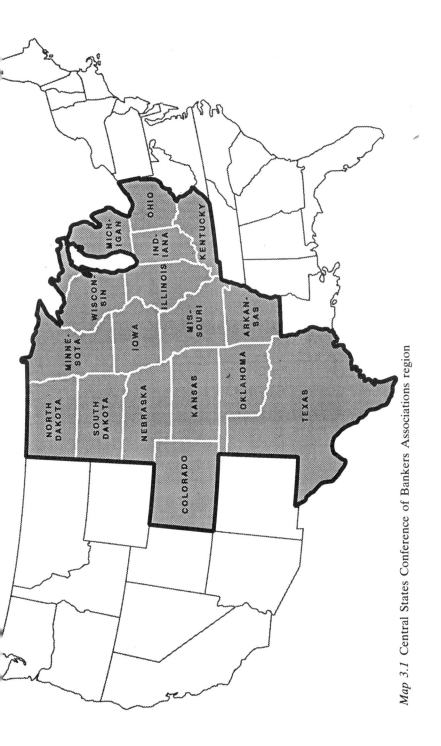

Map 3.1 Central States Conference of Bankers Associations region

This partitioning of the country differs slightly from the US Bureau of the Census divisions: although the Census 'West North Central' and 'East North Central' divisions are included in their entirety in the CSCBA Central Region, Louisiana of the 'West South Central' Census division is excluded and Colorado of the 'Mountain' Census division is included. Thus, data from Census publications will be reaggregated whenever comparisons are made.

PREVIOUS ANALYSES OF VENTURE CAPITAL RECIPIENT FIRMS

It is difficult to find measures and characteristics of VCRFs to use as benchmarks for regional or temporal comparisons with the sample obtained for this study because there have simply been very few systematic empirical studies of such firms to date. Most writers present detailed individual firm case studies, or are content with the 'fast growth/high yield' generalization. Those empirical studies which do exist vary considerably in goals, in format, and in degree of statistical detail. They have tended to emphasize portfolio composition and investment performance rather than the character-istics and later developmental tracks of the recipient firms themselves (Fried and Hisrich 1988). For example, Hutt and Thomas (1985) have looked at the size and composition of individual venture Fund portfolios, while Brophy (1981) has examined the size and composition of the total industry portfolio. Bygrave and Timmons (1985) discuss the factors possibly influencing the aggregate portfolio, such as interest rates and stock market conditions.

Many general summary articles have provided data on investments at the sector or industry level. Fast's (1982: Figure 1) study of 150 leading Funds' 1981 activities shows that 25 per cent of investments were computer related, 20 per cent went to 'other electronics', 10 per cent to 'communications', and 10 per cent to 'health care'. Howse (1988: 39) notes that, of 1986 investment activity, 19 per cent of all venture dollars went to 'computer hardware and systems', 13 per cent to 'other electronics', 12 per cent were 'medical/health care related', and 11 per cent went to 'telephone and data communica-tions'. These kinds of studies supply interesting general information about levels and trends, but the subjective nature of their industrial categories, which are not tied to the Standard Industrial Classification (SIC) system, means that precise statistical analyses and hard conclusions are difficult to make with their data. This can be overcome partially by looking at the individual firm level. Tyebjee and Bruno (1984: 1051), for example, studied ninety deals with forty-one venture capitalists. They found the 'modal venture represented . . . was a start-up in the electronics industry with a production capability in place and seeking \$1 million (median) in outside financing'. However, their sample was of California, Massachusetts, and Texas venture institutions only, and more recent speculation (Lueck 1987) has it that venture capitalists may be shifting their focus away from high technology.

Several studies have examined new ventures from the point of view of individual firm failure rates. Rubel (1972) found a loss rate of 15 per cent in 378 new venture investments. Huntsman and Hoban (1980) found a 17 per cent failure rate in the portfolios of three Funds. DeHudy *et al.* (1981) analyzed 218 investments made by five Funds and found a complete failure rate of 14.7 per cent, with 3.2 per cent of the investments providing 31 per cent of the total return. With regard to specifically high-technology ventures, Taylor (1969) found a 35 per cent failure rate across 279 venture-backed high-technology companies, and Roberts (1970) found a 20 per cent failure rate. These studies confirm that venture-backed companies do have higher rates of survival than businesses in the general economy, where the mortality rate for new firms is commonly quoted as being 80 per cent and 90 per cent (for example, Timmons and Bygrave 1986: 163). However, this differential is not surprising given that venture-backed firms constitute a survivor-sample from a highly selective initial proposal screening process.

Hoban (1981) was interested in whether a set of variables can be identified that can predict whether a given individual new firm will be successful. Using annualized rate of return on the investment realized by the venture capitalist as a dependent variable, along with twenty-four independent variables measuring characteristics of firm management, product, financing, and marketing at the time of venture investment, he made a content analysis of three venture capital Funds' files, focusing on fifty investments made before 1975. It is interesting that the characteristics of his sample at that time do correspond to the stereotypical model of venture capital investments in new small high-technology companies: over half the firms (26 out of 50) were 1 year old or younger at the time of venture investment; over 60 per cent (31 out of 50) received an initial investment of under \$200,000; and 86 per cent (43 out of 50) were classified as having a product which was either 'technical', 'highly technical', or 'extremely technical'. Using a univariate F ratio he found that rate of return was significantly related to the stage of development of the main product, but his stepwise regression could not identify a set of variables predicting success. He concludes that predictors of success are too complex or subjective, and that successful venture capitalism is not a 'science' but an 'art' where the expert's 'feelings' about what will or will not be successful remain important.

Macmillan *et al.* (1987) also used regression, along with factor analysis and clustering, to investigate venture success. They found two significant predictors: insulation from competition and demonstrated market acceptance of the product. They went on to produce a typology of ventures, with three broad classes of 'unsuccessful' ventures and four of 'successful' ones; what made the difference between the two types of classes, they argued, was a flaw in the venture team.

The largest empirical study of venture investments so far has been that carried out between 1982 and 1984 by a group of business researchers based at Babson College, Massachusetts (including Timmons, Pratt, Fast, Khoylian, and Bygrave), and sponsored by the National Science Foundation. The research questions concerned the differences between 'highly innovative' technological ventures (HITVs) and 'least-innovative' technological ventures (LITVs), together with the distinguishing characteristics of these firms and the Funds which invest in them, and the policy implications. Their method was to select at random from the *Venture Economics* database some 1,501 first-round portfolio investments made between 1967 and 1982 (grouped into 4-year periods). They then categorized the investments subjectively for 'degree of innovation', and 464 venture Funds for their 'degree of involvement'. Field interviews then focused on the dynamics of venture capitalist–entrepreneur working relationships. Results have been reported by Timmons *et al.* (1983), Bygrave, Timmons, and Fast (1984), Bygrave and Timmons (1985), Timmons and Bygrave (1986), and Bygrave (1987).

Their study found that investments associated with HITVs increased from a low of 18.8 per cent during the 1971–4 period, to 47.2 per cent during 1979–82. During the latter period there were, in absolute terms, six times as many HITV start-up investments compared with 1967–70, but HITV start-ups as a proportion of total investments declined from a high of 75 per cent during 1971–4 to 49.7 per cent during 1979–82. Expansion financings accounted for 6 per cent of HITV investments during 1967–70, but increased to 26.8

per cent by 1979–82. They also found that HITV investing is a specialized, management-intensive, but not capital-intensive, activity, requiring less capital than LITV investment: the 1979–82 average investment size for HITVs was 74 per cent of that for LITVs. Larger Funds were not significantly more or less involved with HITVs than were smaller Funds, although there was a core group of experienced Funds accounting for a disproportionately large share of HITV investing. These Funds are actively sought out by entrepreneurs because of their reputations for adding value. Their individual venture capitalists then become intensively involved with their ventures, not only in the particular sense of finding other members for the management team, providing credibility with suppliers and customers, and helping shape long-term strategy when management are under pressure of daily tasks, but also in the more general functions of 'catalyzing', 'nurturing', 'bird-dogging', and 'accelerating' development. The researchers also claim to have found definite 'geographical oases' wherein founders, technologists, and venture capitalists cluster: California, New York, and Massachusetts based Funds accounted for over three-quarters of HITV investing in their sample.

These studies emphasize Funds, portfolios, and returns as the units of observation, rather than the recipient firms. They are also characterized by reliance on samples because the in-depth nature of case studies precludes wider attention or limits the access to different sources of data. The studies are thus more useful for illustrating investment types, and for analyzing features of the venture process. They are less useful for producing systematic pictures of the status of VCRFs, or their distribution and characteristics in a given geographical area. Also, they do not go beyond the point of initial investment deals to look at the later evolution of the recipient firms and their interactions with, and impact on, their host regions.

Probably the earliest attempt to look at actual individual recipients, and to incorporate a geographic element more explicitly into the research design, was that by Kieschnick (1979), who was interested in the role of venture capital in firm start-up and urban development. He obtained information from *Dun's Marketing Indicators File* on initial sources of capital and debt-to-equity ratios for sixty-nine firms. These had an average age of under 2 years, and were located in Buffalo, Cincinatti, Atlanta, and Salt Lake City. Contrary to his initial expectations, he discovered a total absence of venture capital start-up investment in his sample of enterprises. On average, personal savings accounted for 81 per cent of initial firm capital, and in three-quarters of the sample, for all of it. He does not address the question of whether this was due to poor sampling, founder preferences, or genuine venture capital shortages.

Brophy (1982) was also interested in the geographically varying availability and terms of local financing, and the effects on the performance of new technology-based firms (NTBFs). He compared two samples of NTBFs which had been incorporated from 1965 to 1970: one was from the Ann Arbor–Detroit area (where there is no well-developed venture capital network), and the other was from the Boston metropolitan area (which has 'well-developed and outstanding access to venture financing', Brophy 1982: 167)). He found that financing was more available, and cheaper, in Boston than in Detroit, and that there is a significant relationship between the availability of capital support for asset acquisition and firm sales growth. He concludes that there are 'fundamental differences in the venture capital supply systems in the two areas' (Brophy 1982: 181).

Finally, only two studies so far, by the US General Accounting Office (US GAO 1982) and Green and McNaughton (1988), have looked at economic impacts to private venture investment in detail. The US GAO tracked development and sales of seventy-two companies which received $209 million of venture capital during the 1970s (US GAO 1982; Pratt 1988). By 1979, total sales from this group were $6 billion, and during the last 5 years of that decade this figure was growing by 33 per cent per annum. These firms were responsible for 130,000 jobs, over $100 million in corporate tax revenues, $350 million in employee tax revenues, and $900 million in export sales. Green and McNaughton (1988) looked at the economic benefits of venture investments in Canada. The sixty-three firms which responded to their mail survey had 16,646 employees in 1986, giving an average firm size of 264 employees. Just over half the jobs were in 'standardized' rather than 'high' technology sectors, though firms in the latter sector did record the highest rate of job creation. Venture capitalists provided almost one-third of the equity capital raised by all firms in the study: for new firms this figure was more than 70 per cent, while for more established firms it was only 20 per cent. The findings of Kieschnick (1979), Brophy (1982), and Green and McNaughton (1988) combine to suggest there may very well be significant geographical differences to venturing outcomes, and that the venture capitalist's theoretical target of potentially high growth/high yield firms is not, in practice, being satisfied by investing in stereotypical small high-technology firm start-ups.

Clearly, only a systematic empirical analysis of a larger number of recipient firms would provide the necessary evidence for this.

DATA SOURCES ON VENTURE CAPITAL RECIPIENT FIRMS

There are no official government data or published complete definitive lists of firms receiving venture capital financing in the United States. The best source from which to attempt to compile such information is the *Venture Capital Journal*, a monthly trade publication for venture capitalists published, like *Pratt's Guide*, by Venture Economics of Massachusetts.

All editions of the *Journal*, monthly, for the 6½ years between August 1983 and February 1989 were searched for the names of VCRFs and their states of residence. Just under 3,000 company names were collected for the whole United States, but it became clear during the search that there are several minor statistical problems with using the *Venture Capital Journal* listings in this way.

First, there is no certainty that the firms found in the *Journal* constitute the universe of venture recipients. The publishers do have the incentive to make, and the expressed intention of making, *Venture Capital Journal* a comprehensive source of information about the venture industry. This is so that the *Journal* will be subscribed to, at its high annual cost of $950, not only by venture capitalists wanting to keep abreast of trends in their own industry, but also by the managers of other types of institutions and Funds who seek the information about venture Fund performances on which they can then base their own investment decisions. However, the *Journal*'s compilers have to rely largely on data supplied by members of the industry. Hence, as with the 'capital under management' data, there are likely to be some Funds who do not wish to disclose their dealings for confidentiality reasons, and others which may, understandably, tend to report their successes and omit their failures. Also, public venture Funds using pension or taxpayer dollars may simply not perceive the need to 'advertise' for their investment dollars in this way, and their portfolio companies (unless they are recipients of coinvestment deals with private Funds) will probably not be mentioned in the *Journal*.

Second, given that it may not be complete, there is also no way of knowing the directions in which it may be biased. It is likely that more is known by the compilers of the *Journal* about the dealings of the larger venture institutions (which often put out brochures naming their portfolio companies) and the Small Business Invest-

ment Companies (whose activities with US Small Business Administration (SBA) funds are more open to scrutiny), and about those
Funds geographically closer to the home base of *Venture Economics*
in Needham, Massachusetts.

Third, although the VCRFs were all mentioned sometime
between 1983 and 1989, no exact information is given about their
dates of founding, incorporation, or start of trading, or even when
the different rounds of venture funding were received. All that can
be said with certainty is that the named firms were venture
recipients and were in some Fund's portfolio at the time of mention.

Fourth, the different major stages of VCRFs – particularly the
initial post-deal restructuring, the later public stock offering, and
the times of buyout, merger, acquisition – are also often points at
which a firm changes its business name. The list of VCRFs compiled
from the *Journal* may thus contain some duplicates.

Fifth, it is not possible to tell which of the firms mentioned have
failed or moved since the time of listing. Thus, the list of names of
VCRFs in a state is not precisely synonymous with actual levels of
venture-backed economic activity. If it were possible to tally the
number of 'definitely existing venture-backed firms in each state at a
given time', then different states would probably make slightly
stronger or weaker showings than they do in this list of 'companies
that at some time in the last six years have received venture capital'.

Sixth, VCRFs were counted only in the states in which they were
headquartered. Some firms, especially those in the retailing and
services sectors, were mentioned as having branches, stores,
franchisees, distributors, or sales offices in other states. These other
places would then also be beneficiaries of venture financing and
indirect beneficiaries of multiplier effects, but this would not be
reflected in their own state's VCRF totals.

Seventh, given that the size of investment in a VCRF is rarely
reported, it is not possible to know how the frequency of mention of
a given company name is related to the volume of dollars
accompanying the reported event.

However, these seven problems are weaknesses only compared
with the ideally desired, but non-existent, perfect information.
Venture Capital Journal is still the only comprehensive and
accessible source available for names of VCRFs across the
organized venture industry, and the inventory that can be culled
from it can stand as a reasonable guide to broad levels of venture-
backed activity in a state.

The individual VCRF names and city or state locations can then be used to find street addresses via several different business directories such as *Standard & Poor's Corporation Records*, Dun's Marketing Services *Million Dollar Directory: America's Leading Public & Private Companies, 1989 Series*, and individual states' own directories of manufacturers and businesses.

The number of VCRFs located through each source are shown in Table 3.1. In the whole Central Region, 348 VCRFs out of 653 (or 53.3 per cent) can be found in one or more of these three main business directory sources. A search of telephone books for all the major metropolitan areas in states where the remaining 305 are believed to be located yields street addresses and phone numbers for another 147 VCRFs. This brings to 495 (or 75.8 per cent of the original 653 firm names) the number of VCRFs with addresses.

Table 3.1 Information sources on venture capital recipient firms

	(a) Total VCRFs	(b) S&P	(c) D&B	(d) State directories	All directories	*(%)*	Phone books	Total from all sources	*(%)*
AR	0	–	–	–	–	–	–	–	–
CO	82	11	22	24	42	50.0	21	63	75.0
IL	71	12	16	26	37	51.4	24	61	84.7
IN	23	3	4	13	14	60.9	3	17	73.9
IA	4	1	3	1	3	75.0	0	3	75.0
KS	6	0	2	5	6	85.7	0	6	85.7
KY	3	1	1	0	2	66.7	1	3	100.
MI	41	5	16	17	23	56.1	9	32	78.0
MN	86	20	31	35	49	57.0	17	66	76.7
MO	13	3	3	2	5	38.5	3	8	61.5
NE	1	0	1	0	1	100.0	0	1	100.0
ND	1	0	0	0	0	0.0	1	1	100.0
OH	64	13	21	17	33	52.4	11	44	69.8
OK	7	3	5	1	6	85.7	0	6	85.7
SD	0	–	–	0	0	100.0	0	0	100.0
TX	224	46	73	30	107	47.8	54	161	71.9
WI	22	7	11	13	20	83.3	3	23	95.9
Relocated[a]	5								
Central states (17)	653	125	209	184	348	53.3	147	495	75.8

Sources: (a) Listings in *Venture Capital Journal*, August 1983 to February 1989; (b) *Standard & Poor's Corporation Records*, New York, March 1989; (c) Dun's Marketing Services *Million Dollar Directory; America's Leading Public and Private Companies*, New Jersey, 1989 Series; (d) individual state directories
Note: [a] Companies with Central states addresses originally, but which now have addresses outside the region.

Information about the type of industry can be taken from the same directories. It is possible to find US SIC code information for 341 VCRFs, or 52.5 per cent of the Central total.

The evaluation of the 'high-technology' status of VCRFs can then be done by comparing their SIC codes with a list of seventeen codes designated as 'high-technology' in a consensus definition based on expert professional understandings within US federal and state high-technology programs and related agencies (Thompson 1987: Table 2) (the 1977 SICs are 283, 2869, 351, 357, 3622, 365, 366, 367, 3693, 372, 376, 381, 382, 382, 384, 386, and 7391).

Information for standardizing the number of VCRFs compared with all other economic activity in a state can be obtained from *County Business Patterns*, which gives the total number of all kinds of industrial establishments per state. It must be remembered, though, that an 'establishment' is 'a single physical location where business is conducted or where services or industrial operations are performed' (US DoC 1984: V). As such, it is not strictly comparable with the enterprise-based VCRF data gleaned from *Venture Capital Journal*: it is not possible to make any direct connection in a legal, ownership, or functional business sense between the different physical locational units within an establishment's data-set. Nor does a numerical comparison of establishments allow for differing establishment sizes, either by industrial sector or by state. Nevertheless, the number of establishments is a reasonable and commonly used indicator of one element of economic activity, and can be used here as a denominator to control for the level of industrialization in a state so long as these important qualifications are borne in mind.

CENTRAL REGION VENTURE CAPITAL RECIPIENT FIRMS

Geographical distribution of Central Region venture capital recipient firms

Table 3.2 shows the geographical distributions of all firms mentioned in *Venture Capital Journal* as having received venture backing some time between 1983 and 1989. In the whole of the United States 2,911 VCRFs are mentioned, with 653 of them (or 22.6 per cent) located in the Central Region.

Texas alone holds 224, or 34.3 per cent, of the Central Region's recipients. The top five Central States of Texas, Minnesota, Colorado, Illinois, and Ohio together contain 527 (or 80.7 per cent)

Table 3.2 Venture capital recipient firms, by area, 1983–1989

Area	(a) Recipient firms	(b) State's rank in Central Region	(c) Share of regional total	(d) Share of US total	(e) Per million population	(f) Per million industrial establish- ments
	(no.)	(no.)	(%)	(%)	(no.)	(no.)
Central states	653	–	100.0	22.4	7.4	21.8
Arkansas	0		0.0	0.0	0.0	0.0
Colorado	82	3	12.6	2.8	25.1	68.3
Illinois	71	4	10.9	2.4	6.1	17.0
Indiana	23	8	3.5	0.8	4.2	12.4
Iowa	4	12	0.6	0.1	1.4	4.7
Kansas	6	10	0.9	0.2	2.4	7.5
Kentucky	3	13	0.5	0.1	0.8	3.0
Michigan	41	6	6.3	1.4	4.5	13.2
Minnesota	86	2	13.2	3.0	20.4	53.8
Missouri	13	9	2.0	0.5	2.6	7.1
Nebraska	1	14	0.2	0.0	0.6	2.0
North Dakota	1	14	0.2	0.0	1.5	5.6
Ohio	64	5	9.8	2.2	6.0	16.9
Oklahoma	7	10	1.1	0.2	2.1	7.7
South Dakota	0		0.0	0.0	0.0	0.0
Texas	224	1	34.3	7.7	13.4	39.8
Wisconsin	22	7	3.4	0.8	4.6	13.3
Relocated[a]	5					
Eastern states	1,139	–	100.0	39.0	10.7	29.9
Massachusetts	407	–	35.7	14.0	69.8	151.0
Rest	732	–	64.3	25.1	7.2	20.7
Western states	1,119	–	100.0	38.4	24.6	72.7
California	966	–	86.3	33.1	35.8	99.3
Rest	153	–	13.7	5.2	8.3	27.0
US total	2,911	–	–	100.0	12.1	34.9

Sources: (a)–(d) Listings in *Venture Capital Journal*, August 1983 to February 1989;
(e) US Department of Commerce Bureau of the Census (1988) *County–City Data
Book*, Table A, col. 2; (f) US Department of Commerce (1989) *County Business
Patterns*, Table 1G, 1986 data
Note: [a] Includes companies with Central states addresses originally, but which now
only have addresses outside the region.

of the region's VCRFs. Both Arkansas and South Dakota have no
recipients named at all, while Nebraska and North Dakota each
have only one. Eight of the seventeen states in the Central region
have fewer than ten recipient firms each. By contrast, Massachusetts
has 407, nearly double the number in Texas, and California has 966,
more than four times the number in Texas and nearly 50 per cent

more again than the entire seventeen-state Central Region.

The absolute numbers of VCRFs can be standardized by considering them relative to the size of state population, and to the number of all industrial establishments. The resulting figures are shown in columns (e) and (f) respectively of Table 3.2.

The Central Region's average of 7.4 VCRFs per million of population is less than that of the Eastern Region's 10.7, and the Western Region's 24.6. Within the Central Region, Colorado, Minnesota, and Texas, the states with the largest absolute numbers of VCRFs, are still the three strongest states when considered relative to population, and are the only Central states with a greater number of VCRFs than the national average of 12.1. Their rank order is now changed from the previous absolute list, however: Colorado has the most VCRFs per capita with 25.1 firms per million of its 1986 population. Minnesota is still second with 20.4, and Texas is now third with 13.4, rather than first. These three states all have more recipients than the Eastern Region average, and Colorado also has more recipients per capita than the Western Region average. Illinois, which was ranked fourth in the Central Region for the absolute number of recipient firms, has only 6.1 VCRFs per million people.

Compared with Massachusetts and California the relative performance of even the top three Central states is less impressive: Colorado has 25.1 VCRFs per million people, but California has 35.8 and Massachusetts, at 69.8, has almost three times as many as Colorado. Nevertheless, it should be noted that the Central Region's average of 7.4 recipient firms per million population is much closer to the averages for the other two regions when Massachusetts and California are excluded from the respective calculations. The Eastern Region's average excluding Massachusetts is only 7.2 firms per million population, which is slightly less than the Central Region's average. The Western Region's average, excluding California, is only 8.3 firms per million population, only slightly higher than the Central Region's.

The average number of Central Region VCRFs per million establishments in all industries is 21.8, which is slightly less than the Eastern Region average of 29.9, and much less than the Western Region average of 72.7. The same three Central states as before show the strongest performance within the Central Region: Colorado has 68.3 VCRFs per million establishments, Minnesota has 53.8, and Texas 39.8. Illinois is ranked a distant fourth, with 17.0. By comparison, Massachusetts and California once again have a much stronger relative showing of VCRFs than the rest of the nation: Massachusetts has 151.0 VCRFs per million industrial establishments, and California has 99.3. However, the Eastern and Western Regions excluding these two states again have averages similar to that of the Central Region.

Age distribution of Central Region venture capital recipient firms

The common perception that venture capital helps start new firms can be tested by examining the dates of founding of VCRFs. Unfortunately, the founding date of a company is not always the same as the start of trading, or the date of legal incorporation, and the same enterprise can be reincorporated many times, often in different states, for a variety of legal and tax reasons. Nevertheless, the date of incorporation is the most 'standard' and comparable date available in different directories. Incorporation dates can be found for 235 (or 36 per cent) of the 653 Central VCRFs, and are plotted in the histogram of Figure 3.1.

Of the 235 firms with incorporation dates available, only 14, or 6 per cent, are 5 years old or younger in 1989. The average age of all 235 VCRFs is 16.8 years, and the median age is 10 years. Altogether, 58 VCRFs, or 24.7 per cent, were incorporated some time during the 6-year study period of 1983–9, and 200 VCRFs, or 85.1 per cent, are under 25 years old. Some 32 firms, or 13.6 per cent, were founded in 1960 or earlier, and the earliest incorporation date in this sample is as long ago as 1829. The peak period for incorporation of VCRFs in the Central Region appears to be 1979–83, with peak individual years being 1982 and 1983. These dates do coincide with the growing volume of venture dollars available at that time.

The apparent tailing-off in VCRFs incorporated from 1984 onwards could be due to several factors. First, there has been a moving away from true seed and start-up situations as the average deal size increases and as established venture capitalists concentrate more on existing firms in their portfolios. Second, it may show a lack of reporting of very young concerns. Third, it may be that in some cases incorporation comes some time after initial venture investment and the functional start of a business. Hence, some enterprises invested in after 1985 may have yet to be legally incorporated, although, given the legal structures insisted on by venture capitalists in their deals, this is unlikely.

The median date of incorporation for the whole Region is the

```
         1829 X
         1857 X
         1887 X X
         1888 X
         1898 X
         1901 X
         1904 X
         1918 X
         1921 X
         1927 X
         1928 X
         1929 X
         1935 X
         1940 X X X
         1946 X
         1948 X
         1953 X
         1954 X
         1956 X X X
         1957 X
         1959 X X
         1960 X X X X X   5
         1961 X
         1962 X
         1963 X
         1965 X X X
         1966 X X
         1967 X X X X X   5
         1968 X X X X X   5
         1969 X X X X X   5
         1970 X X
         1971 X X X
         1972 X X X X X   5
         1973 X X X X X   5
         1974 X X X X X X X   7
         1975 X X X
         1976 X X X X X X X   7
         1977 X X X X X   5
         1978 X X X X X X X X X   9
         1979 X X X X X X X X X X X X X X X X X   19
         1980 X X X X X X X X X X   11
         1981 X X X X X X X X X X X X X X X X   18
         1982 X X X X X X X X X X X X X X X X X X X X X X X X X X X X
         1983 X X X X X X X X X X X X X X X X X X X X X X X X X X X X
         1984 X X X X X X X X X X X X X X X X   16
         1985 X X X X X X X X   8
         1986 X X X X X X   6
```

Year of Incorporation

Total Firms Reporting: 235
X = one VCRF

Figure 3.1 Dates of incorporation for central region VCRFs

Table 3.3 Age of venture capital recipient firms, by state

Central States	Total	VCRFs with incorporation information		Date of incorporation						Median date
				1979–83		1984–9		1979–89		
	(no.)	(no.)	(%)[a]	(no.)	(%)[b]	(no.)	(%)[b]	(no.)	(%)[b]	(year)
Arkansas	0	–	–	–	–	–	–	–	–	–
Colorado	82	30	36.6	21	70.0	1	3.3	22	73.3	1982
Illinois	71	27	38.0	9	33.3	3	11.1	12	44.4	1975
Indiana	23	11	47.8	3	27.3	1	9.1	4	36.4	1976
Iowa	4	2	50.0	1	50.0	0	0.0	1	–	–
Kansas	6	0	0.0	–	–	–	–	–	–	–
Kentucky	3	1	33.3	0	0.0	0	0.0	–	–	–
Michigan	41	17	41.5	9	52.9	2	11.8	11	64.7	1981
Minnesota	86	39	45.3	19	48.7	7	17.9	26	66.7	1981
Missouri	13	4	30.8	0	0.0	2	50.0	2	50.0	1980
Nebraska	1	0	0.0	–	–	–	–	–	–	–
North Dakota	1	0	0.0	–	–	–	–	–	–	–
Ohio	64	25	39.1	7	28.0	4	16.0	11	44.0	1976
Oklahoma	7	4	57.1	1	25.0	0	0.0	1	25.0	1977
South Dakota	0	0	0.0	–	–	–	–	–	–	–
Texas	224	61	27.2	28	45.9	8	13.1	36	59.0	1979
Wisconsin	22	13	59.1	5	38.5	2	15.4	7	53.8	1979
Relocated[c]	5									
Central total	653	234	35.8	103	44.0	30	12.8	133	56.8	1979

Sources: Listings in *Venture Capital Journal*, August 1983 to February 1989, plus directory information

Notes: [a] Percentage of total VCRFs.
   [b] Percentage of VCRFs with incorporation date information available.
   [c] Includes companies with Central states addresses originally, but which now only have addresses outside the region.

year 1979. At the state level, shown in Table 3.3, the median is slightly earlier than this for Indiana, Illinois, and Ohio, and slightly later for Michigan, Colorado, and Minnesota. Minnesota and Texas are the only states in the Central Region with more than five incorporations listed within the last 5 years.

Size distribution of venture capital recipient firms

One corollary of the idea that venture capital backs new firms is that these are probably also 'small'. However, just as the idea of 'new' depends on definitions, so does any judgement on 'small' depend on the observer's chosen upper size limit to 'small'. In the industrial literature, a complete size spectrum of choices is apparent: Barff (1987) uses '15 or fewer' employees for 'small'; Cohen and Berry

Table 3.4 Employment size distribution of venture capital recipient firms

(a) Employee	(b) VCRFs		(c) All industrial establishments 1986			
			Central region		USA	
(no.)	(no.)	(%)	(no.)	(%)	(no.)	(%)
1–4	4	1.2	1,139,448	55.3	3,258,407	56.1
5–9	4	1.2	411,177	19.9	1,133,825	19.5
10–19	22	6.6	250,238	12.1	689,395	11.9
20–49	70	20.9	161,676	7.8	448,769	7.7
50–99	55	16.4	56,271	2.7	156,286	2.7
100–249	81	24.2	30,422	1.5	84,834	1.5
250–499	33	9.9	7,736	0.4	22,164	0.4
500–999	25	7.5	2,932	0.1	8,466	0.1
Over 1,000	41	12.3	1,665	0.1	4,827	0.1
Total	335	100	2,061,663	100	5,806,973	100

Sources: (a) Size classes as in US Department of Commerce *County Business Patterns*) (b) listings in *Venture Capital Journal*, August 1983 to February 1989; (c) aggregated from US Department of Commerce *County Business Patterns*, Table 1G.

(1975) use 'fewer than 20'; Gilmour (1974) uses 'fewer than 25'; Scott (1983, 1984) uses 'fewer than 30'; and Oakey (1984) uses 100 as the upper limit of 'small' firm size. The need to compare VCRF data here with the larger universe of all establishments given in *County Business Patterns* confines analysis to the format used there. Fortunately, those data are arrayed in nine categories, allowing some flexibility in the choice of 'small'.

Information on the number of employees in 335 Central Region VCRFs, or 51.3 per cent of the 653 total, is shown in Table 3.4. The largest size category is 100–249 employees, with almost one-quarter of Central VCRFs: interestingly, this is a size category with more employees than any of the 'small' definitions given above. Fully 61.5 per cent of VCRFs have between 20 and 100 employees, and some 12.3 per cent of VCRFs are very large firms of over 1,000 employees. If 'small' is taken as under ten employees, then under 2.5 per cent of VCRFs are small firms; if twenty is the limit, then still only 9 per cent of VCRFs are small. This is in contrast with the size distribution of industrial establishments, since in both the Central Region and the United States as a whole, over 55 per cent of all establishments have under five employees, and over 75 per cent have fewer than ten employees.

It is possible, therefore, that venture capital is not, on average, being targeted towards 'small' firms. However, this particular size distribution of VCRFs could also have other explanations. First, the 'mortality rate' for new ventures could be exceedingly high in the very early stages of firm life, when there are fewest employees. The size of the 'small' category in this sample could therefore look underrepresented compared with the size of the same category in the general establishment distribution, even though venture capitalists are, in practice, starting up many small firms. Second, if the pool of funds available for venture investments has been growing in waves over time, it is possible that the size category distribution of VCRFs in Table 3.4 reflects a cohort moving up through the size distribution as it ages. Third, statistics could be skewed by the appearance of the one company listed in a directory as having 62,000 employees, which is over five times the size of the next largest company. Since in this particular case the company also refused to participate in a survey because nobody now employed there had any knowledge of venture capital, and that it was unlikely any had ever been needed as the company already had $6 billion in annual sales, this VCRF's employment was removed from the analysis.

Table 3.5 shows employment data for the remaining 330 Central VCRFs (i.e. with the largest company and the outwardly-relocating firms removed from the earlier 335). Central VCRFs with employment data available employ a total of 169,205 people, giving an average of 512.7 employees per firm. For the whole region, this means that there are 5.5 employees in VCRFs for every 1,000 employees in all types of industrial establishments. If the average size of the remaining 323 companies without employment data was the same as that for the known sub-sample, then total employment in the region's 653 VCRFs would be 334,821, or 11.2 employees in VCRFs for every 1,000 employees in all establishments. At the individual state level, Minnesota has the highest ratio of VCRF employees to total employees with 15.1 per thousand, and Colorado is second with 13.9. No other Central state is over 10: Ohio and Texas are 9.7 and 8.0 respectively, and the remaining 13 have fewer than 5.0 each.

Employment in VCRFs is central not only to any description of their characteristics compared with firms in the rest of the economy, but also to their overall economic impact on their host areas. Hence, their employment sizes and growth trajectories, and how these compare with both the rest of the economy and popular

Table 3.5 Size of venture capital recipient firms, by state

Central States	(a) VCRFs			(b)		(c)	(d) Employment in VCRFs	(e)
	Total	With employment information	(%)ᵃ	Total	(%)ᵇ	Mean	Median	In all establishments
	(no.)	(no.)	(%)ᵃ	(no.)	(%)ᵇ	(no.)	(no.)	(no/1,000)
Arkansas	0	–	–	–		–	–	–
Colorado	82	40	48.8	16,662	9.8	416.6	75	13.9
Illinois	71	34	47.9	14,220	8.4	418.2	150	3.4
Indiana	23	14	60.9	4,490	2.7	320.7	152	2.4
Iowa	4	3	75.0	1,832	1.1	610.7	375	2.1
Kansas	6	5	83.3	595	0.4	119.0	175	0.7
Kentucky	3	2	66.7	442	0.3	221.0	–	0.4
Michigan	41	22	53.7	11,912	7.0	541.5	72	3.8
Minnesota	86	49	57.0	24,204	14.3	494.0	100	15.1
Missouri	13	5	38.5	3,025	1.8	605.0	256	1.7
Nebraska	1	1	–	1,800	1.1	–	–	3.6
North Dakota	1	0	0.0	–		–	–	–
Ohio (incl X)	64	31	48.4	98,916	–	3,190.8	215	26.0
(excl. X)		30	–	36,916	21.8	1,230.5	207	9.7
Oklahoma	7	5	71.4	868	0.5	173.6	50	1.0
South Dakota	0	0	0.0	–	–	–	–	–
Texas	224	102	45.5	44,894	26.5	440.1	138	8.0
Wisconsin	22	18	81.8	7,345	4.3	408.1	167	4.4
Relocatedᶜ	5			5				
Central totals:								
Incl. X	653	331	50.7	231,205		698.5	120	7.7
Excl. X		330		169,205	100.	512.7	120	5.5
Extrapolated	653			334,821		512.7		11.2(d)

Sources: (a) *Venture Capital Journal*, August 1983 to February 1989; (b), (c), (d), directories; (e) combined with data from US Department of Commerce *County Business Patterns*, Table 1G

Notes: ᵃ Percentage of total VCRFs.
ᵇ Percentage of regional employment in 330 VCRFs with employment information available.
ᶜ Companies with Central states addresses originally, but which now only have addresses outside the region.
X, single extremely large Ohio company with 62,000 employees listed.

beliefs about the working of venture capital, all merit detailed examination. For example, if venture capital backs small firms with high growth potential, the size of recently incorporated VCRFs should be smaller than the average firm, while older VCRFs should be larger than average.

Table 3.6 shows the employment size class distribution of VCRFs by incorporation period. The average size of all 233 Central VCRFs on which both employment and incorporation data are available is 548.8 employees. This is over thirty-seven times the employment size of all establishments in both the Central Region and the United States as a whole. Even allowing for the statistical incompatibility between 'firms' and 'establishments' as units, it is likely that VCRFs have considerably higher employment levels than the average firm. Again, it should be noted that this average figure can be pulled

Table 3.6 Employment size distribution of venture capital recipient firms, by age

(a) Employees	Total		(b) VCRFs incorporation date					
			1979–83		1984–9		1979–89	
(no.)	(no.)	(%)	(no.)	(%)	(no.)	(%)	(no.)	(%)
1–4	4	1.7	2	2.0	1	3.3	3	2.3
5–9	3	1.3	3	2.9	0	0.0	3	2.3
10–19	11	4.7	5	4.9	3	10.0	8	6.1
20–49	42	18.0	29	28.4	8	26.7	37	28.0
50–99	41	17.6	15	14.7	4	13.3	19	14.4
100–249	60	25.8	25	24.5	6	12.0	31	23.5
250–499	22	9.4	5	4.9	4	13.3	9	6.8
500–999	21	9.0	5	4.9	1	3.3	6	4.5
Over 1,000	29	12.4	13	12.7	3	10.0	16	12.1
Total VCRFs	233		102	43.8	30	12.9	13	56.7
Total	127,860		49,784	39	7,303	5.7	7,087	44.6
Average	549		488		243		433	
Median	135		80		75		80	

Total, all Central Region						Total, USA	
Establishments	2,061,663						5,806,973
Employees	29,932,586						83,380,465
Average		14.5					14.4

upwards by some of the twenty-nine firms in the largest size category, five of which have 5,000 or more employees. The median employment size (which is less distorted by extreme cases) is 135 employees, which is much lower than the 548.8 average, though still larger than 'small'. When the categorical data on firm size are further broken down by incorporation period in Table 3.6, then, as hypothesized, the younger VCRFs are smaller than older ones: VCRFs 5 years old or younger (that is, incorporated in 1984 or later) have an average size of 243.4 employees, while those VCRFs 6–10 years old (that is, incorporated between 1979 and 1983, inclusive) have almost double the average size of the firms 5 years old and younger, at 488.1 employees. Again, though, the median exhibits only a slight increase, from seventy-five to eighty employees.

There are several theoretical hypotheses about this impressive VCRF growth which could help explain these empirical distributions. First, the conventional explanation would be that, although these are different cohorts of the firm population rather than longitudinal observations over time on the same firms, the pronounced average size difference over time confirms the generalization that, on average, successful VCRFs can double in size from their first 5 years of life to their second, and are thus fulfilling the high growth expectations of their stereotype. Second, since even the VCRFs in the category 5 years old or younger have an average size more than sixteen times that of the average US establishment, either employment growth within a VCRF takes place astonishingly early in the life-cycle or venture capital did not go to small start-ups and VCRFs were larger companies to begin with. Third, the fact that the median does not move as much as the mean shows that the growth distribution is skewed: that is, even within this high-growth type of company, there is a further subcluster of super-growth VCRFs whose employment performance has accounted for most of the movement of the mean figure. Fourth, the differences could, after all, just be a statistical artefact of having two different groups of companies in each 5-year cohort and it happens that some very big companies have been included in one group but that analogous firms have been omitted from the other group.

Sectoral and industrial distribution of Central Region venture capital recipient firms

Table 3.7 shows the SIC codes of 341 Central Region VCRFs (or the 52.5 per cent of the Central total on which SIC information was traceable) and compares their sectoral distribution with the distribution of all industrial establishments in both the region and the nation. The most obvious feature of the data is the small total size of the venture-backed sector of the economy: there are 341 VCRFs, but over 1.9 million establishments in all industries in the region (though, again, it must be remembered that there are more establishments than enterprises). At the level of broad industrial sectors, the Central VCRFs are mostly in manufacturing, which has

Table 3.7 Distribution of venture capital recipient firms in Central states, by sector

(a) Sectors and SIC codes	(b) VCRFs in Central Region		(c) Central Region (1986)		(d) USA (1986)		(e) All industrial establishments US growth rates (1982–6)		
							Ests	Emps	Pay
	(no.)	(%)	(no.)	(%)	(no.)	(%)	(%)	(%)	(%)
Agric., forestry, fishing (SICs 00–09)	1	0.3	22,257	1.2	68,076	1.3	+37.0	+28.6	+48.8
Mining (SICs 10–14)	10	2.9	21,455	1.1	34,973	0.7	−0.4	−28.7	16.2
Construction (SICs 15–19)	1	0.3	166,141	8.7	492,132	9.2	+27.5	+18.2	+32.7
Manufacturing (SICs 20–39)	215	63.0	125,473	6.6	355,452	6.6	+8.1	−2.2	+21.4
Transportation and utilities (SICs 40–49)	11	3.2	79,125	4.1	209,920	3.9	+18.9	+5.6	+23.0
Services (SICs 50–99)	103	30.2	1,493,821	78.3	4,196,550	78.3	+18.0	+17.9	+44.4
Total	341		1,908,272		5,357,103		+18.2	+11.2	+33.0

Sources: (a) Office of Management and Budget, *Standard Industrial Classification Manual*, 1972 and 1977 supplement; (b), (d) see Table 3.1, col. (a); (c), (e) aggregated from US Department of Commerce, Bureau of the Census, *County Business Patterns* (various years), Washington, DC: US GPO

Table 3.8 Distribution of venture capital recipient firms in Central states, by manufacturing industry

Manufacturing industry and two-digit SIC code[a]	VCRFs in Central Region		All industrial establishments in SIC code, 1986			
			Central Region		USA	
	(no.)	(%)	(no.)	(%)	(no.)	(%)
20 Food and kindred products	5	1.5	8,226	0.43	21,145	0.39
27 Printing and publishing	10	2.9	20,927	1.10	57,299	1.07
28 Chemicals and allied products	18	5.3	4,520	0.24	12,069	0.23
33 Primary metal industries	5	1.5	3.131	0.16	6,725	0.13
34 Fabricated metal products	14	4.1	15,061	0.79	35,020	0.65
35 Machinery, nonelectrical	66	19.4	22,643	1.19	50,168	0.94
36 Electric and electronic equipment	44	12.9	5,413	0.28	17,374	0.32
38 Instruments and related products	32	9.4	2,548	0.13	8,323	0.16
39 Miscellaneous manufacturing	5	1.5	4,590	0.24	15,830	0.30
Total, above codes	199		87,059	4.56	223,953	4.18
All manufacturing	215		125,473	6.58	355,452	6.64
All establishments	341		1,908,272		5,357,103	

Sources: Office of Management and Budget, *Standard Industrial Classification Manual,* 1972 and 1977 supplement; US Department of Commerce, Bureau of the Census, *County Business Patterns* (various years), Washington, DC: US GPO
Notes: [a] Includes only those manufacturing codes with more than five VCRFs.
[b] 312 out of the total 653 VCRFs (47.7 per cent) did not have their SIC code given in directories; percentages given are of the 341 VCRFs with SICs.

63 per cent of the identifiable regional VCRF total; another 30.2 per cent are in services. This situation is in contrast with the distribution of all industrial establishments, where under 7 per cent in both the region and the nation are in manufacturing, and over 78 per cent in both the region and the nation are in services.

Table 3.8 disaggregates the data in Table 3.7 further by individual industries within manufacturing, listing only those with five or more VCRFs. The most popular industry for firms receiving venture backing in the Central Region is SIC 35 'Machinery, except electrical', with almost 20 per cent of the region's VCRFs, followed by SIC 36 'Electric and electronic equipment', with almost 13 per cent. Table 3.9 does a similar disaggregation, but for services industries. Over half the services VCRFs in the Central Region fall into the 'Other' category, with forty-three out of fifty-six VCRFs there falling into SIC 73 'Business services'.

Table 3.10 shows the finest disaggregation possible, given the data system, and lists in declining order all four-digit codes with more than five VCRFs. SIC 3573 'Electronic computing equipment' is the most popular code in the Central Region, with forty-one VCRFs, or

Table 3.9 Distribution of venture capital recipient firms in Central states, by services industry

SIC code[a] services	VCRFs in Central Region		All industrial establishments in SIC code, 1986			
			Central Region		USA	
	(no.)	(%)[b]	(no.)	(%)	(no.)	(%)
50, 51 Wholesaling	19	5.6	165,735	8.69	439,960	8.21
52–59 Retailing	15	4.4	526,167	27.57	1,441,236	26.90
60–69 Fire[c]	13	3.8	172,042	9.02	504,052	9.41
70–89 Other Ser.	56	16.4	629,877	33.01	1,811,302	33.81
73 alone Bus. Ser.	43	12.6	89,458	4.69	276,557	5.16
Total, All codes	103	30.2	1,493,821	78.28	4,196,550	78.34
All estab.	341		1,908,272		5,357,103	

Sources: Office of Management and Budget, *Standard Industrial Classification Manual,* 1972 and 1977 supplement; aggregated from US Department of Commerce, Bureau of the Census, *County Business Patterns* (various years), Washington, DC: US GPO

Notes: [a] Includes only those service codes with more than five VCRFs.
[b] 312 out of the total 653 VCRFs (47.7 per cent) did not have their SIC code given in directories; percentages given are of the 341 VCRFs with SICs.
[c] Finance, insurance, real estate.

12 per cent of the regional total. This is almost three times the number of VCRFs as there are in the second code, SIC 3841 'Surgical and medical instruments'. SIC 7372 'Computer programming and software' and SIC 3662 'Radio and TV communications equipment' are third and fourth respectively. These four codes together contain eighty-three Central VCRFs, or almost a quarter of the total with SIC information, and are the only ones with more than ten firms. The remaining 258 Central VCRFs are spread across 159 different three-digit SIC codes.

The overall regional distribution of VCRFs between different four-digit codes does not always hold for individual states within the Central Region, as can be seen in Table 3.11. The most popular

Table 3.10 Most prevalent individual SIC codes for venture capital recipient firms in Central states

Four-digit SIC codes and short titles of industries with more than 5 VCRFs	VCRFs in Central Region		All 1986 industrial establishments in code			
			Central Region		USA	
	(no.)	(%)	(no.)	(%)	(no.)	(%)
3573 Elec computing eqpmt	41	12.0	454	0.02	1,980	0.03
3841 Surgical & medical instr	16	4.7	312	0.02	950	0.02
7372 Computer programming & software	15	4.4	3,270	0.20	11,119	0.19
3662 Radio & TV communications eqpmt	11	3.2	601	0.03	2,262	0.04
3674 Semiconductors & related devices	8	2.3	181	0.01	804	0.01
5081 Commercial machines & eqpmt (wholesaling)	7	2.1	8,590	0.42	24,444	0.42
1311 Crude petroleum & natural gas	6	1.8	6,730	0.33	9,087	0.16
3661 Telephone & telegraph apparatus	6	1.8	105	0.01	359	0.01
3679 Elec components nec	6	1.8	875	0.04	3,483	0.06
6711 Holding offices	6	1.8	2,310	0.11	5,887	0.10
7391 Research & Devpt labs	6	1.8	939	0.05	3,582	0.06
7392 Management & public relations	6	1.8	13,521	0.64	45,408	0.78
2834 Pharmaceutical preps	5	1.5	187	0.01	678	0.01
7379 Computer-related ser nec	5	1.5	1,662	0.08	6,309	0.01
Total, above SIC codes	109	40.0	39,737	1.90	116,352	2.00
Total, all SIC codes	341	100.0	2,061,663		5,806,973	

Sources: Office of Management and Budget, *Standard Industrial Classification Manual*, 1972 and 1977 supplement; aggregated from US Department of Commerce, Bureau of the Census, *County Business Patterns* (various years), Washington, DC: US GPO

code at the whole Central Region level is SIC 3573 'Electronic computing equipment', but this is the most popular in only three states: Colorado, Minnesota, and Texas. Elsewhere, SIC 7372 'Computer programming and software' is the most frequent code in Illinois, SIC 3563 'Air/gas compressors' and SIC 3841 'Surgical and medical instruments' are the most popular in Indiana, SIC 3829 'Measuring and controlling devices' tops the list in Michigan, SIC 1311 'Crude petroleum and natural gas' is the most popular in Oklahoma, and SIC 2731 'Book publishing' leads codes in Wisconsin. Moreover, the degree to which a state's VCRFs are concentrated in the most popular code also varies by state, from 8.9 per cent in Illinois to 50 per cent in Oklahoma.

Table 3.11 Primary SIC codes[a] of venture capital recipient firms, by individual Central states, 1983–1989

Area	VCRFs Total	With SIC info	SIC codes Primary	Largest primary code in state	Conc[c] in largest code	
	(no.)	(no.)	(no.)	(SIC#) (short title)	(no.)	(%)
Arkansas	0	–	–	– –	–	–
Colorado	82	40	24	3573 Computing eqpmt	13	32.5
Illinois	71	34	27	2834 Pharmctcl preps	3	8.9
				7372 Programming/soft		
Indiana	23	14	12	3563 Air/gas comprssrs	2	14.3
				3841 Surg/med instrmts		
Iowa[b]	4	3	3	– –	–	–
Kansas[b]	6	5	5	– –	–	–
Kentucky[b]	3	2	2	– –	–	–
Michigan	41	23	19	3829 Meas-contr devs	3	13.0
Minnesota	86	49	32	3573 Computing eqpmt	11	22.4
Missouri[b]	13	5	5	– –	–	–
Nebraska	1	0	–	– –	–	–
North Dakota	1	0	–	– –	–	–
Ohio	64	33	29	2831 Biological prods	2	6.1
				3679 Elec comps nec		
				3825 Instr meas elec		
				7372 Programming/soft		
Oklahoma	7	6	4	1311 Cr petrl/nat gas	3	50.0
South Dakota	0	–	–	– –	–	–
Texas	224	103	63	3573 Computing eqpmt	13	12.6
Wisconsin	22	18	17	2731 Book publishing	2	11.1
Total, Central states	653	341	163	3573 Computing eqpmt	41	12.0

Sources: (a) Listings in *Venture Capital Journal,* August 1983 to February 1989; (b) trade and state business directories; SIC titles from the Office of Management and Budget, *Standard Industrial Classification Manual*, 1972 and 1977 supplement; state directories using the 1987 classification were 'translated' back to 1977 codes for conformity

Notes: [a] Directories sometimes give more than one SIC code for a company; the first SIC code mentioned is conventionally the one yielding greatest sales, and is referred to here as the 'primary' code.

[b] no primary code with more than one VCRF.

[c] Concentration, that is, the number of VCRFs in that state's most popular prime code, expressed as a percentage of all VCRFs with SIC information.

When the individual state breakdown is made, the numbers of VCRFs become too small for sophisticated statistical analysis: nine out of the seventeen states have only ten or fewer VCRFs with SIC information reported. Nevertheless, such data as there are do seem to support several general notions about the outcomes to venture capital investment in the Central Region. First, rather than all venture dollars being piled into a limited number of very high growth activities, there seems to be a wide range of industries (a minimum of 163 could be identified here) whose member firms are capable of attracting venture capital. Second, this diversity of VCRF distribution is most clear in states which themselves are larger and more industrialized. Third, these states are the only ones which have their most popular code corresponding to the venture capitalist's traditionally targeted sectors of computers and medical ventures. In other states which are not quite the power-houses of these high-tech industries, the most popular codes correspond more closely with traditional industries in their area: petroleum in Oklahoma, machinery and instruments in Indiana and Michigan, and publishing in Wisconsin.

Three factors could tentatively be put forward to explain these empirical differences. First, there is a varying degree of maturity in the venture industry in different states. Illinois, Minnesota, and Colorado were established, though minor, centers of venture capital before states like Wisconsin and Oklahoma. The early venture capitalists in any area may opt for stereotypical high-tech ventures, but latecomers in the same geographical areas may have to diverge towards less stereotypical companies and be more specialized in order to compete, or else seek new locations in which they themselves can be early comers. However, venture activity in new environments may encounter problems, like the lack of a tradition of dynamic entrepreneurship, which may restrict their investments to buyouts and the restructuring of existing concerns, while they may also have to be less particular about the choice of industry involved. Second, the 'raw material' for successful entrepreneurship on which the venture capitalists base their judgements about proposals is the experience and quality of the management team. This must mean that, to a large extent, new firms, spin-offs, and buyouts are closely related to the socio-economic environment from which they have sprung. Pre-existing variations can be playing an important role in conditioning later venture outcomes in the Central Region. Third, the varying degree of concentration in primary codes at the state level suggests that there could also be agglomeration effects. States with a larger and more diverse industrial base offer venture capitalists a wider array of opportunities, and hence a greater number of specialized venture capital Funds find reason to be there. These three possible explanations are not mutually exclusive, of course, and contain a common stress on continuity with previous economic environments of the host area.

High-technology status of Central Region venture capital recipient firms

Part of the idea of venture capital as a dynamic, propulsive, and radical force for new industrial growth lies in its presumed association with high-technology industry. Data on the high-technology nature of VCRFs and their employment are given in Tables 3.12–3.14 (using the definition of 'high-tech' provided by Thompson (1987, Table 2), with 'primary' codes).

Table 3.12 gives the high-tech versus non-high-tech breakdown for VCRFs. In the Central Region as a whole, 130 out of 341 VCRFs with available information (or 38.1 per cent) are in high-tech SIC codes. This is far higher than the 0.39 per cent high-tech share of all industrial establishments in the region, though the absolute number is under 2 per cent of total high-tech establishments. At the individual state level for those with ten or more recipient firms, Colorado and Minnesota have the highest proportions of all their VCRFs in the high-tech category, with 65.0 per cent and 63.3 per cent respectively. However, these are the only two out of seventeen states to have the majority of their identifiable VCRFs in high-tech codes. Also, they already have the two highest proportions of all industrial establishments being high-tech.

Table 3.13 gives the high-tech versus non-high-tech breakdown of employment. In the Central Region as a whole, there are 171,405 employees in the VCRFs for which both employment and SIC information is available. Of these employees, 30,417 (or 17.8 per cent) are in VCRFs which are high-tech. At the individual state level for those states with ten or more recipient firms, the most high-tech employees in VCRFs are in Minnesota (with 9,630 employees, or 39.8 per cent of total VCRF employment in the state) and Texas (with 8,515 employees or 18.1 per cent of total VCRF employment in the state). No state with more than ten VCRFs had more than 40 per cent of its VCRF employment in high-tech firms.

Table 3.14 gives the average employment sizes of the 202 non-high-tech VCRFs for which both SIC and employment information is available. For the Central Region as a whole, the average size of all 330 VCRFs is 519.4 employees. For high-tech VCRFs only, the average size is much smaller at 235.8 (Table 3.12), while for non-high-tech VCRFs it is much larger, at 698.0 employees.

Table 3.12 High-tech status of venture capital recipient firms in Central states

Area	(a) Total	(b) VCRFs With SIC code info	(c) In high-tech SIC codes		(d) All 1986 establishments in high-tech SIC codes	
	(no.)	(no.)	(no.)	(%)	(no.)	(%)
Arkansas	0	–	–	–	194	0.37
Colorado	82	40	26	65.0	525	0.55
Illinois	71	34	6	17.6	1,178	0.46
Indiana	23	14	3	21.4	503	0.42
Iowa	4	3	1	33.3	165	0.23
Kansas	6	5	2	40.0	276	0.42
Kentucky	3	2	0	0.0	123	0.16
Michigan	41	23	11	47.8	798	0.41
Minnesota	86	49	31	63.3	577	0.55
Missouri	13	5	2	40.0	357	0.29
Nebraska	1	1	0	0.0	97	0.23
North Dakota	1	0	–	–	16	0.08
Ohio	64	33	13	39.4	1,002	0.43
Oklahoma	7	6	0	0.0	248	0.32
South Dakota	0	–	–	–	33	0.17
Texas	224	103	33	32.0	1,559	0.39
Wisconsin	22	18	2	11.1	398	0.35
Relocated	5	5				
Central total	653	341	130	38.1	8,049	0.39
US total					28,258	0.49

Sources: (a) Listings in *Venture Capital Journal*, August 1983 to February 1989; (b) trade and state business directories; SIC titles from the Office of Management and Budget, *Standard Industrial Classification Manual*, 1972 and 1977 supplement; state directories using the 1987 classification were 'translated' back to 1977 codes for conformity; (c) using 'consensus definition' from Thompson (1987); (d) US Department of Commerce Bureau of the Census, *County Business Patterns*, 1986, Washington, DC: US GPO

SUMMARY OF RESULTS

In this chapter data on the empirical patterns of venture capital recipient firms in a seventeen state Central Region of the United States have been collected, tabulated, and analyzed. For the various reasons presented in the introduction, this area is believed to provide an interesting contrast with the more often studied Coastal venture environments, and may lead to a different model of venturing.

In absolute terms, the Central Region in 1989 has 210 venture sources managing a total of $7,365 million of venture capital; it is also the location of 653 firms which have received venture funding in the 6-year period between August 1983 and February 1989. In relative terms, compared with the Central Region's 38 per cent share of the nation's population, these levels of venture activity are below the averages for the nation and for the Eastern and Western Regions. The Central Region has under 26 per cent of all working professional venture capitalists, just over 23 per cent of all listed venture sources, just over 22 per cent of VCRFs, and only 15.6 per cent of all venture dollars under management in the United States. At the individual state level within the Central Region, Illinois, Texas, Colorado, and Minnesota are the major states for venture activity in absolute terms. Under a variety of other relative measures, Iowa, Ohio, Michigan, and Indiana also occasionally make strong showings. At the other extreme, Arkansas, Kentucky, Nebraska, North Dakota, and South Dakota appear to have negligible venturing activity.

Among the detailed results of analyses of specifically Central Region VCRFs are the following. First, the spatial distribution of VCRFs within the Central Region is very uneven. Texas holds 224, or 34.3 per cent, of the Central Region's 653 total VCRFs. The top five Central states of Texas, Minnesota, Colorado, Illinois, and Ohio together contain 527 (or 80.7 per cent) of the region's VCRFs. Eight of the seventeen states in the Central Region have fewer than ten recipient firms each, while Nebraska and North Dakota each have only one, and Arkansas and South Dakota have no recipients named at all. By contrast, Massachusetts has 407 VCRFs, nearly double the number in Texas, and California has 966, more than four times the number in Texas and nearly 50 per cent more again than the entire Central Region.

Second, VCRFs are at present not 'new' firms, though they may have been close to that when they first received venture funding: the average age of VCRFs in 1989 is 16.8 years, and the median age is 10 years; the peak period for incorporation of VCRFs was 1979–83, with peak individual years being 1982 and 1983.

Third, VCRFs are currently not, on average, 'small' firms, though again they may have been when they received venture funding: only 9 per cent of VCRFs have fewer than twenty employees, compared with over 75 per cent of all establishments in this size class for the

Table 3.13 Employment in high-tech venture capital recipient firms in Central states

Area	(a)	(b) VCRFs	(c)	(d) In high-tech SIC codes			VCRF mean	All 1986 employment in high-tech SIC codes	
	Total	With employment and SIC[a] info	Employees		Share of state total	Share of Central total			
	(no.)	(no.)	(no.)	(no.)	(%)	(%)	(no.)	(no.)	(%)
Arkansas	0	0	0	0	0.0	0.00	0.0	12,386	1.89
Colorado	82	40	26	6,266	37.6	3.66	241.0	79,950	6.66
Illinois	71	34	6	1,574	11.1	0.92	262.3	144,188	3.46
Indiana	23	14	3	492	11.0	0.29	164.0	98,279	5.30
Iowa	4	3	1	57	3.1	0.03	57.0	17,401	2.04
Kansas	6	5	2	360	60.5	0.21	180.0	53,485	6.66
Kentucky	3	2	0	0	0.0	0.00	0.0	17,090	1.69
Michigan	41	22	10	949	8.0	0.55	43.1	57,938	1.87

Minnesota	86	49	31	9,630	39.8	5.62	310.7	41,244	2.58
Missouri	13	5	2	421	13.9	0.25	210.5	79,300	4.36
Nebraska	1	1	0	0	0.0	0.00	0.0	12,543	2.50
North Dakota	1	0	0	0	0.0	0.00	0.0	1,313	0.73
Ohio	64	30	12	1,913	5.2	1.12	159.4	115,580	3.04
Oklahoma	7	5	0	0	0.0	0.00	0.0	27,590	3.02
South Dakota	0	0	0	0	0.0	0.00	0.0	5,139	2.84
Texas	224	102	33	8,515	18.1	4.97	258.0	215,572	3.83
Wisconsin	22	18	2	240	3.3	0.14	120.0	50,620	3.05
Central total	653	330	128	30,417		17.75	235.8	1,029,618	3.44
US total								3,642,212	4.37

Sources: (a) Listings in *Venture Capital Journal*, August 1983 to February 1989; (b) trade and state business directories; SIC titles from the Office of Management and Budget, *Standard Industrial Classification Manual*, 1972 and 1977 supplement; state directories using the 1987 classification were 'translated' back to 1977 codes for conformity; (c) using 'consensus definition' from Thompson (1987); (d) US Department of Commerce, *Country Business Patterns*, 1986, Washington, DC: US GPO
Note: [a] Since SIC and employment information are not always both available for the same firms, the total for this column differs from that in Table 3.12, col. (b).

Table 3.14 Employment in non-high-tech venture capital recipient firms in Central states

Area	Non-high-tech VCRFs		Mean
	VCRFs	Employees	
	(no.)	(no.)	(no.)
Arkansas	0	0	0.0
Colorado	14	10,396	742.6
Illinois	28	12,646	451.6
Indiana	11	3,998	363.5
Iowa	2	1,775	887.5
Kansas	3	235	78.3
Kentucky	2	442	221.0
Michigan	12	10,963	913.6
Minnesota	18	14,574	809.7
Missouri	3	2,604	868.0
Nebraska	1	1,800	1,800.0
North Dakota	0	0	0.0
Ohio	18	35,003	1,944.6
Oklahoma	5	868	173.6
South Dakota	0	0	0.0
Texas	69	38,579	559.1
Wisconsin	16	7,105	441.1
Central total	202	140,988	698.0

region and the nation (although if the upper limit of 'small' is considered to be between twenty and a hundred employees, then over 60 per cent of VCRFs are 'small'). Central VCRFs average 512.7 employees per firm, and probably have a total workforce of over 334,000 employees. There are 11.2 people in VCRFs for every 1,000 employees in all establishments in the region. Minnesota has the highest ratio of VCRF employees to total employees, with 15.1 per 1,000.

Fourth, in terms of their sectoral distribution, some 63 per cent of VCRFs are in manufacturing: within this sector the most prevalent four-digit SIC code is SIC 3573 'Electronic computing equipment', with 41 VCRFs or 12 per cent of the regional total; this is almost three times the number of VCRFs in the second code, SIC 3841 'Surgical and medical instruments'. Some 32 per cent of VCRFs are in services, with the majority of these in SIC 73 'Business services'. Four codes – SIC 3573 'Electronic computing equipment', SIC 3841 'Surgical and medical instruments', SIC 7372 'Computer programming and software', and SIC 3662 'Radio and TV communications equipment' – together contain eighty-three VCRFs, or almost a quarter of the region's VCRFs with SIC information, but these four are the only codes with more than ten firms and the remaining 258 VCRFs are spread across 159 different three-digit SIC codes. The most prevalent four-digit SIC code also varies between individual states. In only three, Colorado, Minnesota, and Texas, is it the same as at the regional level.

Fifth, in direct contrast with Fast's (1982: Figure 1) finding that 70 per cent of venture capital investments were in technology-based businesses in 1981, almost two-thirds (61.9 per cent) of Central Region venture recipients are not high-technology firms. Those which are high technology contain under one-fifth (18 per cent) of all employees in VCRFs, and under 3 per cent of all the region's high-technology employment. Though we might hope that today's high-technology VCRFs represent the seeds of greater employment gains in the associated services, supply, and manufacturing firms for tomorrow, it is clear that the stereotypical image of venture capital as funding new small high-technology companies holds for only a minor part of venture activity on the USA's 'Third Coast'.

CONCLUSIONS AND DIRECTIONS FOR FURTHER RESEARCH

The general conclusion from this study of the spatial distributions of recipient firms is that the Central Region is under-endowed compared with the rest of the country. Yet uneven distributions of venture capital have been documented before: the true import of findings in this instance lies in their being associated with qualitative, and not just scale, differences in outcomes. This, in turn, prompts a venture-specific version of the general debate in economic geography: what is the real significance, as opposed to merely the empirical extent, of uneven spatial distributions? Just what is the causal efficacy of space in venturing phenomena? What does unevenness mean for the prospects of healthy levels of entrepreneurship, for new firm start-ups and early growth, for generation of high-risk, technology-based companies, and ultimately for the Central Region's future economic development and prosperity? And how should the stereotypical model of venture capital being associated with new small high-technology start-ups be modified considering these findings?

These questions can be approached on several levels: the empirical (that is, what is the proper comparative summary evaluation of the distributions as observed?), the conceptual (that is, what do the statistical findings mean for the stereotype model?), the real (that is, what do the findings tell us about the necessary or sufficient conditions for particular outcomes?), and the relevant (that is, to what extent should we be concerned about these findings, given our preferences for certain outcomes?).

With regard to the empirical significance of the findings, several tables showed the Central Region under-endowment to be less pronounced compared with the Eastern and Western Regions if the two venture 'super-states' of Massachusetts and California are each removed from their respective region's figures. Without these two states in the comparisons, the Central Region averages are much closer to the levels of the rest of the country. The particular historical circumstances, current economic positions, and weight of population and political influence of these two 'super-states' of the venture industry are hardly likely to be easily replicated by any other state in the country. It is also worth noting what pre-eminence of California and Massachusetts means for the venturing potential of other neighboring states in the same regions: for if California has 966 VCRFs, or over 86 per cent of all such firms in the Western Region, then this means that eleven other Western states are sharing only 153 companies, or under 14 per cent of the firms, between them. Consequently, one hidden virtue of the pattern of venturing activity in the Central Region may at least be its degree of dispersion compared with the situation in the other two regions. These points thus offer another way of looking at these inter-regional and intra-regional disparities in relative levels of venturing activity which can give cause for greater optimism about the situation in the Central region.

Regarding the question of conceptual significance, it is clear that the stereotypical model of venture capital as being primarily concerned with new, high-technology start-ups, is not supportable in the Central Region. The majority of recipient firms are not new, small, or high-technology, and there are differences across space not only in the quantitative levels of venture phenomena but also in their qualitative nature. This gives strong support to use of the 'adjustments theory' approach, which emphasizes variable individuals and institutions, legacies of past decisions and environments, and local places and contexts (Thompson 1989a). In this framework, venturing is cast as very much a contingent, rather than a mechanistic, phenomenon. The 'Third Coast' venture model could then be one where venture capitalists are more responsive to the more uneven patterns of opportunities presented by existing industrial structure than they are generative of new landscapes: in other words, less gatekeepers than foragers.

This is not to say, of course, that, given the inherently very diverse set of actors and preferences within the venture capital business, there will not be some Funds and individual venture capitalists who will on occasion do something very different with new enterprises in nontraditional industries in new geographical areas. However, the data suggest that the practical possibilities for venture capital to start new industries in completely new locations in the Central Region may be much more limited than the popular journalistic image of venture capital as a dynamic, propulsive, and radical force behind new high industrial growth would lead us to believe. In the Central Region, wherever the raw material of dynamic entrepreneurship is not available, venture capitalists resort to high growth opportunities in non-high-technology fields, and to buyouts rather than start-ups. The real significance of these results thus becomes the rediscovery of the importance of geographical contexts, which had originally been stripped away to form the abstract stereotype.

Finally, with regard to the relevance of the findings, there has to be a preferred outcome against which they can be judged. If this means equal treatment of equals everywhere, it would seem that the relevance of the specific unevenness shown here depends on (1) the significance of the venture-backed sector in the future growth of the economy, (2) the extent to which venture capital matches the spatial patterns of potentially fundable business ideas, and, if it does not, then (3) the extent to which the venture process is inherently bound by geographic constraints to operating close to venture capitalists' nominal home bases. For if the spatial distributions of fundable business ideas and actual new firm start-ups do not match, and if venture capital is not mobile over space to redress a poor match, then organized professional venturing is unlikely to be fulfilling the main criterion for capital market efficiency, which US Congressional Joint Economic Committee researchers expounded in a 1984 review of the venture capital business:

> A regional gap problem would exist if the regional disparities resulted in entrepreneurs in the venture capital poor regions being at a competitive disadvantage in competition with entre-preneurs in venture capital rich regions for venture capital financing, for otherwise comparable deals.   (JEC 1984: 52)

In other words, proposals which are equally risky in business terms should stand an equal chance of being funded everywhere.

Obviously, there is a limit to how well this condition can be evaluated from aggregate statistics alone, since these could mask important individual-level and qualitative differences, which can be satisfactorily approached only at the level of the firm. For example, it cannot be known merely from the date of incorporation of VCRFs how long it took firms in different places to secure venture financing. Similarly, which explanation of the three suggested alternatives is most relevant to the noted size distribution of VCRFs can only be found by questioning the company managers involved about what precise stage in their firm's life-cycle and employment history they first received venture capital.

Thus, the next step in the on-going research project of which this chapter is a part (Thompson and Bayer 1989a, b, 1990) will be to explore further this 'spatial interfacing' problem between entrepreneurship (which could be thought of as the 'demand' for business financing) and venture capital (which could be thought of as the 'supply' of one type of finance for new businesses). The main vehicle for this will be a survey of managers and founders of VCRFs. For while economists and geographers have developed a large corpus of theory and evidence on how the mature firm as an economic entity behaves under a variety of conditions commonly found in market economies (Watts 1987), rather less is known about real constraints within the firm founding process, the very early stages of entrepreneurship, the types of people who successfully attract venture funding, and the uses to which such capital is put within the firm. Above all, there is a need to address venture capital's precise role not only in the generation of new firms, but also in the phenomena which this chapter's results concerning age and size of Central Region VCRFs hint it may be more closely associated with: the restructuring and relocation of existing enterprise.

ACKNOWLEDGEMENTS

The author wishes to thank the Prochnow Educational Foundation and the University of Wisconsin-Madison Graduate School Research Committee for financial support (UW grant #133-P162) and Professor Milford Green, Dr Ron Hustedde, Professor Glen Pulver, Richard Doolittle, Bob Klockars, and Joan Pfister, for advice; Kristin Bayer provided valuable research assistance and Gail Grothaus took part in data collection. Empirical research for this chapter was carried out in Summer 1989 under the sponsorship of the Prochnow Educational Foundation Inc., of the Graduate School of Banking Inc., One East Main, Madison, WI 53703, USA. Nothing herein should be taken as reflecting the views or policies of the Foundation, and any opinions, errors, or omissions remain the responsibility of the author.

4 Regional patterns of venture capital investment

Richard Florida, Donald F. Smith Jr and Elizabeth Sechoka

INTRODUCTION

Venture capital investment is a critical component of high-technology economic growth. Although investment is perhaps the most important dimension of venture capital activity, there is virtually no literature on it. The academic literature has generally focused on the concentration and distribution of venture capital resources and firms, largely because of unavailable or unreliable data. While most studies assert that venture capitalists tend to invest within 200 miles of the home office, none have systematically reviewed many of the considerations that make geography such an important factor in a venture capitalist's investment decision. This may stem from the fact that most academic studies suffer from over-aggregation, convey only regional totals or state-wide aggregates, which prevents an in-depth analysis of state or metropolitan level flows of venture capital.

In this chapter, we overcome these problems by basing our analysis on a new, comprehensive database on venture capital investment. This database is derived from information published by *Venture Capital Journal* over the 3-year period 1984–87, and provides a 40–45 per cent sample of all venture investment made over that period. The database provides 'micro-level' information on venture capital investments in actual companies. This enables us to look closely at investment flows at the micro level, thereby overcoming the shortcomings of previous studies.

Our major findings can be summarized as three major points. First, venture capital investments are highly concentrated by region. Just two regions – the Northeast and the Pacific – accounted for almost 75 per cent of the venture capital invested in 1986. Second, at the state level, just two states – California and Massachusetts –

accounted for over 50 per cent of all venture capital invested in that year. And third, venture capital investments are highly concentrated within most states. According to our data, the San Francisco–Silicon Valley area accounted for 58 per cent of all venture capital investments made in California, and 23 per cent of all venture capital investments made nationwide; the Route 128 area around Boston received 95 per cent of the venture capital investments in Massachusetts and 14 per cent of the national total (Map 4.1). Moreover, this pattern is also observable in states that are not leading centers of venture capital. A prime example of this is Georgia – almost all the venture capital investments in that state are concentrated in the Atlanta area.

Together, these three findings lead us to conclude that venture capital investments flow to areas with established concentrations of high-technology businesses. Many researchers have explored the following 'chicken or the egg' question: Does venture capital attract high-technology industry or does high-technology attract the venture capital dollars? Our research supports the latter interpretation. An area is much more likely to be a recipient of venture capital if it is home to high-technology firms.

Although a logical assumption might be that venture capital investments tend to concentrate in areas that possess venture capital resources, our findings indicate that this is only partly true. Venture capital mainly flows to the nation's premier high-technology centers, most notably California's Silicon Valley and Route 128 around Boston. In contrast, venture capital centers like Chicago and New York City receive a relatively minor share of venture investments.

This chapter proceeds as follows. The first section explores the major trends in the concentration of venture capital investment. The second section provides detailed analyses of venture capital investments within regions at the level of state and metropolitan area. In this section we also present some rough comparisons between venture capital investments and the location of high-technology businesses.[1]

CONCENTRATION OF VENTURE CAPITAL INVESTMENTS

The geographic distribution of venture capital investments is highly uneven and tightly clustered. As Table 4.1 illustrates, venture capital investment is concentrated at the regional level, exhibiting pronounced 'bi-coastalism'. The Pacific and Northeast Regions together attracted almost three-fourths (74 per cent) of the $2.9

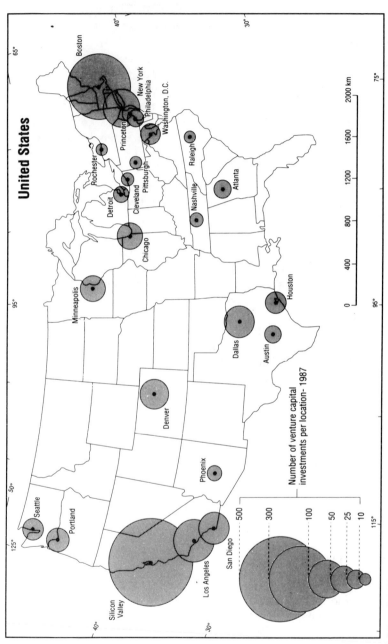

United States

Boston
New York
Princeton
Philadelphia
Washington, D.C.
Rochester
Detroit
Cleveland
Pittsburgh
Raleigh
Nashville
Atlanta
Chicago
Minneapolis
Houston
Dallas
Austin
Denver
Phoenix
Seattle
Portland
Silicon Valley
Los Angeles
San Diego

0   400   800   1200   1600   2000 km

Number of venture capital
investments per location– 1987

500
300
100
50
25
10

65°   40°   30°   75°   95°   50°   95°   125°   115°   30°   40°

Map 4.1 Venture capital investments, 1987

billion funds invested by the venture capital industry in 1986. The Pacific Region is led by California, which dominates the rest of the nation in its ability to attract venture capital. The Northeast Region is placed a distant second behind the Pacific. Within the Northeast Region, Massachusetts attracts the majority of this region's venture investments. However, its dominance over the rest of the Northeast Region is far less than that of California's in the Pacific Region.

The Midwest Region has seen a precipitous decline in venture capital investments. A report prepared for IBM by S.M. Rubel (Rubel and Company 1975) in the mid-1970s presented findings that, in the 1968–75 period, states in the Midwest had attracted almost 20 per cent of the total share of venture capital investments. By 1981, the Midwest's share had declined to a mere 8 per cent of the national total. For the past decade, the distribution of venture capital throughout the United States has remained relatively constant. The only possible exception is the South Region which has shown a steady increase, from 6 per cent in the early 1970 period to 9 per cent in 1986.

As Table 4.2 shows, among states, California attracted the 'lion's share' of the investment dollars, with $1.1 billion or 38 per cent of the national total in 1986. Massachusetts was second, receiving approximately $400 million or 14 per cent of the total venture capital invested, while New York, Texas, and New Jersey attracted $200 million, $170 million, and $140 million respectively. No other state drew more than $100 million in venture capital investments. Although in recent years California and Massachusetts have commanded the majority of the venture capital industry's disbursements, this pattern of investment did not always hold. In the period prior to the industry's boom of the late 1970s the combined share of investments for these two states was only 35 per cent.

Venture capital is also highly concentrated within states. Silicon Valley receives more than two-thirds of all venture capital investments made in California, with investments tightly clustered in the cities of Sunnyvale, Santa Clara, and San Jose. These cities received 30 per cent of the California total, and 12 per cent of total investments. Of the states, only Massachusetts received more venture capital investments than this three city area. A similar level of concentration is noticeable in the Route 128 area. The eighteen cities and towns along the Route 128 corridor received almost 75 per cent of that state's investments. And just three communities, Newton, Waltham, and Woburn, received 62 per cent of the Route 128 investments – almost 3 per cent of the national total of venture capital investments.

Table 4.1 Venture capital disbursements, by region, by total dollar amount (in millions), and by percentage of total

Region	1968–75	1980	1981	1982	1983	1984	1985	1986	1987
Pacific	213	365	648	875	1,071	1,035	1,118	1,066	1,638
	(28)	(36)	(46)	(48)	(51)	(45)	(43)	(41)	(42)
Northeast	246	275	352	474	525	552	702	858	1,092
	(28)	(27)	(25)	(26)	(25)	(24)	(27)	(33)	(28)
Midwest	154	92	113	146	147	184	234	182	312
	(20)	(9)	(8)	(8)	(7)	(8)	(9)	(7)	(8)
South	46	92	71	91	147	184	182	234	468
	(6)	(9)	(5)	(5)	(7)	(8)	(7)	(9)	(12)
Gulf Coast	57	133	155	146	105	230	208	156	234
	(7)	(13)	(11)	(8)	(5)	(10)	(8)	(9)	(6)
Mountain	31	68	71	91	105	115	156	104	156
	(4)	(7)	(5)	(5)	(5)	(5)	(6)	(6)	(4)
US total	747	1,025	1,409	1,822	2,100	2,300	2,600	2,900	3,900

Sources: 1968–75 data from Rubel (1975); 1980–2 data from OTA (1984); 1983 data from *Venture Capital Journal*, May 1984; 1984 data from *Venture Capital Journal*, May 1985; 1985–6 data from *Venture Capital Journal*, May 1987; 1987 data from *Venture Capital Journal*, May 1988.

Table 4.2 Venture capital disbursements – leading recipient states, by dollar amount (in millions), and by percentage of total

State	1968–75	1980	1981	1982	1983	1984	1985	1986	1987
California	201 (26)	345 (34)	587 (42)	829 (46)	987 (47)	1,012 (44)	1,014 (39)	988 (38)	1,521 (39)
New York	82 (11)	66 (7)	45 (3)	135 (7)	105 (5)	115 (5)	130 (5)	182 (7)	117 (3)
Massachusetts	66 (9)	123 (12)	180 (13)	224 (12)	252 (12)	322 (14)	338 (13)	364 (14)	429 (11)
Illinois	57 (7)	29 (3)	32 (2)	–	42 (2)	46 (2)	78 (3)	78 (3)	117 (3)
Texas	57 (7)	108 (11)	140 (10)	142 (8)	105 (5)	184 (8)	182 (7)	156 (6)	234 (6)
Colorado	25 (3)	54 (5)	44 (3)	67 (4)	63 (3)	69 (3)	78 (3)	78 (3)	117 (3)
Michigan	22 (3)	–	14 (1)	15 (2)	–	–	–	–	–
Minnesota	20 (3)	–	21 (1.5)	33 (2)	42 (2)	69 (3)	–	–	–
New Jersey	31 (4)	24 (2)	35 (2.5)	38 (2)	42 (2)	46 (2)	78 (3)	130 (5)	234 (6)
Ohio	24 (3)	–	37 (3)	–	–	–	–	–	–
Pennsylvania	23 (3)	42 (4)	30 (2)	30 (2)	42 (2)	46 (2)	52 (2)	52 (2)	78 (2)
State total	608 (79)	791 (77)	1,165 (80)	1,532 (84)	1,680 (80)	1,909 (83)	1,950 (75)	2,028 (78)	3,042 (78)
US total	747	1,025	1,409	1,822	2,100	2,300	2,600	2,600	3,900

Sources: 1968–75 data from Rubel (1975); 1980–2 data from OTA (1984); 1983 data from Venture Capital Journal, May 1984; data from Venture Capital Journal, May 1985; 1985–6 data from Venture Capital Journal, May 1987; 1987 data from Venture Capital Journal, May 1988

Interestingly, this pattern is also true of states that control only minor amounts of venture capital. Atlanta, Georgia, which was the leading recipient of venture capital in the South Region, has been evolving a high-technology industrial base in recent years. A similar trend was especially evident in Colorado where the distribution of venture financings went primarily to high-technology firms located along Interstate 25, a corridor that is becoming a well-known center for technology-intensive defense industries.

REGIONAL ANALYSES OF VENTURE CAPITAL INVESTMENTS

This section provides detailed analyses of venture capital investment in five major regions: the Northeast, Pacific, Midwest, Sunbelt, and Mountain Regions. It provides data on gross investment dollars adopted from *Venture Economics* sources and supplements this with data on the number of venture capital investments and coinvestments in each state of a region derived from our micro-level database.

The Northeast Region

The Northeast Region has long been recognized as one of the nation's premier centers of venture capital. During the 1970s it received almost 32 per cent of the nation's venture capital investments, the largest percentage of venture capital of any region. Since then, the Northeast has fallen to second place, behind the Pacific Region. Table 4.3 shows that the growth in venture capital dollars invested in the region increased 127 per cent from 1981 to 1986 in real dollar terms. In recent years the Northeast Region attracted roughly one-fourth of the venture capital industry's investments.

Venture capital in the Northeast is concentrated mainly in two states: Massachusetts and New York. Massachusetts accounted for $406 million or 14 per cent of venture capital investments in 1986, while New York accounted for $203 million or 7 per cent of the total. Here it is quite evident that New York fails to attract a level of venture capital investment. Clearly, New York is not a leading center of venture capital investment comparable with the level of venture capital resources it controls.

It is slightly surprising that the remaining Northeast states have attracted so little in the way of venture capital investment. Even

Table 4.3 Venture capital investments in the Northeast

State	1968–75			1981			1986			Change
	$ million	% natl	% regional	$ million	% natl	% regional	$ million	% natl	% regional	% 1975–86
Northeast	246.2	31.8		348.0	24.8		957	33		289
New York	82.3	10.6	33.4	45.0	3.2	12.9	203	7	21.2	147
Massachusetts	66.2	8.6	26.9	181.0	12.8	52.0	406	14	42.4	513
Connecticut	–	–	–	38.0	2.7	10.9	87	3	9.1	–
Pennsylvania	23.3	3.0	9.5	29.0	2.1	8.3	58	2	6.1	149
New Jersey	31.1	4.0	12.6	35.0	2.5	10.1	145	5	15.2	366
Rhode Island	5.2	.7	2.1	–	–	–	–	–	–	–
Other	38.1	4.9	15.5	20.0	1.4	5.7	58	2	6.1	52

though these states are located in relatively close proximity to two of the major venture capital centers, Boston and New York, and many boast research-oriented universities, they have not attracted a significant amount of venture capital. Our analysis does reveal that the distribution of venture capital investments in these states is concentrated in centers of high-technology businesses.

Massachusetts

The dramatic evolution of Route 128 as one of the premier high-technology centers in the world has thrust Massachusetts into the national limelight. The state's extraordinary rise from a period of prolonged economic decline in the 1970s to one of rapid growth and expansion has caught the attention of many of the country's leading economic development experts as they try to duplicate the 'Massachusetts Miracle' in other depressed regions.

The striking reversal in the economic fortunes of Massachusetts has been traced directly to its transformation into a center for high-technology industry. Venture capital has played a vital role in that transformation. Despite the bleak economic outlook during the last decade, venture capitalists have continued to invest much of their venture capital dollars in firms located in Massachusetts. In real dollar terms, Massachusetts has experienced a 71 per cent increase in venture capital investments from 1975 to 1981, and an 85 per cent increase from 1981 to 1986 (Table 4.3).

In recent years, Massachusetts has led the other states located in the Northeast Region in venture capital investments. In 1986, Massachusetts received 42 per cent of the Northeast Region's share of venture capital investments and 14 per cent of the US total. On a national level, Massachusetts ranked second behind California in the amount of venture capital investments received in the period from 1980 to 1986.

The distribution of venture capital investments in Massachusetts is mainly concentrated in the Route 128 complex, which accounted for a remarkable 95 per cent of the 282 venture capital financings we recorded for Massachusetts. Within this general area, the Boston–Cambridge area (which includes cities such as Somerville and Revere) accounted for 24 per cent of the state's total venture capital investments; the towns that lie directly along Route 128 accounted for roughly one-third of the state's venture investments (Newton, Woburn, and Waltham alone drew 20 per cent of the state's total); and the Route 495 area accounted for 18 per cent; communities that fall between the Route 128 and Route 495 boundaries received 21 per cent. Other areas within Massachusetts received very little venture investment, despite the Dukakis administration commitment to dispersing economic development activity.

The distribution of venture capital investments in Massachusetts follows the distribution of high-technology companies. The Route 128 complex has 67 per cent of the state's high-technology companies. Newton, Waltham, and Woburn alone were home to 47 per cent of the high-technology firms located in the Route 128 complex, 13 per cent of the state total, and 1 per cent of the national total for high-technology firms.

New York

As we have seen, New York is a major center of venture capital resources. It would thus seem reasonable to expect New York to be a center for venture capital investments. This is not the case, however. New York has been unable to attract a large percentage of the venture capital industry's investment. In fact, in recent years New York's share of venture capital investments has hovered between 5 and 7 per cent of the national total (Table 4.3). Simply put, in recent years the state's own venture capitalists have chosen to invest their capital elsewhere.

Still, venture capital investments in New York State are quite concentrated, mainly around existing clusters of high technology. According to our database, New York City received 40 per cent of the state's venture capital investments. According to Sommerfield (1986), $66.8 million of venture capital, half of the total invested, was placed in twenty-seven firms located within a 25-mile radius of the Statue of Liberty in 1985. When combined with its suburbs in Long Island and White Plains, the New York City Metropolitan Region received approximately 72 per cent of New York State's venture capital investment. This follows the pattern of the state's high-technology companies, of which 68 per cent are located in this area.

Rochester, Albany–Troy, and Buffalo attract a minor share of venture capital investment in New York. According to our database, the greater Rochester area received almost 9 per cent of New York's venture investments, and it is home to approximately 7 per cent of the state's high-technology firms. The Albany–Troy area accounted for almost 16 per cent of the state's venture capital investments, while the area's share of high-technology firms was

4 per cent. Finally, Buffalo's share of the state's venture capital investments was 3 per cent and its share of high-technology firms was 7 per cent.

New Jersey

During the 1940s and 1950s, New Jersey was considered a leading state for technological innovation. AT&T's Bell Labs can perhaps be considered primarily responsible for putting New Jersey on the map as a center for cutting-edge technology. With inventions like the transistor in the 1950s and fiber optics in the 1970s, Bell Labs has revolutionized the communications industry. But perhaps even more important than the inventions at Bell Labs was the development of a large number of scientists who spun off from Bell and went on to found their own, highly successful high-technology firms. Not least among these scientists was William Shockley, considered by many to be the father of Silicon Valley's semi-conductor industry.

In recent years, New Jersey has regained some of its status as a high-technology state. For example, in 1985, over 10 per cent of the state's labor force was employed in the high-technology sector (Malecki 1985). And over the past decade New Jersey has experienced a dramatic increase in venture capital investments. Between 1981 and 1986, New Jersey's share of venture capital investments increased from 2.5 to 5 per cent of the national total, a real dollar increase of 250 per cent. At the same time, its regional share rose from 10.1 to 15.2 per cent (Table 4.3).

The northeast portion of the state received the major share of venture capital investments. According to our database, this region accounted for 55 per cent of the state's venture investments.[2] Princeton received 25 per cent of the venture capital investments for New Jersey. Princeton is home to Princeton University and to the Princeton University Forrestal Center, one of the most successful research parks in the United States. The Forrestal Center has over fifty tenants, including divisions of Xerox, IBM, and Siemens AG (Glazer 1987).

Connecticut

For the past several years, Connecticut has received 2–3 per cent of venture capital investment dollars, and approximately 10 per cent of the Northeast Region total (Table 4.3). The state experienced a 90 per cent increase in terms of real dollars invested during this period.

According to our database, 77 per cent of venture capital investments in Connecticut were located along the Route 95 corridor, and more specifically were to companies located between New Haven and the New York border. Stamford and its suburb Darien were the major focus. Together, they received almost 30 per cent of the state's venture capital investments. Coupled with the investments for Fairfield, Westport, and Norwalk (Stamford to Fairfield is a distance of 22 miles along Route 95), the percentage of investments received for this area increases to almost 50 per cent of the state total. The Waterbury–Hartford area received 13 per cent of the state's investments and, as such, was the only other section of Connecticut to receive a significant number of venture capital investments.

Venture capital investment follows the distribution of the state's high-technology companies. Almost 77 per cent of the state's high-technology firms are located in cities along the Route 95 corridor. The Stamford–Fairfield corridor contains one-fourth of the state's high-technology firms. In addition, one fourth of Connecticut's venture capital offices are located in Stamford, and another 13 per cent are in Hartford. The greater Waterbury–Hartford area housed approximately 15 per cent of the state's high-technology firms.

Pennsylvania

At one time, Pennsylvania was fairly successful in attracting venture investments. For example, during the period from 1968 to 1975, Pennsylvania received almost 10 per cent of the venture capital investments made in the Northeast Region, and 3 per cent of the national total. However, during the 1980s, the state's share of venture investments has declined to about 2 per cent of the national total (Table 4.3). Part of the reason for the lack of growth in venture investments in Pennsylvania is the investment orientation of the state's venture capitalists. For example, although the number of venture capital firms in Pittsburgh increased from four to seventen between 1980 and 1987, almost 75 per cent of the capital invested by these firms in 1986 went to companies located outside the state (Enterprise Corporation of Pittsburgh 1987).

According to our database, the Philadelphia area received 44 per cent of the state total of venture capital investments, while firms in the Pittsburgh area received over 30 per cent. The Philadelphia and

Pittsburgh Regions were home to the majority of the state's high-technology firms. The greater Philadelphia Region has 50 per cent of the state's high-technology firms, while the greater Pittsburgh Region contains 35 per cent. Pennsylvania provides yet another example of the close association between existing high-technology centers and investments of venture capital.

Other Northeast States

New Hampshire, Vermont, Maine, and Rhode Island have all been generally overlooked by the venture capital industry, receiving only a minor portion of venture investments. Indeed, during the past decade, these states together received less than 2 per cent of the national total of venture investments, and only 6 per cent of the regional total. Rhode Island and New Hampshire each received somewhat more than 2 per cent of the region's financings, while Maine received slightly less than 1 per cent. These investments were primarily directed to the major city of each state. According to our database, over 60 per cent of Rhode Island's investments were in Providence, over 75 per cent of Maine's investments were in Portland, and close to 50 per cent of those for New Hampshire were in Manchester and Nashua. Comparing the areas of investments with the location of high-technology firms for these states, once again a close parallel can be found. A third of Rhode Island's high-technology firms are in the Providence area, one-sixth of Maine's high-technology firms are in Portland, and 25 per cent of the New Hampshire high-technology firms are in Manchester and Nashua.

The Pacific Region

The Pacific Region now accounts for the largest amount of venture capital investments (Table 4.4). In 1986, it received $1.2 billion or 41 per cent of the national total. California is unquestionably the leading state in this region and in the nation as well, capturing a huge share of total venture capital investments. In 1986 California received 38 per cent of the total amount of the nation's venture capital investments, which was 93 per cent of the total amount invested in the Pacific Region.

Silicon Valley can claim responsibility for the unprecedented success of this region as one of the world's leading centers of high-technology and venture capital investment. It receives 23 per cent of the national total of venture investments. The success of Silicon

Table 4.4 Venture capital investments in the Pacific

| State | 1968–75 | | | 1981 | | | 1986 | | | Change |
	$ million	% natl	% regional	$ million	% natl	% regional	$ million	% natl	% regional	% 1975–86
Pacific	213.2	27.5		621	44.1		1,189	41.0		458
California	201.3	26.0	94.4	588	41.7	94.7	1,102	38.0	92.7	447
Oregon	–	–	–	–	–	–	58	2.0	4.9	–
Other	11.9	1.5	5.6	33	2.3	5.3	29	1.0	2.4	144

Valley is regarded as a model for many other communities that hope somehow to duplicate its phenomenal rise from orchards to high-technology mecca.

As Table 4.4 shows, the Pacific Region has experienced tremendous growth in venture capital investment. During the early 1970s, it received 28 per cent of the venture industry's investment dollars, though it controlled only 10 per cent of the total amount of venture capital resources. By the end of the decade, it had taken over the lead as the leading recipient region in the country. In 1980, the Pacific Region laid claim to 36 per cent of the venture capital industry's investments and by 1986, its share was 41 per cent of national venture capital investments.

California

California is undeniably the major player in the Pacific Region. California has a long history as a home for high-technology and venture capitalists and their investment dollars. Even when its own venture capital industry was in its early development stages during the late 1960s and early 1970s, California still managed to attract significant amounts of venture capital. Between 1968 and 1975, California attracted over $200 million in venture capital investments, an amount double that of its venture capital resources and two and a half times the amount of investments received by any other state. Since then, the state's ability to attract investments has only increased.

Venture capital investments are strikingly concentrated within California. Silicon Valley is the main center for venture capital investment. Twenty-three per cent of the venture capital investments in our database are in this region. Cities that lie just outside the Silicon Valley area attract much smaller amounts of venture capital. For example, the greater Oakland area (which lies just across the bay from San Francisco) received a mere 7 per cent of the California total of venture capital investments, while the Sausalito area managed to attract only 2 per cent of the state's total venture financings. This pattern of venture capital investments maps nicely onto the distribution of high-technology firms in the San Francisco area. The San Francisco Region contained 44 per cent of the state's high-technology firms, with the greater San Jose area accounting for roughly half this total.

In recent years, California venture capitalists have shifted some of their investment focus to the greater Los Angeles and San Diego areas. Both cities are home to major universities, have a growing number of venture capital offices, and contain a significant number of high-technology firms. Firms in the Los Angeles area received 18 per cent of the California venture capital investments, 7 per cent of the national total. San Diego attracted 9 per cent of the California investments. In short, 98 per cent of venture capital investments in California go to companies located in Silicon Valley, Los Angeles, or San Diego, areas that are home to 95 per cent of the state's high-technology firms.

Other Pacific States: Oregon, Washington, and Alaska

Oregon has increased its share of the venture capital industry's investments from 1.1 per cent in 1981 to 2 per cent in 1986 (Table 4.4). According to our database, roughly 90 per cent of Oregon's venture capital investments went to firms located in Portland and its suburbs. Portland is a growing high-technology center, home to Sequent, a top computer company, and other high-technology companies.

Washington has experienced a relative decline in its share of venture capital investment dollars. Its share of the regional total fell from 5.3 per cent in 1981 to 2.4 per cent in 1986 (Table 4.4). According to our database, almost 87 per cent of the venture capital investments in Washington went to the Seattle–Tacoma area, a region with 80 per cent of the state's high technology firms.

Alaska is perhaps an extreme example of the difficulties that an individual state faces as it explores the use of high technology as a way to diversify its economy. Like Texas, Alaska has been highly reliant on the oil industry for its economic base. It has received an extremely small number of venture investments. The *Corporate Technology Information Service Directory* (1987) counts only five high-technology firms in the entire state. Alaska has tried to address its weakness in high technology with a variety of programs. Between 1978 and 1985, the state sponsored Alaska Resource Corporation invested $40 million, primarily in existing fishing and timber companies that were facing severe financial difficulties. The state corporation registered $4.5 million in losses, and in 1984 the legislature ordered it to terminate its operations and phase out its equity investments by 1988 (Farrell 1985). Currently, the state is contemplating founding another investment corporation whose focus will be almost solely on financing high technology enterprises. Summing up Alaska's problems, one commentator noted that 'the prospects for developing a "Silicon Tundra" on any large scale will remain bleak until the basic infrastructure required by high-technology industry is in place.' (Dixon 1985).

The Midwest Region

The Midwest has experienced a significant decline in venture capital investments over the past two decades. Between 1968 and 1975 the Midwest Region attracted 20 per cent of the venture capital investments, ranking third behind the Northeast and the Pacific Regions; the region also contained four of the top ten venture capital recipient states in the nation. By 1980, Illinois was the only Midwestern state to be listed among the top 10 states, ranking seventh. By 1986 the Midwest's share of venture capital investment had dropped further to 7 per cent (Table 4.5).

According to our database, venture capital investments in the Midwest are primarily concentrated in Chicago and the Minneapolis–St Paul area. Together, these areas accounted for almost 50 per cent of the Midwest's venture investments. These areas also have the region's highest concentrations of high-technology firms. Almost one-fourth of the Midwest's high-technology firms are found in Chicago or its suburbs, and over 12 per cent are in the Minneapolis–St Paul area (*Corporate Technology Information Service Directory* 1987).

Despite its reputation as a center for traditional manufacturing, the Midwest does possess something of a high-technology base. Nearly 20 per cent of the nation's high-technology firms are located there, and more than half of these companies are concentrated in Illinois, Ohio, and Minnesota (*Corporate Technology Information Service Directory* 1987). Illinois, Ohio, and Michigan also rank among the top 10 states for new business starts in 1987, according to the Dun and Bradstreet listings. The Midwest was responsible for almost 20 per cent of the nation's new business starts in 1987 (Dun and Bradstreet 1988). In addition, the region has a strong university base with six of the nation's top twenty universities in terms of corporate sponsored research and development (O'Connor 1988).

Illinois

Illinois, the leading center for venture capital in the Midwest, attracted just 3 per cent of all venture capital invested in 1986 (Table 4.5). This is a sharp drop from the 1960s and 1970s when

Table 4.5 Venture capital investments in the Midwest

State	1968–75			1981			1986			Change
	$ million	% natl	% regional	$ million	% natl	% regional	$ million	% natl	% regional	% 1975–86
Midwest	153.8	19.8		108.5	7.7		203	7.0		32
Ohio	23.7	3.1	15.4	36.0	2.6	33.2	–	–		–
Illinois	56.5	7.3	36.7	33.0	2.3	30.4	87	3.0	42.9	54
Michigan	22.3	2.9	14.5	–	–		–	–		–
Minnesota	19.8	2.6	12.9	–	–		–	–		–
Other	31.5	4.1	20.5	39.5	2.8	36.4	116	4.0	57.1	268

Illinois accounted for over 7 per cent of the national total. Like New York City – another major financial center – many of the state's venture investments went to areas outside the state and, indeed, outside the Midwest Region. The Chicago area is the leading site for venture capital investment in the Midwest Region. According to our database, the Chicago area accounted for 26 per cent of the region's investments, and 88 per cent of the Illinois total. The greater Chicago area accounts for 87 per cent of all high-technology firms in Illinois, and 22 per cent of those in the Midwest. However, according to a recent article, Chicago's high-technology and venture capital environments are in dismal shape (Moberg 1988). Moberg noted that 'the common complaint [about Chicago] is that there aren't enough like-minded people around to create a vibrant high-tech community – not just entrepreneurs and engineers, but also knowledge investors and venture capitalists and consultants who often help shepherd young companies through infancy' (Moberg 1988: 88).

Minnesota

Minnesota has a rather interesting pattern of venture capital investment. Although it is a small center, it tends to retain a large share of its venture capital, capturing roughly 25 per cent of the region's venture investments recorded in our database. Venture capital investments and high-technology firms are highly concentrated in the Minneapolis–St Paul area. All the venture capital investments that we recorded for Minnesota and 92 per cent of the state's high-technology companies were in this area. The twin cities are the national center for supercomputing with Control Data Corporation, Cray Computer, and a host of new start-ups. Of all the potential areas in the country, we believe that the Minneapolis–St Paul area has the best chance of duplicating the Silicon Valley–Route 128 experience – a belief echoed in numerous interviews with Silicon Valley venture capitalists and entrepreneurs.

Michigan

Michigan ranked a distant third behind Illinois and Minnesota in venture capital investments in the Midwest. Michigan received almost 11 per cent of the Midwest Region's venture financings. The state is also home to 15 per cent of the region's high-technology firms. Over 75 per cent of Michigan's venture capital investments were in the Detroit–Ann Arbor area, which also contains two-thirds of the state's high-technology firms. Not surprisingly, many of the high-technology companies in the Detroit–Ann Arbor area manu-facture products that are of importance to the automobile industry (Glazer 1987).

Ohio

Ohio receives a small and declining fraction of venture capital investments. Its share of venture capital investment dollars has declined from 3.1 per cent of the total investments in the 1968–75 period to less than 2 per cent in 1986 (Table 4.5). According to our database, it received slightly over 8 per cent of the Midwest's total of venture investments in recent years. Venture investments in Ohio were distributed among several areas, following the distribution of the state's high-technology firms. The Cleveland area, which is home to one-third of the state's high-technology firms, had roughly 30 per cent of the state's venture investments. The Columbus area had 15 per cent of the state's high-technology companies, and received 20 per cent of Ohio's venture capital investments. Cincinnati was home to 12 per cent of the state's high-technology firms and received 18 per cent of the venture investments.[3]

The Sunbelt

The Sunbelt comprises two subregions: the South (that is, Delaware, Maryland, Virginia, West Virginia, Kentucky, Washing-ton, DC, Tennessee, South Carolina, North Carolina, Georgia, Florida, Arkansas, and Mississippi); and the Gulf Coast area (that is, Texas, Louisiana, and Oklahoma). The Sunbelt accounts for roughly 15 per cent of all venture capital investments.

The South

The South is an 'up and coming' region for venture investments. Between 1981 and 1986, investments in the region increased 127 per cent, in real dollar terms. In 1986, the South accounted for $261 million in venture capital investments, 9 per cent of the national total (Table 4.6).

Georgia has been the major recipient of the venture investments in the South. In 1986, the state received one-third of all Southern venture capital investment. Georgia is followed by Florida,

Table 4.6 Venture capital investments in the South

State	1968–75			1981			1986			Change
	$ million	% natl	% regional	$ million	% natl	% regional	$ million	% natl	% regional	% 1975–86
South	46.0	5.9	–	95.0	6.7	–	261	9	–	467
DC	6.8	0.9	14.8	–	–	–	–	–	–	–
Georgia	–	–	–	–	–	–	87	3.0	33.3	–
Tennessee	–	–	–	–	–	–	–	–	–	–
Virginia	–	–	–	–	–	–	–	–	–	–
Other	39.2	5.0	85.2	66.0	4.7	69.5	174	6.0	66.7	344

Tennessee, Virginia, Maryland, and North Carolina. The remaining states in the region have been far less successful in attracting venture capital investment funds. Delaware, Mississippi, Kentucky, West Virginia, and South Carolina each received less than 2.5 per cent of the South Region's venture capital investments. Again, the distribution of venture investments throughout the South Region is toward areas with high concentrations of technology-intensive businesses.

Georgia

In 1986, Georgia led the South in the dollar amount of venture capital investments received, attracting 3 per cent of the national total and one-third of the region's total (Venture Economics 1989c). Georgia's success has been a relatively recent phenomenon, and according to a 1987 article in *Datamation*, little of the increase in high technology and venture capital activity occurred before 1982 (Schatz 1987). Atlanta's first high-technology-oriented venture fund was not established until 1983.

A large part of Georgia's emergence can be directly attributed to Atlanta's recent rise as a center for high-technology. Our database provides evidence of the importance of Atlanta to Georgia's high-technology economy. Indeed, 96 per cent of the venture investments in Georgia were clustered in the greater Atlanta area, 71 per cent in the city itself. In addition, Atlanta is home to the state's ten venture capital firms (Morris 1988).

The geographic distribution of venture capital investment follows that of the high concentration of high-technology firms in the greater Atlanta area (*Corporate Technology Information Service Directory 1987*). More than 90 per cent of Georgia's high-technology firms are located in the Atlanta area, with almost 65 per cent situated in either Atlanta or Norcross, a northern suburb of the city. While Atlanta contains many of the elements that have been cited as crucial to the success of both Route 128 and Silicon Valley as high-technology centers, it remains to be seen whether it can emerge as a high-technology center itself.[4]

Florida

It is somewhat surprising that Florida has only about 1 per cent of national venture capital investment (Table 4.6). The geographic distribution of venture capital investments in Florida is less concentrated than in other states. According to our database, venture capital investments were distributed across the Miami area and Tampa–St Petersburg area, which received 39 per cent and 17 per cent of Florida's venture investments respectively, and Orlando, Jacksonville, Titusville, and Melbourne. Once again, the distribution of venture capital investments follows that of the state's high-technology firms. The Miami area is home to 38 per cent of Florida's high-technology firms, Tampa–St Petersburg 23 per cent, and the greater Orlando Region 16 per cent. Florida trails Georgia in venture capital investment within the South Region, despite ranking well above Georgia in total number of high-technology companies and being one of the principal sites for new business start-ups, falling just behind California, Texas, and New York.

Florida has developed its active high-technology base with only a small contribution from the venture capital industry. According to a study by Maidique (Suran *et al.* 1986), this is due in large part to the sizable amount of government defense funding invested in the state, especially by NASA for the US space program based at Cape Canaveral. This study also cites the decision by IBM in 1981 to headquarter its personal computer business in Boca Raton as instrumental in the establishment of other non-defense related high-technology firms in the state, via the service and supplier networks (Suran *et al.* 1986).

Tennessee

Tennessee receives roughly the same number of venture capital investments as Florida, even though it has one-fifth the number of high-technology firms (*Corporate Technology Information Services Directory* 1987). Unlike most other states, the geographic distribution of venture capital investments in Tennessee does not closely follow that of the state's high-technology firms. According to our data, the Nashville area of Tennessee received the majority of Tennessee's venture capital financings (11 per cent of the South Region total). While Nashville is the primary recipient of venture capital investments in the state, it has only 25 per cent of the state's high-technology companies.

Virginia

The proximity of Virginia to Washington, DC, and therefore to the Pentagon and other federal agencies has enabled the state to capture a respectable share of the venture capital investments. Virginia accounted for 12 per cent of the South's venture capital investments, with the greater Alexandria area responsible for almost three-quarters of those investments. The majority, 68 per cent, of Virginia's high-technology firms are also located in the greater Alexandria area. The greater Richmond area received 13 per cent of the state's venture financings, and is home to 11 per cent of Virginia's high-technology firms.

Maryland

Maryland also benefits greatly from its location near Washington, DC. The region of Maryland that borders Washington, DC, an area which contains 57 per cent of the state's high-technology firms, received almost 40 per cent of the state's venture capital investments. The greater Baltimore Region led the state in the total number of financings with 54 per cent of the state total. Baltimore has seven of the state's twelve venture capital funds.

North Carolina

North Carolina received 9 per cent of the venture capital investments made in the South Region (Table 4.6). According to our database, 64 per cent of these investments were located in the Raleigh–Durham (Research Triangle) area of the state, and 28 per cent in the Burlington–Greensboro region. This distribution follows the distribution of the state's high-technology firms. The Raleigh–Durham area has 39 per cent of North Carolina's high-technology firms, while the Greensboro region contains just 9 per cent of the state's high-technology firms. However, Charlotte, which has 26 per cent of the state's high-technology firms, received only a minor amount of North Carolina's venture capital investment. North Carolina has a long history of investment in high-technology industry, as evidenced by the state-supported Research Triangle Park which opened in 1959. Although many commentators point to the North Carolina Research Triangle as a potentially successful model for public policy aimed at stimulating high-technology development, we are less sanguine. As Luger (1984) has pointed out, many of the high-technology firms in the Research Triangle Park are divisions of larger corporations such as IBM and General Electric. In our own interviews, we came across one high-technology company which, in fact, had relocated from the Research Triangle to Silicon Valley (De Geus 1988).

Other Southern States

Alabama, Delaware, Mississippi, Kentucky, and West Virginia received the remaining 15 per cent of venture investments in the southeast region. Almost all the investments were to firms located in the major cities of those states. We recorded no venture capital investments for South Carolina in our database.

The Gulf Coast

The Gulf Coast Region was the only region to experience a negative growth rate in terms of real investment dollars between 1981 and 1986 (Table 4.7). This is especially interesting since, as late as 1980, the region appeared to be an up and coming site for venture capital investments, having received 13 per cent of the venture capital industry's investment dollars, ranking third behind the Pacific and the Northeast Regions.

Texas leads the Gulf Coast Region as its center for venture capital investment. As the economy of Texas has faltered in recent years with the declining price of oil, so did venture capital investments in the region. While prior to 1986 Oklahoma and Louisiana both received a small share of the industry's dollars, in 1986 Texas received all the investments for the region.

Texas

Venture capital investment in Texas peaked in 1980, when Texas received almost 11 per cent of the nation's investments, and has fallen off since then (Table 4.7). By 1986, the state's share was only 6 per cent of the total industry's investments. Still, Texas remained among the top five states for venture capital investments, receiving between 5 per cent and 8 per cent of the industry's investments between 1981 and 1986. Part of the reason for this is the decline in the oil-related economy in Texas. Still, Texas remains a center for high-technology. Texas Instruments, one of the foremost electronics companies in the country, was founded in Dallas. Compaq Computer, originally financed with venture capital funds, was founded in Texas and continues to manufacture there. Texas is also home to Sematech and the MCC research consortium. In addition, Texas has 5 per cent of the nation's high-technology companies, which places it among the top five states in the country (Corporate Technology Service Directory 1987).

Table 4.7 Venture capital investments in the Gulf Coast

| State | 1968–75 | | | 1981 | | | 1986 | | | Change |
	$ million	% natl	% regional	$ million	% natl	% regional	$ million	% natl	% regional	% 1975–86
Gulf Coast	56.9	7.3	–	162.0	11.5	–	174	6	–	206
Texas	56.9	7.3	100.0	139.0	9.9	85.8	174	6	–	206
Other	–	–	–	23.0	1.6	14.2	–	–	–	–

Within Texas, the Dallas–Fort Worth area was the major site for venture capital investments and high-technology companies. Dubbed 'Silicon Prairie', the Dallas–Fort Worth area contains over 50 per cent of the state's venture capital investments and a similar 50 per cent share of its high-technology companies. The Houston area received 27 per cent of venture capital investments in Texas. Houston also accounts for 22 per cent of the high-technology firms in the state. The corridor between Austin and San Antonio was the third most popular area for venture capital investments in Texas, with 18 per cent of the state's venture capital investments.

The Mountain Region

Of the six regions, the Mountain Region has consistently received the smallest share of venture capital investment dollars (Table 4.8). The Mountain Region has received on average 4 per cent of the venture capital industry's investments over the past three decades. The region's growth rate in real venture capital investment dollars was 45 per cent between 1981 and 1986. Only the Gulf Coast Region experienced a slower growth rate in investments. The rate of venture capital investment in the Mountain Region over the past decade has not even kept pace with the growth of venture capital resources there.

Most venture capital investment in the Mountain Region is concentrated in Colorado, which also controls the largest share of the region's venture capital resources, and has the largest number of venture capital offices. Indeed, the combined share of venture capital investments for the other states in the Mountain Region has been less than 2 per cent of the venture capital industry's investments.

Colorado

Colorado is a growing center for high-technology industry. In recent years, several Silicon Valley firms have located along 'Silicon Mountain', a corridor that stretches along Interstate 25 from Boulder to Colorado Springs (Malecki 1987). Part of this is clearly linked to Colorado's standing as a center for the defense and nuclear industries. According to regional scientists and geographers, like Edward Malecki and Ann Markusen, defense spending is an important determinant of high-technology concentration. As Malecki has noted, 'The second major influence on high-technology

Table 4.8 Venture capital investments in the Mountain Region

State	1968–75			1981			1986			Change
	$ million	% natl	% regional	$ million	% natl	% regional	$ million	% natl	% regional	% 1975–86
Mountain	30.5	3.9	–	66.0	4.7	–	116	4	–	280
Colorado	24.5	3.2	80.3	43.0	3.1	65.2	87	3	75.0	255
Arizona	–	–	–	10.0	0.7	15.2	–	–	–	–
Other	6.0	0.8	19.7	29.0	1.0	25.0	29	1	25.0	383

geography is defense spending' (Malecki 1985). This has been especially true in recent years for the Mountain Region. Interstate 25, which winds through Colorado and New Mexico, is fast developing into a leading center for high-technology. Many of the high-technology firms have substantial ties with the defense industry. A complex composed of hundreds of high-technology companies, military installations, and government laboratories devoted to the Strategic Defense Initiative (SDI) and nuclear weapons research line Interstate 25. In 1987, 30 per cent of all US defense and energy dollars was spent on facilities located along this stretch of road. Half of this ($4.3 billion) was spent in Colorado (Associated Press 1988).

In the past few years, Colorado has received a significant share of the venture capital industry's investments, averaging 3 per cent of total venture investments, placing it among the top five states in the country. Colorado received approximately 62 per cent of the Mountain Region's venture capital investments recorded in our database. Two-thirds of these were in the Boulder area and 91 per cent were in the Boulder–Denver complex. All of Colorado's venture capital offices are located in either Boulder, Denver, or Englewood (a suburb of Denver). Colorado is home to 41 per cent of the region's high-technology firms, the majority of which are located in the Boulder–Denver Region.[5]

Arizona

Arizona received 18 per cent of the total venture capital investments made in the Mountain Region (Table 4.8). Of these, 95 per cent were in the Phoenix–Scottsdale area, also known as 'Silicon Desert'. Ninety-six per cent of the state's high-technology companies are located in either the Phoenix–Scottsdale area or Tucson, once again demonstrating that venture capital investments tend to cluster in areas noted for high-technology activity. Bill McKee, president of FBS Venture Capital Company, notes the lack of a venture capital infrastructure linking entrepreneurs and venture capitalists as one of the major problems his company and other venture capitalists face in Arizona (Johnston 1985). According to McKee, 'One of our challenges is making contact with the entrepreneur. Phoenix is an early-stage economy with regard to venture capital. Venture capital is not particularly well-known or well-defined, and there aren't enough players in the market' (Johnston 1985).

New Mexico

Venture capital investments have been few in number in New Mexico. The majority of venture capital investments in New Mexico were located in Albuquerque, which accounts for roughly 75 per cent of New Mexico's high-technology firms, with a majority of the remaining high-technology companies located along Interstate 25 (*Corporate Technology Information Service Directory* 1987). Part of the reason for sluggish venture investment can be found in the defense orientation of the New Mexico economy. In 1987, the Sandia National Laboratory – a major nuclear weapons and energy research facility – spent $280 million in the Albuquerque area, and $575 million total in contracts with the private sector (Associated Press 1988). Some estimates suggest that the government has awarded almost $1.6 billion in contracts for 'Star Wars' research to the state (Associated Press 1988). According to Brian McDonald, director of the University of New Mexico Bureau of Business and Economic Research, 'The federal government is the major industry in New Mexico. It accounts for 15 per cent of all jobs in the state' (Associated Press 1988). Although scores of private companies have spun out of the government nuclear weapons laboratories (Los Alamos and Sandia National Laboratories and the White Sands Missile Range, to name but a few), few have been backed by venture capital, since they have had sizable defense grants and contracts.

SUMMARY

The distribution of venture capital investments closely follows that of high-technology firms, on regional, state, and intra-state levels. The Pacific and Northeast Regions capture over 50 per cent of total venture capital investments and high-technology firms. Among states, California and Massachusetts were the leaders. And within states, the distribution of venture investments was again concentrated, flowing mainly to areas with large concentrations of high-technology businesses. This is true for the major recipient states of venture capital, such as California and Massachusetts, and for states that receive only a minor share of the venture industry's investments, like Georgia. Technology-oriented businesses are the primary factor that draws venture capital investment. The geographic distribution of venture capital investments is extremely concentrated. Places like Chicago and New York City, which are major financial centers for venture capital resources, are relatively minor centers of venture capital investment.

NOTES

1 Information on high-technology firms is taken from the *Corporate Technology Information Service Directory* (1987). This directory isolates firms by high-technology product classification, and thus includes only those firms that make what most of us consider leading-edge high-technology products. In this regard, it overcomes some of the shortcomings of other databases which define high technology by research and development (R&D) intensity (that is, the amount of money spent on R&D or the share of scientists engaged in R&D) and therefore end up with companies producing guided missiles, airplanes, and even oil refineries in their listings.

One of the major problems in analyzing the high-technology industrial structure in general is the quality of the data. There is an absence of adequate longitudinal information. The US Census of Manufacturers provides 5-year totals of companies and establishments, but does not allow one to get a handle on how many plants opened and closed during those intervals. While the firm level information based on Dun and Bradstreet files available from the Small Business Administration provides a way around this, it does not provide an adequate time series.

In addition, there is little consensus on how to define 'high technology' companies for analytical purposes. Most analysts use a working definition based on R&D intensity (measured either as percentage of revenues directed to R&D or share of employees engaged in R&D). But this kind of definition aggregates a wide variety of types of companies, and therefore makes it impossible to isolate the small entrepreneurial companies that are so much a part of the Silicon Valley/Route 128 phenomenon. We do not wish to get involved in the debate over these thorny statistical and analytical issues. We have pointed them out to make the reader aware of the inherent limits of the data. We believe that we can get a reasonable picture of high technology industrial organization by drawing from a range of data sources, and this is basically how we proceed. Good discussions of the way high technology companies are defined can be found in OTA (1984) and Markusen (1986).

2 However, unlike some of the other states that we examined, these investments showed no clear pattern of clustering, but instead were distributed fairly evenly throughout the region. This portion of New Jersey also accounted for almost 65 per cent of the state's high technology firms, according to the *Corporate Technology Service Directory* (1987). The high technology firms within this area were also distributed fairly evenly throughout the region. Clifton, Englewood, Parsippany, Secaucus, and Newark, which together accounted for one-fourth of the area's high technology companies, provide the only example of concentration. The remaining 75 per cent of the high-technology companies in this area are distributed among more than 100

other cities and towns.

3 Ohio's Thomas Edison Program is geared to generating new innovations and stimulating high technology development. See Malecki (1987a).

4 According to Schatz (1987) much of Atlanta's recent rise as a high technology center can be attributed to the strong ties that industry has established with the Georgia Institute of Technology.

Evidence of Atlanta's close business–university association can be found in a recent National Science Foundation study which showed that in 1986 Georgia Technology ranked second only to MIT in the amount of industry sponsored R&D expenditures for all universities and colleges in the United States. (In comparison, Stanford ranked a surprising sixteenth in corporate sponsored R&D spending, although it ranked sixth in total R&D expenditures.) According to Said Mohammadioun, who founded his own office automation manufacturing firm in Atlanta in 1982, 'Technology is **the** catalyst in making Atlanta a high-technology center . . . Technology brings students to Atlanta and creates engineers. Atlanta keeps them' (O'Connor 1988: 600).

5 Most of these companies are found along Interstate 25, two-thirds of which are in the Boulder–Denver area. Another 10 per cent were located in Colorado Springs, which is currently constructing a $100 million center for SDI research and was recently selected by Cray Research Inc. as the production site for Cray-3, the next generation of supercomputers. Fort Collins, which is also located along Interstate 25, is home to 8 per cent of the state's high-technology firms.

ACKNOWLEDGEMENTS

We would like to thank Martin Kenney for his assistance in framing many of the ideas reflected in this chapter and Mark Clark for assistance with data analysis. We would also like to thank the US Economic Development Administration for funding.

5 What do we know about the geography of US venture capitalists?

Chris Thompson

Many studies have discussed the critical need for capital in the early start-up and development stages of new high-technology enterprises (Robinson 1980; Anderson and McElveen, 1982; JEC 1982; Rothwell and Zegveld 1982; US GAO 1982; Obermayer 1983; Timmons *et al.* 1983; Horvitz and Pettit 1984; Pettit 1984; Timmons *et al.* 1984; Rothwell 1985; Hisrich 1986). Venture capital, in particular, has been highlighted as a driving force in the development of such companies and, by extension, their host areas – the so-called 'technology regions' (Florida and Kenney 1988b), 'creative regions' (Malecki 1987b), 'innovative environments' (Aydalot and Keeble 1988), and 'new Silicon Valleys' (Tatsuno 1986). Consequently, much has been written on venture capital with regard to its historical origins (Hussayni 1959; Kenney 1986: 132–75; Doerflinger and Rivkin 1987), the venture investment process (Bean *et al.* 1975; Cooper 1977; Coutarelli 1977; Tyebjee and Bruno 1981, 1984; JEC 1984; Kozmetsky *et al.* 1985; Venture Economics 1985), the geographical distribution of venture institutions (Green 1989 and Chapter Two of this volume), and the spatial flows of venture funds (Venture Economics 1983; Haslett 1984: 45–7; Leinbach and Amrhein 1987).

However, there has so far been little systematic analysis of the key personnel at the very heart of this important business: the individual professional venture capitalists themselves. In this chapter, some theoretical reasons as to why venture capitalists are individually important and worthy of study are reviewed. Then, possibly for the first time, some simple systematic spatial analyses are made of personal biographical data. Geographical patterns in career life-paths are explored, and the results are used tentatively to address the validity of the prevailing conventional model of venture capital as a phenomenon exhibiting a deterministic process of simple spatial diffusion driven by growth in total supply. As well as extending our knowledge of venture capitalists in particular, this study hopes to make a minor contribution to the wider current debate about the extent to which natural 'trickle-down' forces can be relied upon to generate equilibria when more direct government actions against polarizing tendencies are politically eschewed.

WHAT AND WHO ARE 'VENTURE CAPITALISTS', AND WHY ARE THEY SO IMPORTANT?

Haslett (1984: 41) lists the key attributes of venture capital as being a long-term investment requiring up to 10 years for return, and involving potential equity participation for the venture capitalist whose experience and specialized skills add value through active involvement. Coutarelli (1977: 20) adds that investment is specifically in growth-oriented small or medium sized businesses, that new capital be injected for growth and not merely for acquisition of outstanding shares, and that the deal be deliberately structured so as to obtain 'a very high return on investment if everything turns out according to plan'. Premus (JEC 1984) quotes portfolio analyses of venture capital firms as indicating that they anticipate a minimum rate of return of 30 per cent per annum on investments. The typical rate of return follows the so-called 'J-curve' or 'hockey stick' pattern where, in the early years of the investment, the cumulative rate of return is actually negative, but by about the third year it turns positive and trends upward (OTA 1984: 42; Derven 1987).

The term 'venture capitalist', as used in such literature, implicitly refers to any financial institution, corporation, or Fund making investments on this basis. The corporate typology of the venture industry is usually portrayed as a fourfold division, comprising 'public companies' (which are larger than average and traded on stock exchanges), 'private companies' (limited partnerships for investing in venture situations), 'bank-related companies' (set up to allow banks to respect laws about owning small businesses), and 'large corporate venture companies' (venture capital subsidiaries of major industrial corporations). Over 350 venture capital companies are licensed with the Small Business Administration (SBA) (Gladstone 1983: 4), and about another 100 venture capital pools are not affiliated with the SBA but are members of the National Venture Capital Association. For 1988, some 750 US venture Funds appear in *Pratt's Guide to Venture Capital Sources* (Morris 1988) – the venture industry's own definitive directory.

Statistical tabulations on shares of total resources controlled by different types of venture institution vary according to the classification used. Haslett (1984: 42) estimated in 1984 that 58 per cent of the organized US venture capital pool was in the hands of private firms, with another 25 per cent in corporate subsidiaries, and the rest with Small Business Investment Companies (SBICs). A more recent breakdown in *Venture Capital Journal* (Venture Economics 1989c: 10–11) shows 83 per cent of 1988 venture capital dollars in the hands of the 'independent private and public firms' (including both institutionally and non-institutionally funded firms, family groups and affiliated SBICs); 9 per cent with 'venture capital subsidiaries and affiliates of financial corporations' (including banks and insurance companies and their affiliated SBICs); 7 per cent with 'venture capital subsidiaries and affiliates of industrial corporations' (and their affiliated SBICs); and finally, just over 1 per cent with 'other venture capital SBICs' (including unaffiliated, privately and publicly held SBICs).

Rarely, if at all, however, is the term 'venture capitalist' used to refer to the actual individuals supplying the venture dollars or managing the Funds' portfolios. Yet within venture capital institutions nearly all investment operations are performed by a limited number of officers who are, for all intents and purposes, the functional venture capitalists.

An individual professional venture capitalist has to generate for consideration a flow of proposals, often through personal contacts with bankers, lawyers, accountants, and business consultants. On average, a US venture capital Fund received 470 formal business proposals in 1983 (JEC 1984). He or she then prescreens these initial submissions: the majority of proposals (and sometimes over 95 per cent) cannot meet initial requirements and go unfunded after only very brief consideration, often much to the frustration of the potential entrepreneur for whom the proposal may represent the culmination of years of effort. Doubtless this has contributed to some of the recent disenchantment with 'vulture capital' in the United States (Kotkin 1984; Kierulff 1986). Venture capitalists themselves commonly reply that the high initial rejection rate says more about the poor quality and preparation of many proposals, some of which are constantly recycled, and about inappropriate routing advice from referral sources who do not understand venture capital – a point supported by the research of Pulver and Hustedde (1988). The few more promising proposals are then put through intense due diligence, background checking, and feasibility studies, during which the venture capitalist may again call on a personal network of technical experts and industry specialists.

For proposals eventually judged as deserving of investment, the venture capitalist may then act as an advocate before the Board of Directors of the venture capital institution, as well as personally negotiating the structure and terms of the investment deal. In the majority of deals, the venture capitalist in the 'lead' role will invite counterparts at other venture institutions to participate in a 'coinvesting' arrangement so as to spread the risk, enlarge the pool of money available, and gain access to other expertises. As part of the final deal, the lead venture capitalist is then often appointed to the board of the investee, not merely to safeguard the interests of the investors, but primarily as a way of monitoring progress, helping steer development, and adding value to the company. This active personal participation usually includes frequent contact by phone and site-visits, sometimes at a rate of more than once a week in the early stages. The venture capitalist also plans an 'exit' strategy: over 60 per cent of portfolio companies are expected to be liquidated by going public or merging upwards (JEC 1984: XII and 2), giving exit profits in typically 5–7 years. During all this work with individual investments, the venture capitalist must also keep an eye on the venture institution's overall portfolio, and may be involved in raising new venture dollars and soliciting new limited partners for the next round or for a successor Fund, often largely on the basis of his or her personal track record.

Of course, it is not unusual in the banking and financial services industries for positions of central importance in investment decision-making to be held by a limited number of key individuals, and yet their personal characteristics and behavior still may not have a great influence on investment outcomes. What makes venture capitalist individuals especially significant in this case are five key features of the venture investment process.

First, there is a limited number of individual venture capitalists: in 1988, $31 billion of US venture capital was being managed by probably under 2,500 people (Venture Economics 1989c: 11). The archetypal professional venture capitalist is someone with graduate business or financial training, plus usually several years' prior experience within conventional business or investment finance, plus preferably some investing experience in, and technical or market knowledge about, the Fund's preferred industries. Venture institutions will rarely have more than five such full-time professionals on staff and frequently have only one or two (Fells 1984: 77). Each individual venture officer will then typically handle only about six to twelve active projects at a time, and as Haslett (1984: 43) notes, 'when a firm concentrates on early stage and start-up investments, there are even fewer portfolio assignments per professional, since such investments usually involve more substantial involvement and time'. Consequently, Haslett (1984) notes the sheer amount of venture capital being managed in a region will not necessarily increase the amount of investment activity there, citing as evidence that the relationship between capital raised and companies financed between 1972 and 1983 varies markedly at the state level. Instead, he argues that

> a healthy investment climate in a region requires the existence of a cadre of professionals and managers in key institutions who understand the venture investment process and the requirements, particularly the risk-taking element, of the entrepreneurial and business-development process.
>
> (Haslett 1984: 46)

The major continuing constraint on the expansion of venture capital activity may thus be the industry's limited human resource base.

Second, this limited supply of professionals adds greater significance to any uneven spatial distribution, because there are also geographic constraints inherent to the venture investment process. Haslett, for example, asserts

> some venture capitalists cite, as an informal rule, that they do not wish to look at seed or start-up situations more than 250 or 300 miles from their office. Thus a focus on seed and start-up situations will necessarily confine investments to the region where the venture firm is located.
>
> (Haslett 1984: 43)

Third, the non-routine nature of venture decision-making, and the 'search for golden apples', brings opportunities for the individual's subjective judgements to play an important role. Classically, venture capitalists search for the next Apple Computers: with backing by venture capitalist Arthur Rock, this company made history by moving into the *Fortune 500* list within just 5 years of being founded. In practice, however, roughly only two out of every ten venture deals may be 'winners', while another two are 'losers', and the remaining six become the 'living dead' whose operations are viable but not capable of yielding significant profits (Fells 1984: 74). The individual venture capitalist thus faces the question of how to pick winners from the enormous numbers of proposals crossing his or her desk each year.

Lungren (1984) notes that venturing is 'idea based' rather than 'collaterized', and in such a situation there are no ready formulae or conventional bank loan eligibility criteria for selecting proposals which anyone with limited financial training could apply. Yet financial and business research studies, like those of Hoban (1981) and Macmillan *et al.* (1987), have generally not been very successful at identifying objective measurable indicators which could be used to predict project outcomes in specific cases. Hoban (1981) is forced to conclude that correlates of 'success' are too complex or subjective, and that successful venture capitalism is not a 'science' but an 'art', where the expert's 'feelings' about what will or will not be successful remain important. Though assisted by due diligence studies and background checking, the individual venture capitalist eventually has to make an evaluation of prospects using his or her own professional, but nevertheless subjective, judgements about the quality of the proposed management team, plus his or her previous personal experience of that industry, and often simple 'gut feelings'.

Fourth, venture capitalists typically have a very wide spread of responsibilities within their Funds. Except in the very large and diversified financial institutions, the venture investment process is not usually a series of discrete decisions and tasks which can be parceled out to different offices and individuals so as to take advantage of intra-organization specialities and divisions of labor. Rather, the process is usually more of an evolving organic whole, with the individual venture capitalist being intimately involved from start to finish in all aspects of the investment. Most venture capitalists are proud of their 'hands-on', 'do-it-all', function and cite it as a reason for entering this business as opposed to traditional banking. In addition, unlike the situation with pension fund or mutual fund managers, a judgement of the individual venture capitalist's 'performance' can only really be made after several years of investment activity. This may be close to the end of the lifetime of a Fund, because many are set up as partnerships for a defined period of, commonly, 10 years. Consequently, until then there is the opportunity for considerable unsupervised independence and freedom in decision-making, which gives room for the development of varying personal styles of dealing and managing.

Finally, there is the intensely personal nature of the whole venture process. To a greater extent than conventional bank finance, venturing is centered on personal relationships and all that they imply about openness, trust, respect, shared goals, complementary skills, and 'workability'. The key relationships are between the venture capitalist and the working managers or entrepreneurs, who must become long-term partners in the funded concern; between the venture capitalist and any coinvestors; and between the venture capitalist and the referral sources and technical advisors. Venture capitalists often use terms such as 'comfort-level' or 'excitement-level', or mention their stock of accumulated experience that comes from repeatedly working with particular coinvestors, when explaining how they weigh up potential deals.

For these five reasons, venture capitalists are individually very important in the venture capital investment process, and they have even been cast by Florida and Kenney (1988b) as veritable 'gatekeepers' for a form of finance crucial to the growth and development of the new 'technology regions'. Yet most previous academic research has not dealt directly with them as individuals, but instead has revolved around a more impersonal concept of venture capital involving the location of office entities and the spatial flows of dollars. Even when some abstract consideration of venture capitalists' personal characteristics has been made – as, for example, by Hambrecht (1984), Janeway (1986), Rock (1987), and Brunning (1988) – this has often been at a stereotypical or anecdotal level, wherein they are portrayed journalistically as having 'the guts of a riverboat gambler combined with discipline, prudence, and industry knowledge to pull it off' (Hambrecht 1984: 81). According to this genre, the stereotypical venture capitalist simply works in Boston or San Francisco, is a male of late middle-age, and has an MBA from Harvard Business School.

There is thus a need to document and analyze more systematically such limited information as is available on these key individuals, to see whether this stereotype holds in practice and in all places. With the results it should then be possible to make some evaluation of the conventional working model of the evolution of the venture capital industry, which currently guides the official hands-off policy towards the phenomenon. In this, the so-called Haslett–OTA/Premus–JEC model (Thompson 1989a: Table 1), differences in the availability of deals, in the geographic concentration of firms, and in risk-taking by institutional investors, are the suggested factors underlying 'regional gaps' in venture funding (JEC 1984; OTA 1984). Premus thus recommends improving the total supply of venture capital available, since this would result in a filtering down of investment both to lagging regions and to earlier stage firms. Examination of a segment of the actual career life-paths of individual venture capitalists, defined by the point locations of their education and workplace, should thus provide some tentative empirical support or otherwise for the notion of achieving equilibrium through diffusion and filtering down, for the first time using this novel personal dimension.

METHODOLOGY

The only personal biographical data on named venture capitalists is in *Who's Who in Venture Capital* (Silver 1984), which has information on 636 individuals. Given the need for venture capitalists to maintain high personal visibility towards referral sources and potential entrepreneurs (for maintaining proposal flow), and towards other venture capitalists (for potential coinvesting), it is likely that this constitutes a relatively complete list – or at least the most complete documentation available – of active, professionally employed, venture capitalists for that time. Though now slightly dated, it does include the period 1980–82, which witnessed the highest rate of increase in new venture capital institutions ever and a doubling of the amount of venture capital committed to investing firms (Leinbach and Amrhein 1987; *New York Times* 1987).

However, it probably does not include the personally wealthy 'angel' investors, who traditionally maintain a more discreet profile and concentrate on private networking (Seymour and Wetzel 1981; Krasner and Tymes 1983; Wetzel 1983). It should also be noted that the information is often presented in qualitative biographical format, and individual entries vary in their degree of completeness and level of detail. Nevertheless, there is still probably more information available from this directory than could be gathered by a conventional customized mailback questionnaire survey, which other venture capital studies indicate may have a response rate, in this arena, of only some 20–35 per cent (Green and McNaughton 1988; Thompson and Bayer 1989b).

RESULTS

Compiling, sorting, tidying, recoding, and cross-tabulating these data, allows the following spatial patterns of age, education, and workplaces to be uncovered for about 600 individual US venture capitalists on whom relatively complete information is available.

The estimated ages of venture capitalsts by 1989 range from 30 to 75, with an average of 48.7 years. The average number of years of working experience (of all kinds) was 26.8 since their first degree, and 21.7 since the second. Of the 574 venture capitalists for whom some educational data are available, 97 per cent have one Bachelor's degree and 5 per cent have two. Bachelor's degrees are split between 42 per cent in the arts and 33 per cent in the sciences; 8 per cent are identifiable separately as being in some kind of engineering and 5 per cent are in business (though there were probably more of both hidden in the general Bachelor categories, depending on how different colleges label their undergraduate degrees). There are nineteen undergraduate law degrees, and twenty-five graduate law degrees.

The 540 first degrees which have educational institution identified were obtained from 211 different colleges or universities. However, within this large total the educational background is highly concentrated. Harvard provided forty-one first degrees, Princeton thirty, Yale twenty-one, and MIT sixteen: these 'Big Four' schools of the 'eastern' educational establishment thus produced 20 per cent of all the first degrees held by this particular occupational group. Stanford graduated another sixteen, Cornell thirteen, and the University of Pennsylvania twelve. No other college or university graduated more than ten.

About 85 per cent of these venture capitalists also have graduate degrees. An MBA is held by 337, or 59 per cent of those with second degree information given; 110 of these, or 18 per cent of the 609, have their MBA from Harvard. There are also sixty-one with MSs and twenty-eight with MAs, and twelve with Masters degrees identified separately as engineering. Not counting those with two degrees at the same level (that is, double Bachelor's or two Master's), some 17 per cent of 574 venture capitalists have three educational qualifications: twenty-one have PhDs, and there are fourteen with accountancy certifications (either CPAs or CFAs).

The 440 second degrees came from 126 different establishments, but again extreme concentration is evident: only nine of these colleges or universities graduated more than ten venture capitalists. Harvard alone provided ninety-six with their second degrees, followed by the University of Pennsylvania with thirty, Stanford with twenty-four, and Columbia with twenty. Also making an appearance in this list are New York University, which provided fifteen, and the University of Chicago and Northwestern University, with fourteen each. MIT provided eleven, and the University of Michigan ten second degrees.

Table 5.1 Locations of venture capitalist educations

	Share of total US pop 1986	Place of education for				
		1st degree		2nd degree		3rd degree
	(%)	(no.)	(%)	(no.)	(%)	(no.)	(%)
Census regions and states[a]							
North Central[b]	24.7	105	20.8	85	20.8	10	12.3
IL	4.8	30	6.0	35	8.6	8	9.9
OH	4.6	24	4.8	13	3.2	1	1.2
Northeast	20.7	265	52.6	240	58.7	47	58.0
MA	2.4	86	17.1	131	32.0	29	35.8
NY	7.4	69	13.7	56	13.7	13	16.0
NJ	3.2	36	7.1	4	1.0	1	1.2
PA	4.9	31	6.2	37	9.0	3	3.7
CT	1.3	24	4.8	8	2.0	0	0.0
South	34.2	71	14.1	31	7.6	8	9.9
West	20.2	63	12.5	53	13.0	16	19.8
CA	11.2	39	7.7	46	11.2	16	19.8
US total		504		409		81	
Joint Economic Committee regions							
Bicoastal states[c]	43.5	317	62.4	269	65.3	70	84.3
Interior states[d]	56.5	191	37.6	143	34.7	13	15.7
Coterminous US total		508		412		83	

Sources: Silver (1984), US DoC (1988, Table A, col. 2), JEC (1986) and author's calculations

Notes: [a] States shown have educated more than twenty at first degree level.
[b] Also referred to as 'Midwest' in some Bureau of Census publications.
[c] ME, NH, VT, NY, MA, CT, RI, NJ, DE, DC, MD, VA, NC, SC, GA, FL, CA, as defined in JEC (1986).
[d] All other states, excluding AK and HI.

These institutions of higher education for first, second, and third degrees are ranked in Table 5.1 by region and by each state educating more than twenty venture capitalists. Three striking patterns emerge. First, the prominence of the Northeast as a region of venture capitalist education is clear: it provides the majority of all kinds of degrees, and within it just Massachusetts and New York together generate over 30 per cent. Second, this concentration increases with the transition from undergraduate to graduate level, particularly in the case of Massachusetts, which alone is the location for almost one-third of all second degrees. Third, while the North

Table 5.2 Top ten concentration of venture
capitalists, by state

State rank	Working venture capitalists	
Absolute	(no.)	(% of USA)
1 New York	141	23.2
2 California	97	15.9
3 Massachusetts	77	12.6
4 Illinois	50	8.2
5 Connecticut	32	5.3
6 Minnesota	22	3.6
7 Texas	21	3.5
8 (New Jersey) (Ohio)	18	3.0
10 Florida	16	2.6
US total	609	100.0
Relative		(per 1,000,000 of 1986 pop.)
1 Massachusett		13.2
2 Connecticut		10.0
3 New York		7.9
4 Vermont		5.6
5 Minnesota		5.2
6 Rhode Island		5.1
7 Illinois		4.3
8 California		3.6
9 Colorado		2.8
10 New Jersey		2.4
US total		2.5

Sources: Silver (1984), US DoC (1988), Table A,
col. 2), and author's calculations

Central and West Regions maintain their share of the total between
first and second degrees, the South, whose share of first degrees was
already considerably below its share of population, slips further,
providing just 7.6 per cent of second degrees. The location of
venture capitalist work addresses is available for 609 individuals,
and is tabulated in Tables 5.2–5.4 in both absolute and relative
terms, for states, Metropolitan Statistical Areas (MSAs), and
individual named cities. Regional groupings are given in Table 5.5.

The Northeast Census Region has 47 per cent of the nation's
venture capitalists working there, the North Central Region 20 per

Table 5.3 Top ten concentration of venture capitalists, by Metropolitan Statistical Area

MSA rank	Working venture capitalists	
Absolute	(no.)	(% of USA)
1 NY/North NJ/Long Is. CMSA	144	23.6
2 Boston–Lawrence–Salem CMSA	69	11.3
3 SF–Oakland–San Jose CMSA	66	10.8
4 Chicago–Gary–Lake C. CMSA	45	7.4
5 LA–Anaheim–Riverside CMSA	20	3.3
6 Minneapolis–St Paul MSA	18	3.0
7 Philadel.–Wilm.–Trent. CMSA	16	2.6
8 Milwaukee–Racine CMSA	11	1.8
9 (Dallas–Ft Worth CMSA) (Houston–galv.–Brazoria CMSA)	8	1.3
US total	609	100.0
Relative	(per 1,000,000 of 1986 pop.)	
1 Boston–Lawrence–Salem CMSA	17.0	
2 SF–Oakland–San Jose CMSA	11.2	
3 NY/North NJ/Long Is. CMSA	8.0	
4 Minneapolis–St Paul MSA	7.8	
5 Milwaukee–Racine CMSA	7.1	
6 Chicago–Gary–Lake C. CMSA	5.5	
7 Columbus MSA	4.6	
8 Providence–Pawtckt.–Fall R CMSA	4.5	
9 Denver–Boulder CMSA	2.7	
10 Houston–Galv.–Brazoria CMSA	2.2	
US total	2.5	

Sources: Silver (1984), US DoC (1988, Table A, col. 2), and author's calculations

cent, the West 19 per cent, and the South 13 per cent. Thus, compared with regional population shares, the North East has over double the concentration of venture capitalists, while the North Central and West are more balanced. The South, however, has only just over a third the concentration of venture capitalists as it does population.

Altogether, venture capitalists' 1984 workplaces are spread across 130 cities in 38 states, but there is pronounced concentration within this apparently dispersed distribution. As can be seen in the absolute figures of Table 5.4, New York City alone has 128 working there, or 21 per cent of the nation's total, and this is almost double

Table 5.4 Top ten concentration of venture capitalists, by individual city

City rank	Working venture capitalists	
Absolute	(no.)	(% of USA)
1 New York, NY	128	21.0
2 Boston, MA	66	10.8
3 Chicago, IL	45	7.4
4 San Francisco, CA	37	6.1
5 Minneapolis, MN	18	3.0
6 (Los Angeles, CA)	17	2.8
(Menlo Park, CA)		
8 Stamford, CT	16	2.6
9 Milwaukee, WI	10	1.6
19 Princeton, NJ	9	1.5
US total	609	100.0
Relative		(per 1,000,000 of 1986 pop.)
1 Princeton, NJ		635.1
2 Menlo Park, CA		623.2
3 Chevy Chase, MD		326.8
4 Stowe, VT		310.6
5 Sausalito, CA		261.1
6 Carlisle, MA		246.3
7 London, KY		236.4
8 Saddle Brook, NJ		217.9
9 Hudson, OH		214.6
10 Painesville, OH		183.5
US total		2.5

Sources: Silver (1984), US DoC (1988, Table A, col. 2), and author's calculations

the number in the second ranked city, Boston, which has sixty-six; Chicago has forty-five and San Francisco thirty-seven. This means that 276 venture capitalists, or 45 per cent of the nation's total, work in just these four cities.[1] The next largest venturer groups are those in Minneapolis, Los Angeles, Menlo Park (CA), Stamford (CT), and Milwaukee (WI), all with between ten and eighteen present. The 121 other cities have fewer than ten venture capitalists each, and sixty-seven cities, or just over half, have only one working venture capitalist there. When concentrations are expressed relatively, however, none of the top ten individual cities in absolute terms appears in a ranking ordered by the number of venture capitalists

Table 5.5 Regional distributions and characteristics of venture capitalists

Region of Workplace	Share of total US pop. 1986 in region	Venture capitalists		Characteristics Age	
	(%)	(no.)	(%)	(mean)	(s)[d]
Census regions					
North Central[a]	24.6	123	20.2	47.8	10.54
Northeast	20.7	289	47.5	49.1	8.92
South	34.4	78	12.8	50.5	9.82
West	20.2	119	19.5	47.7	8.17
US total	100.0	609	100.0	48.7	9.24
Joint Economic Committee regions					
Bicoastal States[b]	43.5	413	67.9	49.2	9.06
Interior States[c]	56.5	195	43.2	47.7	9.59
Coterminous US total	100.0	608	100.0	48.8	9.25

Sources: Silver (1984), US DoC (1988, Table A, col. 2), JEC (1986), and author's calculations.
Notes: [a] Also referred to as 'Midwest' in some Bureau of Census publications.
[b] ME, NH, VT, NY, MA, CT, RI, NJ, DE, DC, MD, VA, NC, SC, GA, FL, CA, as defined in JEC (1986).
[c] All other states, excluding AK and HI.
[d] (s) = Standard deviation.

per million of population: the highest is Boston, ranked only seventeenth. This is because the 'relative' calculation arithmetically favors smaller places with few venturers but also low population denominators. (Half the individual cities shown in the top ten relative concentrations in Table 5.4 have only one venture capitalist working there, and all ten cities have populations of under 30,000 people.)

Many cities in both absolute and relative sections of Table 5.4 are in any case only parts of larger functional metropolitan areas, and in these cases the whole MSA may be a more appropriate spatial unit. The four Consolidated Metropolitan Statistical Areas (CMSAs) of which New York, Boston, San Francisco, and Chicago are the main respective cities have 324 venture capitalists, or 53 per cent of the nation's total, compared with their 15 per cent aggregate share of the nation's total population. In Table 5.3, the top three CMSAs in absolute terms also appear at the top under the relative measure, although their order changes. In addition, the Minneapolis--St Paul

Table 5.6 Distribution and characteristics of working venture capitalists, by order of center

Center and state of work	Venture capitalists (no.)	(% of total)	Characteristics Age (mean)	(s)^c	With MBA (no.)	(%)	With Harvard MBA (no.)	(%)	With eastern degree (no.)	(%)
Primary	365	59.9	48.7	9.06	218	59.7	80	21.9	143	39.2
NY	141	23.2	50.4[a]	9.12	69	48.9	24	17.0	51	36.2
CA	97	15.9	48.2	8.58	67	69.1	22	22.7	33	34.0
MA	77	12.6	48.6	8.79	47	61.0	28	36.4	48	62.3
IL	50	8.2	44.9[a]	9.33	35	70.0	6	12.0	11	22.0
Rest of USA	244	40.1	48.9[a]	9.51	329	54.0	110	18.1	196	32.2
Secondary	127	20.0	50.6	9.83	54	42.5	15	11.8	29	22.8
CT	32	5.3	48.1	9.00	16	50.0	4	12.5	7	21.9
MN	22	3.6	52.4	11.64	9	40.9	0	0.0	2	9.1
TX	21	3.4	49.4	7.64	7	33.3	2	9.5	3	14.3
NJ	18	3.0	49.5	8.81	10	55.6	4	22.2	9	50.0
OH	18	3.0	53.1[a]	10.60	6	33.3	2	11.1	4	22.2
FL	16	2.6	55.3[a]	12.40	6	37.5	3	18.8	4	25.0
Tertiary	40	6.6	45.1[a]	9.37	24	60.0	5	12.5	7	17.5
WI	11	1.8	44.5	11.72	6	54.5	1	9.1	1	9.1
MI	10	1.6	46.6	14.21	5	50.0	1	10.0	2	20.0
PA	10	1.6	46.9	7.11	6	60.0	2	20.0	2	20.0
CO	9	1.5	43.0	4.90	7	77.8	1	11.1	2	22.2
Lower order (24 states)	77	12.6	47.8	8.39	33	42.9	10	13.0	17	22.1
Total[b]	609	100.0	48.7	9.24	329	54.0	110	18.1	196	32.2

Source: Silver (1984) and author's calculations.
Notes: [a] Sample mean significantly different from total mean at 95 per cent level.
[b] Cases for which there is complete information varies.

MSA moves up, while the Los Angeles–Anaheim–Riverside and Philadelphia–Wilmington–Trenton CMSAs disappear from the top ten, to be replaced by the Columbus (OH) MSA and the Providence–Pawtucket–Fall River CMSA.

At the state level in Table 5.2, New York has 141 working venture capitalists in total, California ninety-seven, Massachusetts seventy-seven, and Illinois fifty. As can be seen in Table 5.6, these four states account for the workplaces of almost 60 per cent of the nation's total number, which is a similar, but less pronounced, degree of concentration than the 75.2 per cent calculated by Haslett (1984: Table 13) for the same four states in the case of venture dollars. In terms of the 'order' of center for working venture capitalists, these four states can thus be thought of as the 'primary' centers. Below them in the rankings are Connecticut, Minnesota, and Texas: these, plus New Jersey, Ohio, and Florida, have 127 venture capitalists, or 20 per cent, and constitute the 'secondary' centers. Wisconsin, Michigan, Pennsylvania, and Colorado, have almost 7 per cent of the total between them, and constitute the 'tertiary' centers. A final group of nineteen states with between two and six venture capitalists working in them, and five states with only one, constitute the low order centers. The remaining twelve states have no venture capitalists working in them at all.

This categorical rank ordering of centers gives one hierarchy of importance for different states in terms of working venture capitalist concentration. Arrayed in this fashion, these results merely confirm what is already known about geographical unevenness in venturing phenomena. However, when weighted with simple geographic differences this hierarchical dimension can be a key reference point for assessing the spatial diffusion and filter-down implications of the conventional theoretical venture model. Specifically, this model would suggest the following four hypotheses relating the locational distributions of venture capitalist workplaces to earlier educational establishments (where these two points are taken to define a simple measure of career life-paths, and hence migratory flows, of individual venture capitalists, and the life-paths are indicative of the evolution of the industry).

First, if the conventional model holds in reality then the spatial pattern of workplaces should be different from that of place of education for the same individuals. The locations of working venture capitalists should have been influenced by their having migrated away from the falling rates of return produced by venturer overcrowding in the early, higher order centers. These centers are

Table 5.7 Venture capitalist education and work locations

Spatial scale	Venture capitalists working in the same location as							
	1st degree		2nd degree		3rd degree		Any degree	
	(no.)	(%)	(no.)	(%)	(no.)	(%)	(no.)	(%)
Same city	30	5.7	43	10.0	10	11.5	68	12.2
Same state	157	29.6	151	35.1	32	36.8	244	43.8
Same div.	232	43.8	184	43.0	38	43.7	325	58.3
Same reg.	311	58.7	256	59.5	55	63.2	401	72.0
US total	530		430		87			

Source: Silver (1984) and author's calculations

also the educational seedbeds and are concentrated very much in the classical 'eastern' locations, while the lower order centers elsewhere supposedly offer the new unexploited opportunities for high returns. The empirical evidence for differences in the two spatial distributions appears at first supportive. Table 5.7 gives the percentages of venture capitalists who work in the same location as they obtained their degrees. Results indicate a high degree of professional mobility, at least at the city scale. Only 12 per cent work in the same city as any of their degrees and only 44 per cent in the same state (though 72 per cent do stay in the same region). Even Massachusetts, the biggest single 'educating' state at the key graduate level, is a net 'exporter' of venture capitalists, retaining only 30 per cent of in-state graduates. The overall retention rate at the state-level is only 31 per cent for first degrees and 37 per cent for second degrees. In Table 5.8, only two individual states – New York and California – out of the twelve which are significant 'educators' (that is, states 'graduating' ten or more venture capitalists) have a higher than average retention rate at both first and second degree level.

The distribution of workplaces for individual venture capitalists thus seems very different from the distribution of educational locations at the city and state level, though less so at the regional level. However, while educations and workplaces may exhibit different geographies, they are not dissimilar down the hierarchy, and individual career paths defined by these two points do not show much evidence of the hypothesized filtering down. When orders of center for education and workplace are cross-tabulated for the graduate (second) degree, as in Table 5.9, a slight majority of all

Table 5.8 State education retention rates of working venture capitalists

State where educated[a]	Venture capitalists working in same state as					
	1st degree			2nd degree		
	G	W	R	G	W	R
	(no.)	(no.)	(%)	(no.)	(no.)	(%)
Texas	14	10	71.4			
California	39	24	61.5	46	28	60.9
New York	69	30	43.5	56	28	50.0
Massachusetts	86	33	38.4	131	39	29.8
New Jersey	36	6	16.7			
Ohio	24	4	16.7	13	5	38.5
Illinois	30	14	13.3	35	16	45.7
Pennsylvania	31	4	12.9	37	4	10.8
Indiana	10	1	10.0	12	1	8.3
Colorado	11	1	9.1			
Connecticut	24	0	0.0			
Michigan				11	4	36.4
Sub-total for states education 10+	374	127	34.0	341	125	36.7
Other educating states	135	30	22.2	71	25	35.2
Total	509	157	30.8	412	150	36.4

Source: Silver (1984) and author's calculations
Notes: [a] Ranked by first degree retention rate.
G, graduated, W, working, R, retention.

cases (210 out of 411, or 51 per cent) fall in the one cell linking primary levels. This means that slightly more than half of all venture careers follow a path which at both ends involves a center at the primary level. In addition, as can be seen in Table 5.10, 84 per cent of all paths from a second degree to a workplace were to a center either at the same or at a higher level. Only 16 per cent involved a move down the hierarchy and only 5.1 per cent of all moves were from one of the three higher levels into centers at the lowest level – supposedly those most in need of venture capitalists and offering the most untapped opportunities and the least competition. Even the majority of venturers (59.6 per cent at the graduate level) educated in those lowest order centers moved up the hierarchy for work, while the level contributing most working venture capitalists to low order centers was the lowest order itself.

Second, if diffusion and filtering has been going on, it should be possible to detect differences in venture capitalist ages between the

Table 5.9 Itra-hierarchical paths of venture capitalists

Education center	Later workplace center								Total	
	Primary		Secondary		Tertiary		Low			
	1st degree	2nd degree	1st degree	2nd degree	1st degree	2nd degree	1st degree	2nd degree	1st degree	2nd degree
	(%)	(%;)	(%)	(%)	(%)	(%)	(%)	(%)	(no.)	(no.)
Primary	77.7	78.4	12.9	12.7	3.1	3.4	6.3	5.6	224	268
Secondary	49.9	40.0	34.5	52.5	7.3	5.0	9.1	2.5	110	40
Tertiary	51.7	53.6	15.0	14.3	21.7	23.2	11.7	8.9	60	56
Low	48.1	29.8	23.1	23.4	3.8	6.4	25.0	40.4	104	47
Total (no)	309	270	100	74	32	27	57	40	498	411

Source: Silver (1984) and author's calculations

Table 5.10 Direction of intra-hierarchical paths of venture capitalists

Degree	Venture capitalists with degree		Workplace in center of Higher order	Same order	Lower order
	(no	(%)	(%)	(%)	(%)
First	498	100.0	34.5	50.4	15.1
Second	411	100.0	20.0	64.0	16.1
Third	83	100.0	14.5	67.5	1.2

Source: Silver (1984) and author's calculations

different orders of center. The major centers, being longer established, would have older venture capitalists, while the second and third order centers, to which later-educated competing venture capitalists should, in theory, have had to spill over, would have younger ones. However, there should not be any differences between individual states within the same given level, since in the conventional abstract model geographical location is less important than hierarchical position. This is, of course, making the gross assumption that all venture capitalists qualify at generally the same age and younger ones can be identified as newer entrants. This is probably least tenable for older individuals, since educational tracks for this specialized profession were likely to have been less organized prior to the mid-1970s.

Table 5.11 shows mean ages by order of center and states. Contrary to this second hypothesis, there are no statistically significant differences between mean ages in the primary level and those in the entire rest of the country. Yet there are significant differences between individual states within the primary level: New York has significantly older venture capitalists than the US total, and Illinois younger. Moreover, the venture capitalists in just secondary centers are, on average, older than those in primary centers. If there is any association between age and center in the direction suggested by the hypothesis, it is that younger venture capitalists are found in, and therefore may have been going to, the tertiary centers. However, as these still hold under 7 per cent of total venturers the impact of this particular flow upon the whole system is slight. In fact, when the venture capitalist age distribution is broken up by decades, it can be seen to vary by geographic region of workplace, rather than by level in the hierarchy: 68.7 per cent of venture capitalists working in the West are in their thirties or

Table 5.11 Venture capitalist educations and work locations, by degree and age

Age Group	Number (no.)	(%)	Venture capitalists working in the same city City (no.)	(%)	State (no.)	(%)	Division (no.)	(%)	Region (no.)	(%)
as 1st degree										
30–39	69	16.5	4	6.0	17	25.4	28	41.8	38	56.7
40–49	178	42.6	5	3.0	39	23.4	65	38.9	91	54.5
50–59	110	26.3	6	5.8	28	26.9	48	46.2	68	65.4
60–69	50	12.0	7	14.6	23	47.9	25	52.1	31	64.6
70–79	11	2.6	1	10.0	3	30.0	4	40.0	7	70.0
30–79	418	100.0	23	5.8	110	27.8	170	42.9	235	59.3
as 2nd degree										
30–39	57	18.2	7	12.3	19	33.3	24	45.6	30	52.6
40–49	148	47.3	10	6.8	52	35.1	67	45.3	88	59.5
50–59	76	24.3	10	13.2	26	34.2	34	44.7	53	69.7
60–69	31	9.9	4	12.9	13	41.9	14	45.2	18	58.1
70–79	1	0.3	0	0.0	0	0.0	0	0.0	0	0.0
30–79	313	100.0	31	9.9	110	35.1	141	45.0	189	60.4
as 1st, 2nd or 3rd degree										
30–39	69	16.5	11	15.9	28	40.6	42	60.9	48	69.6
40–49	178	42.6	15	8.4	74	41.6	106	59.6	126	70.8
50–59	110	26.3	16	14.5	47	42.7	67	60.9	84	76.4
60–69	50	12.0	7	14.0	26	52.0	28	56.0	34	68.0
70–79	11	2.6	1	9.1	3	27.3	4	36.4	7	63.6
30–79	418	100.0	50	12.0	178	42.6	247	59.1	299	71.5

Source: Silver (1984) and author's calculations

forties, compared with 56.5 per cent in the Northeast and only 47.9 per cent in the South.

Third, if venture capital is a spreading surface, there should be no differences between orders of center in terms of 'type' of venture capitalist working there (using educational background as a surrogate here for 'type'). Table 5.6 contains information on the level of MBAs, Harvard MBAs, and Big Four 'eastern' college background. Contrary to this third hypothesis, there is considerable variation in the educational make-up of venture capitalists between different levels. The primary centers have, on average, a higher representation in all these kinds of degrees than do the secondary ones. The tertiary centers do have a relatively higher representation than the secondary ones, but again the small absolute figures involved limit the significance of this for the whole system.

Fourth, because spatial diffusion and filtering down are supposed to be working to even out earlier imbalances, their present operation implies a still immature distribution, wherein venture capitalists should be relatively more numerous in larger cities than in smaller ones, and the proportion of cities of a given size which do not have a venture capitalist present should increase down the city-size hierarchy. Furthermore, this dimension to filtering should be evident regardless of geographical location.

Table 5.12 gives the number of venture capitalists by city-size category and shows some evidence for the predicted top-heavy

Table 5.12 Distribution of venture capitalist workplaces, by city size category

City-size 1986 population	Cities		Venture capitalists			
	Number in USA	With VC	No.	% of US tot	per 1 million pop.[a]	Pop. per VC[b]
Over 1 million	8	7	216	35.5	11.4	87.9
500,000–1 million	15	12	137	22.5	17.5	57.2
200,000–500,000	52	22	59	9.7	7.7	130.6
Less than 200,000	–	74[2]	166	27.3	39.2	25.5
Locatable sample		115	578	95.1	14.9	67.1
Unlocatable		15	30	4.9		
US total		130	608	100.0		

Sources: Silver (1984), US DoC (1988), and author's calculations
Notes: [a] Excludes cities with no venture capitalist.
[b] Includes Minor Civil Divisions and Townships in some states.
VC, venture capitalist.

distribution. Nearly all large US cities of over half a million inhabitants have venture capitalists, but under half of all US cities in the 200,000–500,000 range have any. In addition, the number of venture capitalists per million of population is over three times as high in larger cities than it is in cities of under 200,000 people. However, the distribution is also very uneven: there are seventy-four cities of fewer than 200,000 people with a venture capitalist, but thirty-four cities of over 200,000 population without any venture capitalists. In this group of thirty-four, thirteen cities are in the South, eleven in the West, and four in the North Central Regions. In 1984 eight of these cities lacking a venture capitalist had more than the 396,000 people and would, on average, be associated with the presence of a venture capitalist if the 609 were distributed between cities throughout the United States in proportion to population. None of these eight cities is in the Northeast or North Central Regions, but half are in the South.

A later *Pratt's Guide* (Morris 1988) shows that twelve of these thirty-four cities nevertheless did have a venture capital Fund present by 1988. When all thirty-four are ranked by population, the newly established Funds are found in nine out of the seventeen larger cities in the top half of the distribution, but in only three of the seventeen smaller cities in the lower half. This suggests that some filtering down of venture capitalists may indeed be under way, but is still in its early stages. However, it should also be noted that six out of the twelve cities acquiring a presence since 1984 are in the West, and eleven out of the twenty-two cities still lacking a venture capitalist by 1988 are in the South, indicating that even this limited filtering may be a spatially biased process.

DISCUSSION

Before attempting any conclusions to this analysis, some important caveats should be mentioned.

First, the spatial displacement between just two points – degree location and city of institutional workplace – is, of course, a very simple summary of overall career life-paths for what is certainly a high income, and therefore highly mobile, occupational group whose members probably undergo several relocations during their working lifetime. For example, it may instead be the case that for some individuals their later workplace is really the same as their pre-educational 'origin', while their education place was not an 'origin' but merely a temporary departure. Nevertheless, this

is the only geographical vector constructable out of what constitutes the only systematically collected data available for such an
analysis.

Second, it must be emphasized again that this data-set covers only
the professionally employed venture capitalists, and omits the angel
investors. An OECD (1986: 44) survey estimates that US venture
capital raised by informal sources equalled 10–20 per cent of the
volume raised by specialist venture firms in 1983. During the earliest
stages of a venture's life the relative role of informal sources is
probably even more substantial. This makes it all the more
significant that so little is known about the locations of informal
investors themselves, the decision models they employ, and the
information networks that link them (Wetzel 1986: 104).

Third, it assumes a superior position and role for individuals
within the venture investment process: they are location choosers
and opportunity generators, rather than atomistic responders to
work positions flowing from previously determined venture institution addresses. This is not unrealistic, given recent conditions.
There was a massive increase in the volume of dollars pouring into
venture Funds in the late 1970s and early 1980s, which, by inside
accounts, may have outstripped the limited number of professionals
truly qualified to manage it. Experienced individual venture
capitalists are in relatively short supply and may be able to pick and
choose between job offers and work locations. Also, many
individual venture capitalists are themselves partners in their Fund
or Presidents of their SBICs: in these cases they do have
considerable decision-making power over the institutional entities
within which they work.

CONCLUSIONS

This study is the first systematic attempt to analyze the spatial
distributions of individual venture capitalists' educational and work
locations, as opposed to the office location of venturing institutions
and the spatial flows of funds. It uses the empirical results from
analyses of biographical data contained in a professional directory
source to address hypotheses which flow from the conventional
model of the venturing space-economy. The drawbacks to the data-
set require that these results be viewed as suggestive rather than
confirmatory, and that any conclusions be stated very tentatively.
Nevertheless, given the blind enthusiasm with which trickle-down
theories have sometimes been adopted to justify hands-off policies,

this caution can be seen as a strength and virtue of the approach and results, rather than a weakness.

The popular stereotype of the venture capitalist as a late-middle-aged accountant of East Coast origin with an MBA from Harvard Business School is not found to be generally the case in reality: very few have accountancy training and most are under 50, though a significant minority do possess the other traits in some combination. The Northeast Region – and within it particularly the states of Massachusetts and New York – is a prominent educational center for these people. This area, plus Illinois and California, are important working centers, while the South Region seems under-represented on both counts.

Comparison of education and workplaces for the same individuals offers only limited empirical support for the conventional model's hypothesized outcomes. The spatial distributions of educations and workplaces are different at the city and state scale, but geographically so, and not hierarchically so. Age differences do not vary by order, as would be the case if later graduates had to set up business outside the traditional centers. There are also systematic differences between the characteristics of venture capitalists found at different levels in the hierarchy, which would not be the case with a neutral spreading surface. Venture capitalist career life-paths do not track away from areas of venturer overcrowding and towards different and more sparsely ventured territory, but instead primarily from high-order venturing places to other or the same high-order venturing places. There does appear to be some movement down the size hierarchy for individual cities, but its total impact is limited, and even here spatial biases remain.

As with many other 'natural' trickle-down effects relied upon to even out initial imbalances, the evidence that such is actually occurring in this case is very limited. The overall implication of these detailed results is that the evolution of venturing is a much more complicated and internally differentiated process than a neo-classical equilibrium-based model of spatial diffusion and hierarchical filtering driven by increases in total supply would suggest. What would be more consistent with the empirical findings would be an alternative geographical model, with the following process elements incorporated from current known real trends in venturing.

First, increases in the total supply of venture dollars have come mostly from a surge in interest in this kind of investment by insurance and pension funds. Though now willing to invest a small proportion of their capital in venture Funds with high risks, pension fund managers are still generally risk averse and prefer placements in those larger venture Funds with a longer demonstrated track record of success. These Funds are more likely to be located in the older primary venture centers, like New York and Chicago. The supply increment, and hence the additional employment opportunities for more venture capitalists to dispose of it, thus accrues disproportionately across space.

Second, the favored larger venture institutions likewise show internal conservative preferences in the 'type' of individual venture capitalist they take on to manage these extra funds. Hence, in general, 'blue chip' venturers continue to be concentrated in the primary centers, while diverse (but probably no less functionally effective) venturers locate elsewhere.

Third, when spatial diffusion of venture capitalists away from the older original centers does occur, it is generally towards other places which manifest the same type of working environment (in terms of institutional supports and the type of deals available) because these are the parameters within which such professionals already feel most comfortable. These preferred conditions are more likely to be found in other primary venture centers, or in places where expansion in the kinds of industries and deals venture capitalists favor is demonstrably imminent; less innovative environments are still shunned.

This geographical model gives a more fitting explanation of the empirical patterns uncovered during analysis of biographical data. It achieves this because it does not merely see the supply of venture dollars, the surface over which they are spread, and the individual venturers themselves as neutral components of a system governed by physical or geometric laws. Rather, it allows individuals to be willful actors who are influenced by institutional and behavioral constraints, and who exist in an economic landscape made of real and uneven places and contexts.

This is not to say, of course, that the spatial diffusion and hierarchical filtering envisaged under the conventional model could not occur: rather, it is support for the view that any such movement would not necessarily be a predetermined, exclusive, or simple outcome. Instead, it would be only one particular way that the system could behave. Knowledge about which particular conditions influence different types of non-neutrality, and hence real outcomes, is now needed to flesh out this model more fully.

For example, are the spatial unevennesses and concentrations demonstrated here necessary or sufficient conditions for other venturing differences? Do investment decisions vary systematically by age of venture capitalist because of changing personal energy level and appetite for risk? How may distinct – and often geographically based – 'identities', such as the 'eastern' educational heritage, influence subsequent investment through, for example, their early influence on building the necessary personal networks for later coinvestments? How do venture capitalist distributions initiate, follow from, or reinforce spatial differences in entrepreneurship? Do continuing uneven spatial distributions constitute 'market failure' and justify direct public venture programs in some places and not others, rather than the present reliance on ubiquitous, passive, indirect, aggregate policies? In short, what is the real causal efficacy of space-based contexts in the evolution of venturing phenomena?[2]

Finally, the empirical results of this paper can also make a contribution to a current related policy discussion – or 'war', as Venture Economics (1989a) dubbed it – over capital gains tax. Previous reductions in the capital gains tax rate – particularly the 1978 Hansen–Steiger Amendment reducing the maximum rate from 49 to 28 per cent – together with changes to pension fund regulations (Silver 1984), combined to create at the end of the 1970s and early 1980s a window of opportunity for increasing the total supply of venture dollars. Suggestions have been made about how the trick might be repeated today, not only in proposals put forward by President Bush but also in five different capital gains reform bills introduced by members of the Senate by June 1989 (Venture Economics 1989a, b, d; Kasten 1989).[3]

While it is true that a change in capital gains tax rate would again affect individual angel investors personally, it is open to debate whether it would now affect the total volume of the professional venture capital pool to the same degree. In 1978, independent venture Funds obtained 32 per cent of their venture capital from individuals, but by 1988 this had declined to only 8 per cent. Meanwhile, some 67 per cent of new venture dollars in 1988 came from pension funds, insurance companies, endowments, and foundations (compared with 40 per cent 10 years earlier), and many of these institutions do not pay the tax (Poterba 1988; Henderson 1989a: 66). Some reports indicate that pension funds may in any case be losing their earlier interest in venturing, perhaps because of the complexity and uncertainty in past Labor Department rule changes on the ERISA prudence standards, and in particular the clause about 'looking through' to pension holdings of venture capital securities (Zock 1984: 141–3; Coburn and Patton 1989).

Nevertheless, this has not stopped Senator Robert Kasten (Rep., Wisconsin) from proposing his 'Entrepreneurship and Productivity Growth Act' (Kasten 1989), under which capital gains would be cut again. His proposed measure is distinctive because one of his justifications is that the same policy in 1978 and 1981 'sparked a stunning explosion of venture capital' which, if repeated, would 'make the spring of 1989 a season of growth for all Americans'. Unfortunately, not taking a geographical view, he fails to consider that in the short term an abstractly conceived aggregate policy is unlikely to change the pre-existing uneven spatial patterns of venturing to a significant degree. There is a hint in some of the distributions examined here that increases in supply may yield some spatial diffusion and filtering-down. For the most part, however, the empirical results to these analyses of individual venture capitalists' career life-paths strongly suggest that Kasten's 'growth for all Americans' is very unlikely to mean 'all Americans in all places'.

NOTES

1 Furthermore, it should be remembered that these are cities taken from mailing addresses and are not wider MSAs.
2 Work is presently under way pursuing some of these questions through personal interviews of venture capitalists and recipient firm founders (Thompson and Bayer 1989a, b).
3 These were: Rudy Boschwitz (R-MN), Dale Bumpers (D-AR), Alan Cranston (D-CA), Dennis DeConcini (D-AZ), and Bob Kasten (R-WI). Substantive details of their suggestions are compared in Venture Economics (1989d: 4-6).

ACKNOWLEDGEMENTS

The author wishes to thank the Prochnow Educational Foundation and the University of Wisconsin-Madison Graduate School Research Committee for financial support (UW grants #101-3098 and #133-P162) and Professor Milford Green and Kristin Bayer for helpful advice. Nothing herein should be taken as reflecting the views or policies of the sponsors, and any opinions, errors, or omissions remain the responsibility of the author.

6 The rise and fall of venture capital in New Zealand

Martin Perry

The history of venture capital in New Zealand has been unusual. Other case studies in this volume at least partly support the role of venture capital as a key influence in the innovation process and over the emergence of new, industrial core regions. In New Zealand, venture capital has not only failed to influence economic restructuring, it has itself experienced decline as part of a recent wider demise in the financial services industry.

The progress of New Zealand's venture capital industry can be divided into three main stages. Before 1984 institutional sources of venture capital were limited to one publicly-owned agency. Between 1984 and 1987, the industry grew rapidly in the context of economic policy reforms which allowed new activities and freed the access to financial markets. At its peak in 1987, the New Zealand Venture Capital Association (NZVCA) recorded almost NZ$100 million[1] of annual investment by over twenty investing agencies. In the wake of the collapse of share market values in October 1987, the industry experienced an equally rapid decline. In mid-1989, no institutional sources of venture capital existed and it was estimated that only NZ$30 million of venture capital remained invested.[2].

The dramatic shifts in the supply of venture capital in New Zealand require explanation and this will be the task of the first part of this chapter. This explanation is addressed in two stages: first, the economic context and its transformation under a program of economic liberalization is considered; second, the institutional character of the industry that arose before 1987 is examined. In the second part of the chapter, the character of the investment undertaken during 1985–7 is evaluated, and this is followed by a wider discussion of the opportunities for and importance of reviving the supply of venture capital.

PRODUCTION, INNOVATION, AND ECONOMIC POLICY IN NEW ZEALAND

New Zealand is a small country (population 3.3 million) most widely known as an agricultural economy (Map 6.1). In terms of employment, this farming image is difficult to justify. By 1970, agriculture employed about the same share of the total labour force in New Zealand as it did in western economies and much less than the share in poorer nations. What makes agriculture of more economic significance in New Zealand than in most OECD countries is its productivity and importance in export earnings. Between 1960 and 1970, the farm and agricultural processing sectors had the highest productivity performance resulting from techno-logical innovation amongst all major sectors (Easton 1988). In 1985, about 60 per cent of export earnings came from categories linked to the agricultural sector. New Zealand agriculture is not a relic feature surviving through tolerance and subsidy; rather it is the key component of the national economy. Thus, although the long-term trend in the local economy has been towards diversification, most of this expansion has been contained within the land-based sector. Businesses developing information technology and advanced elec-tronic equipment remain insignificant in terms of employment and output. The computer software industry has been identified as a potential growth industry on the basis of several early successes (Kaiser 1986), but this promise has yet to be realized in the face of increasing market dominance by multinational firms (Perry 1989). In further contrast with countries with expanding venture capital industries, small manufacturing firms have a lower rate of job generation than large and medium sized companies (Harper and Bollard 1985).

New Zealand's agriculture is remarkably efficient by world standards and, while this results from the rapid adoption of new production practices and technologies, individual producers remain risk averse (McLean 1978). In New Zealand, the risks associated with agricultural production are severe by world standards. Low or no support prices for most products have not maintained farm incomes in times of surplus production and the form of grassland farming is particularly susceptible to climatic conditions. Thus efficiency has derived mainly through reducing the labor input per unit of production, rather than by increasing output per unit area of land. This pattern of development led to declining agricultural production and limited opportunities for outside investment, particularly as innovation was concentrated in the research programs of government bodies and freely disseminated to individual producers (McArthur 1988).

Moreover, by the 1970s the availability of new technologies slowed down and along with this new investment stagnated (McLean 1978). These historical conditions militated against the use of venture capital, but in the 1980s development patterns changed. An increase in corporate ownership, diversification into new high-value products, such as exotic meats and horticulture (partly encouraged by a period of government incentives) and advances in biotechnology have generated more opportunities for investment finance (Pryde 1988). Wider changes in the direction of economic management created additional stimulus to the demand for finance from land-based and other sectors of the economy.

Up to 1984 the New Zealand development model pursued by the government consisted of industrialization financed by the export earnings from the agricultural sector (Le Heron 1988). The slow growth in local output and international demand for agricultural products, compounded by increasing difficulties in gaining access to former major markets, most notably the UK market, forced a change in economic management. Since 1984, a new Labour government has instituted a watershed in the state response to deteriorating economic conditions (Britton and Le Heron 1987). The economy has been exposed to more international competition through the elimination or reduction of import controls and tariffs; industry regulation has been relaxed to enable easier entry and exit and the state sector is being remodelled through privatization and corporatization (Bollard and Buckle (1987) provide an overview of these changes).

While no part of the economy has been left unaffected by the reform program, the financial sector has experienced the most dramatic transformation. As late as 1984, the market for finance was supplied by institutions subject to rigid and pervasive controls on their balance sheet structure, interest rates, exchange rates, foreign exchange, and credit growth (Harper 1986). For example, there was close control of the range of investment that banks and other financial institutions could undertake. This regulatory regime restricted the supply of venture capital for several reasons. The 1956 Trustee Act limited the range of investments open to trustee funds (banks, insurance companies, pension funds) and this excluded the possibility of establishing venture capital subsidiaries. Perhaps more important, however, was the small scale of the market for all forms

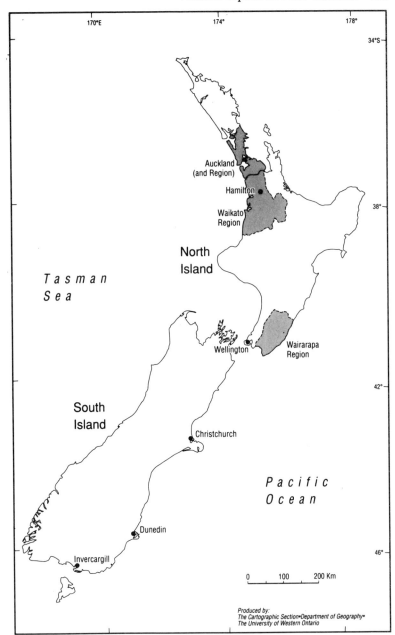

Map 6.1 New Zealand

of commercial finance. Strict border controls on the movement of capital, high tariff barriers, and licensing control over many industries created an industrial sector which, like the land-based sector, was characterized by a preponderance of small firms with low levels of investment and innovation (Le Heron 1979). The exposure to the competitive forces of the global economy has forced the restructuring of all productive activities and encouraged the diversification of the financial sector. For example, the Bank of New Zealand did not establish a commercial banking division until 1980. Between 1957 and 1978 the share market index grew by an annual average of less than 10 per cent; between 1979 and 1984, the annual average growth jumped to 60 per cent (Wheeler and Nash 1989). After 1984, the number of financial institutions serving the business sector multiplied. Harper (1986) identified twelve new merchant and investment banks and fifteen new foreign exchange dealers established during 1984–6.

While the market for commercial finance remained small, one publicly owned agency was the sole source of venture capital. The Development Finance Corporation (DFC) was established in the early 1960s to provide loans to the government's priority sectors and to administer loans and grants under its regional development program. In 1972, DFC Ventures was formed and this division became the country's main source of venture capital funds up to 1987. In the wake of financial deregulation, the agency diversified into various money market and foreign exchange activities while its development agency functions were wound down as part of a government ordered preparation for transferring the agency to private ownership. Its subsequent history was not a success. In October 1989 the DFC was placed into receivership by its new owners, becoming another casualty in the investment industry collapse.

Venture capital in New Zealand does not, therefore, owe its origins to the liberalization of economic activity, but it grew rapidly in the newly deregulated environment. The NZVCA was formed in 1985 with twenty members and NZ$20 million of invested funds. By 1987, membership had doubled and invested funds had grown to over NZ$100 million. The NZVCA established itself as an effective lobbying organization, campaigning successfully for changes in the trustee legislation to allow trustee fund managers to invest a proportion of their funds as venture capital. The NZVCA was instrumental in working with the local stock exchange to establish a second board for companies without the capital required for listing on the main board. The second board was regarded as a major step forward for the venture capital industry because of the 'exit route' provided for the realization of mature investments. The euphoria surrounding the industry was then abruptly altered by the worldwide drop in share market values in October 1987. Subsequently the NZVCA and the second board have been disbanded and the supply of venture capital has reduced to nothing. Of course, New Zealand was not unique in experiencing a share market crash, but elsewhere it does not seem to have affected the venture capital industry except in reducing the value of second-board companies (Thompson 1989a). To understand why the crash has been so influential in New Zealand, the structure of the industry that developed during 1985-7 and the particular severity of the fall in share market values need explanation.

VENTURE CAPITAL INSTITUTIONS

Four main types of venture capital provider can be distinguished: 'captive' funds, independent funds, publicly listed companies and public sector funds. Captives are venture capital groups that are owned by larger investment and/or financial services organizations which use their own resources to establish venture funds. Independent funds are concerned solely with the management of the venture fund for the institutional and/or individual investor(s) which provide the resources for the fund. Publicly listed companies, like independent funds, concentrate solely on the provision of venture capital but obtain their resources through a public share issue. Public sector funds vary in character and sometimes may be a captive fund where the venture capital is supplied by a body with other funding programs, as happened with the DFC.

The unusual characteristic of the New Zealand venture capital industry was its dominance by captive funds. During 1985–6, captive funds (including the DFC) accounted for roughly 95 per cent of the venture capital investments recorded by the NZVCA. The minor role played by publicly listed funds was not atypical, but compared with international experience independent funds were underrepresented. Publicly listed funds are a minority in most countries because early failures in the investment portfolio tend to depress share values and frustrate the development of the fund. In the UK, private independent funds were responsible for 37 per cent of total venture capital investment by value in 1985 BVCA (British Venture Capital Association 1985): in the United States, they controlled 75 per cent of available venture capital in 1986 (New Zealand Venture Capital Association 1987). In the case of the United States, Leinbach and Amrhein (1987) have emphasized the significance of independent funds in spreading the spatial distribution of venture capital. The New Zealand experience highlights the importance of a diversified supply base to enhance the industry's continuity.

Most of the captive funds were linked to financial institutions that, to varying degrees, were affected by the October 1987 sharemarket crash. The New Zealand market lost 36 per cent of its value in that month, and while several countries fared worse, New Zealand has experienced the most prolonged fall (Wheeler and Nash 1989). By mid January 1988, 57 per cent of the market's pre-crash capitalization value had been eroded and by July 1989 the market remained over 40 per cent below its peak value. A government examination of the prolonged severity of the market decline concluded that the role played by investment companies was the single most important cause of the sustained recession.

The program of economic policy reforms commenced in 1984 required the widespread restructuring of business activities in the face of new competitive conditions. Investment companies played a major part in this change through the purchase and reorganization of firms, which generated high levels of equity trading. Investment companies are particularly vulnerable to a decline in share market values because of (1) the use of shares as security for debt and the tendency to have higher than average debt to equity ratios and (2), as a result of (1), their own share values shift disproportionately to the overall movement of the share market.[3] In December 1986, seven investment companies accounted for 33 per cent of the market capitalization of the top thirty companies. When the decline commenced, the dominance of investment companies hastened and steepened the drop in values.

The sustained depression in the share market had several consequences for the venture capital industry. Most directly, several captive venture funds were owned by investment companies that are now bankrupt. More generally, financial institutions have reappraised their investment strategies and concentrated on their core activity of providing secured debt finance rather than equity to new and high-risk ventures. This reappraisal has both ended the flow of capital to new proposals and caused the withdrawal of support to existing investments. Two publicly listed funds have survived, but with no resources to expand their investment portfolios which comprised less than ten investments in August 1989. The drying up of venture capital has been one part of a general reduction in equity finance in New Zealand. There were no successful new share issues through the stock exchange for 2 years after the crash.

Former prominent members of the NZVCA (the NZVCA is another casualty of the crash) argue that a more diversified venture capital industry would have survived as independent funds are more 'committed' because they do not have the option of shifting their investment focus (King 1988). The emphasis on the relative risk avoidance strategies of captive and independent venture funds may be less important than the atmosphere in which investment occurred during 1985–7. The scope and rapidity of the liberalization of the financial sector was unequalled in the OECD (Deane 1985). The sudden increase in the access to investment funds when demand was increasing and new institutions were vying for dominance led, in some institutions at least, to a relaxation of more usual investment criteria.[4] Poor management and doubtful investment practices were revealed through the collapse of investment companies such as Judge Corporation and Equiticorp. Instability amongst captive funds may not, therefore, have been as significant as the lack of experience amongst financial institutions. In the United States, for example, captive funds had increased in importance before the crash but Thompson (1989a) identifies no significant impact on the supply of venture capital caused by the share market fall in this country.

The decline in normal investment standards during the post 1984 euphoria surrounding the deregulation of the financial market implies that the disbursement of venture capital during 1985–7 exaggerated the 'true' demand. The latter possibility can, in part, be examined from the pattern of investment undertaken during 1985–7. It is to an examination of venture capital in this period of growth that the chapter now turns.

VENTURE CAPITAL 1985–7

The evidence in this section is derived from a survey of the members of the NZVCA undertaken by a member organization. Some comments on these data are required. The definition of venture capital adopted by the NZVCA was fourfold: (1) the investment should represent a long-term commitment of funds; (2) the investor(s) should participate in the management of the recipient companies; (3) the investment should be made at an early stage of a company's growth or at the commencement of an expansionary phase, and at the time of the investment the recipient should not be a listed company; (4) the investor(s) should divest once the growth phase is completed. The criteria meet international standards but, unfortunately, were not adhered to as the survey organizers were anxious to inflate the significance of their industry. The present author has reduced the recorded investment compared with the results published by the NZVCA, but there remains some over-recording. More positively, the survey received a 100 per cent coverage of known venture capital suppliers.

The survey covered the period from 1985 to the early part of 1987 (depending on when individual returns were received). The industry was changing rapidly over this period, and so the following discussion concentrates on the 2 years of full data and comments on the evolution of investment. Where the regional distribution of funds is discussed, the 1987 data have been included.

During 1985–6 total venture capital investment increased from NZ$19.5 million to NZ$77.2 million with the number of ventures assisted increasing from thirty-seven to seventy-eight. Alongside the general growth in investment, the average size of individual investments increased but remained small by international standards. The median investment in 1987 was NZ$0.55 million or about one-third of that in the United Kingdom (Mason 1987b). The industry was never more than a minor component of total business funding. Trading bank and major finance company loans to private business amounted to NZ$9,000 million in 1986 (*New Zealand Reserve Bank Bulletin* 1986) and new share issues raised roughly NZ$3,500 million (Buttle Wilson 1987) so that at its peak venture capital was less than 1 per cent of total business funding.

The investment was small but nonetheless important in being directed at the early stages of new ventures. In 1986, early stage funding to support the initiation of production and/or marketing accounted for over one-half the investments made, while in the United Kingdom and the United States it accounted for about 10 per cent of investment (Leinbach and Amrhein 1987; Mason 1987b). In these more established venture capital markets, second stage and expansion funding was the dominant type of investment.

Internationally, a major reason for venture capital growth was the interest in technology related enterprises. Investment in computer communications, other electronics related activities and industrial automation accounted for over 60 per cent of US investments in 1981 (Leinbach and Amrhein 1987). Venture capital in the United States has played a significant role in developing productivity-improving technologies, such as robots and other methods of industrial automation. In the United Kingdom it has been suggested that venture capitalists have a 'lack of appetite' for the higher risks associated with new technologies, but they still accounted for 27 per cent of investments by number in 1984 (Mason 1987b).

The New Zealand industry, in sharp contrast, invested just 3 per cent of its venture capital in electronics and computer related activities (Table 6.1). Entertainment and primary sector activities have absorbed over half the venture capital investments made during 1985–6. While the former was a reflection of the specialization of the national economy, the latter was a more idiosyncratic phenomenon associated largely with one venture capital house that gained international recognition as a funder of theatrical productions. A further atypical feature of the New Zealand venture capital industry was the level of investment in financial services which, adding to the distinctiveness, were usually overseas-based venture funds.

By number, two-thirds of the investment was in New Zealand productive activities related to the primary sector and manufacturing. The primary products and services supported were predominantly

Table 6.1 Venture capital investment, by industry, 1985–1986

Industry	Number of investments	Amount invested		
		(NZ$'000)	(%)	(% abroad)[a]
Primary products and services	38	27,835	28.8	0
Industrial products	22	13,313	13.8	12.4
Foods and beverage	18	9,107	9.4	7.7
Entertainment	17	28,108	29.1	72.0
Computer related	9	1,756	1.8	0
Financial services	5	3,050	3.1	100.0
Tourism	4	3,940	4.1	0
Electronics	3	1,615	1.6	69.0
Medical health	3	2,400	2.5	0
Transportation	2	2,822	2.9	0
Communication	2	700	0.7	28.5
Energy and mining	1	2,000	2.0	100.0

Source: New Zealand Venture Capital Association (1987)
Note: [a] Ventures with a New Zealand and overseas operating base are included; this amounts to $10.2 million of the investment shown in the table.

new ventures in expanding activities, such as deer and goat farming, bloodstock, and horticultural products. More innovative ventures were less common but examples included prawn farming and biotechnology products. Similarly in the industrial category, there were no cases of industrial automation, robotics, or 'advanced materials' being supported. Projects tended to be on a smaller scale, involving the enhancement of existing products: examples of this are a company designing and manufacturing high speed printers and another company manufacturing sophisticated weighing machinery for the agricultural industry.

The existence of taxation incentives allowing generous capital write-offs in the year of expenditure, rather than over the life of the investment, encouraged the investment in horticulture, deer farming, and bloodstock. These incentives were not available for the manufacturing sector and were withdrawn entirely in April 1987. The emphasis on leisure and entertainment was also partly induced by taxation. The attraction was the ease of exploiting leisure and particularly film ventures to obtain tax advantages through use of 'special partnerships' (see below); sometimes the project was incidental or irrelevant.

A further indication of a shortage of genuine investment opportunities in New Zealand was the high proportion of funds invested offshore. Of the total investments during 1985–6, 26 per cent was in overseas operations. Two large venture funds accounted for most of the overseas investment; DFC Ventures and Strada Holdings Ltd (specialists in theatrical funding) made 98 per cent of the overseas investment by value. For Strada, overseas investment was inevitable given their funding niche. In the case of DFC Ventures, a subsidiary office was opened in the United States, partly to access local investment opportunities, but also to improve the corporation's equity funding expertise by participation in the world's largest venture capital market (DFC 1986). After the United States, the most popular overseas investment location was Australia with the other main international destination of New Zealand venture capital being the United Kingdom. In comparison with New Zealand's experience, the United States was a net importer of venture funds while the United Kingdom invested around one-fifth of their venture capital overseas in 1983 (Mason 1987b).

The geographical distribution of venture capital investments within New Zealand was characterized by marked inequalities between regions (Table 6.2). The Auckland region, encompassing the country's largest and fastest growing city, was the major

Table 6.2 Regional distribution of venture capital

Region	Percentage of investments 1985–7 received by		Number of venture capital firms
	Value	*Number of investments*	
Auckland	32.4	39.5	9
Wellington	15.6	15.1	7
Waikato	13.0	10.9	1
Wairarapa	0.4	5.9	1
Other North Island	13.2	7.6	–
Christchurch	7.2	11.7	1
Other South Island	4.9	5.9	–
Nationwide	12.1	3.4	–

Source: New Zealand Venture Capital Association (1987)
Note: Two organizations maintain more than one office.

beneficiary. Auckland accounted for 32.4 per cent of venture capital investments by value and contained 39.5 per cent of the recipient enterprises; the remainder of the North Island took a further 42.2 per cent of the funds invested and 38.3 per cent of the venture-backed enterprises. In addition, firms with more than one location (3.4 per cent of the investee companies) claimed 12 per cent of the funds. The spatial equity of the venture capital investments can be gauged partly by comparison with the distribution of working proprietors, on the assumption that the latter are a reasonable indicator of locally controlled enterprise (there are no published data identifying small firms in New Zealand). In 1987, Auckland accounted for 30 per cent of the total working proprietors and Wellington 6.5 per cent (Department of Labour, 1987), whereas they had 39.5 per cent and 15.1 per cent respectively of the enterprises receiving venture capital. In contrast, the South Island contained 26.2 per cent of working proprietors and 17.6 per cent of the receiving enterprises. Christchurch, the main center in the South Island, was relatively well treated in this comparison, having 6.5 per cent of the total working proprietors and 7.6 per cent of the venture capital recipients.

It is possible that the distribution of venture capital during 1985–6 was unrepresentative because earlier investment had temporarily exhausted opportunities in the rural regions. The DFC was the only significant source of venture capital before 1985 and its more recent investment showed no marked contrast with earlier years. Indeed, during 1985–6 the South Island accounted for 27 per cent of the DFC's new business approvals (by value) compared with 22 per cent for the 1973–86 period (DFC 1985, 1986). As a result, the spatial pattern of investment does not seem to have been distorted by investment before the survey.

Further evidence on the extent of spatial conservatism is provided by the relationship between the location of venture capital offices and recipient regions. Of the funds invested, 42 per cent of the value was retained by recipients in the same region as the investor's location; in terms of the number of investments made, 57 per cent have been regionally contained.

Inter-regional investment flows were dominated by transfers between Auckland and Wellington and by Auckland-controlled venture capital invested in Waikato based enterprises (the region adjoining Auckland's southern boundary): these flows accounted for 35 per cent and 23 per cent respectively of non-local investment value. North Island venture capitalists lodged just 4 per cent of their funds in South Island enterprises. Moreover, investments outside the two main North Island centers of Auckland and Wellington depended mainly on the DFC. DFC Ventures accounted for 81 per cent of the investment in the South Island and was the only venture capital firm located in the South Island. In the North Island, the Hamilton office of DFC Ventures accounted for roughly 90 per cent of the invested funds in enterprises located outside Auckland and Wellington.

There are two possible explanations for the concentration of venture capital investments in Auckland and the North Island. On the one hand it may reflect the preponderance of suitable investment opportunities and willing investment recipients in this part of the country. On the other hand, it may be that venture capital funds were less willing to consider proposals distant from their office base for reasons of administrative convenience and/or, less certainly, of the economic environment of distant locations.

Indirectly there is evidence that investment flows were in agreement with demand. A study of applications to patent inventions in New Zealand (Taylor 1977) found that more than two-thirds originated in the four main centers, with 36.9 per cent from Auckland, 16.7 per cent from Wellington, 11.3 per cent from Christchurch, and 3.1 per cent from Dunedin. A strong concentration of inventive activity was also identified in the Waikato region, centered on the region's capital Hamilton, and into the Wairarapa adjacent to Wellington. Whilst Taylor's study related to different economic circumstances, the pattern of inventiveness was linked to employment and institutional influences that remain strong. Further evidence suggesting that the distribution of venture capital reflected demand is provided by changes in the number of working proprietors. During the period 1980–6, a shift-share analysis shows that Auckland, Waikato, Wairarapa, and Christchurch experienced above expected levels of growth in the number of working proprietors in manufacturing (Perry 1987).

A different source of evidence on the appropriateness of the present distribution of venture capital funds relates to the subsequent performance of investee companies. The NZVCA survey found that of the 119 indigenous investments, twenty-six (22 per cent) had already failed, forty-eight (40 per cent) had equalled expectations, thirty-seven (31 per cent) had exceeded expectations, whilst in eight cases it was 'too early to judge the outcome'. Successes and failures were recorded amongst all types of activity, although the primary sector was distinguished by a high proportion (60 per cent) of investments exceeding expectations. Regionally, the provincial North Island had the greatest share of investments exceeding expectations (Table 6.3), with a perhaps surprisingly similar performance amongst other investment localities. More contemporary data on the performance of investee companies derived from discussions with government officials monitoring the industry and former members of the NZVCA showed that no notable success stories had emerged by mid-1989 and that the failure rate was now at least 66 per cent.[5] The cause of failure was not always the quality of the project, as the collapse of venture funds and an unwillingness by surviving funds to advance further support were sometimes contributory causes of failure. The break-up of the NZVCA and the end of most venture funds frustrates a more detailed analysis of

Table 6.3 Investment outcomes and locations, 1987

Location of investee company	Percentage of investee companies	
	Above expectations	Failed
Auckland	25	28
Wellington	17	22
Other North Island	57	14
South Island	20	25
Total	31	22

Source: New Zealand Venture Capital Association (1987)

investment outcomes, and so the remaining discussion focuses on the pattern up to 1987.

Table 6.4 shows the relationship between the failure rate and the locations of venture company offices and their investments. The interpretation of Table 6.4 requires caution because of the small sample involved and the later history of the industry, but two tentative conclusions may be drawn. First, the high failure rate (29 per cent) of local investments in the Auckland region compared with no failures outside the region suggests that a two-tier investment strategy was followed: a lower level of risk is required of regional projects whilst the demand from Auckland based ventures remained strong. Second, the high failure rate (42 per cent) of ventures supported in Dunedin and Invercargill may be indicative of a genuine shortage of practicable projects in the far south of the South Island. Also, Tables 6.3 and 6.4 provide no clear evidence that projects outside the main centers were less practicable than those in Auckland and Wellington.

The alternative interpretation of the disbursement of venture capital emphasizes the conservatism of investors. The New Zealand financial system operates largely from Wellington and Auckland. Those concerned with economic development in the regions have expressed concern that the concentration of financial control causes investment opportunities available elsewhere in the country to be overlooked, either through a lack of awareness or, less kindly, because of a lack of interest. A recent consultancy study for Northland Regional Development Council (a North Island region with one venture capital recipient during 1985–7) suggested that a regional venture capital organization is required to support local projects.[6] An unrelated survey in Northland examined the experience of new and small businesses in raising debt finance and found that almost half had experienced some form of 'capital stress', although the proportion ultimately denied credit was much less (Perry 1988b). Several respondents to the latter survey specifically suggested that the region's distance from Auckland was an influence in reducing the availability of debt finance, even though most lending institutions had at least one branch in the region.

One influence thought to shape the disbursement of funds is the practice of venture capital funds to place one of their managers on the board of the investee company. This reason has been given as a cause behind the marked spatial concentration of venture fund recipients in the United Kingdom's southeastern corner, close to the financial capital of London (Mason 1987b). In New Zealand,

Table 6.4 Outcome of venture capital investments, 1987, by location of investment and investee

| Location of venture capital office | Proportion of failed investments (%) (number in parentheses) Location of investee enterprise | | | | |
	Auckland	Wellington	Other North Island	Christchurch	Dunedin Invercargill
Auckland	29 (11)	0	0	–	–
Wellington	20 (2)	16 (2)	40 (2)	0	–
Other North Island	–	–	15 (2)	–	–
Christchurch	–	100 (2)	–	22 (2)	42 (2)

Source: New Zealand Venture Capital Association (1987)

directors were appointed in eighty-eight of the 119 indigenous investments. The need to maintain direct management contact, coupled with the multiple directorships held by venture company nominees, places a strong premium on geographical proximity. A shortage of experienced venture capital executives exacerbated the difficulty of managing investments in distant regions. These considerations militated against investments away from venture company headquarters in Wellington and Auckland. Although venture capital lenders have disputed the claim that distance had deterred their investment (Department of Trade and Industry 1988), the importance of regionally based offices, such as those in Christchurch and Hamilton, in spreading the disbursement of venture funds was evident in the NZVCA survey.

THE FUTURE OF VENTURE CAPITAL IN NEW ZEALAND

Thompson (1989a) provides two models of the venture capital industry: a conventional model and a geographical model. The conventional model encapsulates venture capital as a potent force in economic development, mobilizing new high-technology industries with rapid growth and substantial profit potential and diffusing these benefits widely as the total flow of funds increases. The geographical model is more skeptical of the distinctive characteristics of venture capital compared with other forms of business finance and emphasizes how the supply of funds is managed by human and institutional actors behaving in a constrained fashion concerning the spatial and industrial distribution of their funds. The New Zealand experience, while not entirely consistent with either model, fits closest within the more critical, geographic framework.

The growth of venture capital was not experienced equally around the country. The main beneficiary was Auckland which received over 30 per cent of the invested funds, while the less developed regions received little or no new investment. Investment outside the main metropolitan centers resulted largely from the DFC's regional network of offices and, at that stage, a remit to assist regional development. The sectoral distribution of investment was also in conflict with the conventional model. Venture capital was not significant in commercializing research and development, innovation, or technology transfer. Entertainment, leisure, and the primary sector were the principal recipients with technology-based projects accounting for less than 5 per cent of the invested funds. Of course, these characteristics partly reflected the structure of the economy, but the availability of taxation incentives, rather than the search for the super-normal profits associated with innovation, was an important influence on the investment in the primary and entertainment sectors.

On the other hand, roughly one-third of the invested funds went overseas, showing some spatial flexibility in the industry. The importance of early stage funding, where risk is generally highest, is also more consistent with the conventional model. However, both these attributes need qualification. The short life of the local venture capital industry was influential in encouraging these more conventional characteristics. The DFC was the main investor overseas and this was partly motivated by the need to gain experience in equity funding, rather than a long term strategy (DFC 1986). The preponderance of early stage funding reflected the lack of opportunities for second stage or expansion funding. The balance of evidence tends, therefore, to endorse Thompson's geographical model.

The demise of the industry post-1987 does not permit further elaboration of these models in New Zealand, although the rapid withdrawal of funds does provide further support for the geographical model in view of the risk-averse strategy adopted by former venture capital providers. Two issues of practical significance remain: first, the extent to which a shortage of venture capital is constraining economic development; second, the measures that would revive the supply of venture funds. These questions are the subject of the final part of this chapter.

Based on the size of the US and UK venture industries as a proportion of all business finance, it has been estimated that New Zealand could accommodate annual investment of NZ$15–20 millions across fifteen to twenty projects[7]. This estimated rate of investment is below that experienced in 1985–6, although as taxation incentives and over-recording in the NZVCA survey exaggerated the true demand, the future estimate is more realistic. Even the more modest estimate may be too great as it assumes that the rate of new firm innovation is similar between New Zealand and the United Kingdom and United States, which is doubtful. New Zealand lacks research-intensive industries and academic institutions whose combination has stimulated new technology-based regions overseas. The liberalization of the New Zealand economy is expected to lead to a concentration of economic activity in a small number of major enterprises in support of the experience of other small nations (Savage 1986). In line with this expectation, Harper and Bollard (1985) found that small firms in New Zealand were less significant than medium and large sized firms in generating new jobs.

On a more micro scale, the demand for government incentives also shows a lack of growth in the small-firm sector. The government's main scientific organization – the Department of Scientific and Industrial Research (DSIR) – has two grant schemes to help the application and development of new technology but less than fifty grants have been disbursed after 3 years. According to administrators of the program a shortage of worthwhile projects is the main cause behind the low use of the schemes.[8] Another DSIR policy initiative is a training program for new entrepreneurs (New Zealand New Ventures) which for several years has failed to attract any independent entrepreneurs; instead all participants have been middle managers in large companies or public corporations.

A survey of venture capital recipients revealed that most had used this form of finance only after being denied credit from lending institutions (Department of Trade and Industry, 1988). Despite the 'lifeline' provided by venture capital many recipients were critical of their venture partners. The causes of this dissatisfaction were stated as 'unrealistic' levels of reporting, the level of shareholding demanded relative to the capital invested and demands for security against the investment. Several recipients argued that it would have been more effective to form a joint venture with another company than use venture capital. Of course, without the context of these comments it is difficult to judge their substance, but they do emphasize how venture capital is not the only source of equity finance for private companies or necessarily the most effective.

The past ineffectiveness of venture capital to influence innovation and economic development decisively does not preclude its future importance. If international levels of investment were achieved, the cumulative success of investments would be significant. Former members of the NZVCA argue that the number of worthwhile projects now outstrips the supply of finance but that the availability of venture funds will require taxation reforms to encourage small, independent funds. Without such reform, it is argued, supply will depend on investment companies and merchant banks overcoming past losses and re-establishing captive funds. The specific taxation reform sought would allow investors in independently managed funds to offset losses, which are considered inevitable in the early years, against other personal or business income. Such 'special partnership' legislation was withdrawn in New Zealand in 1985 because of its widespread use solely for tax avoidance. In the United Kingdom and United States, tax avoidance has been dealt with specifically and independent funds remain important. Venture capitalists in New Zealand argue that the same can be achieved here, particularly now that trustee funds can invest in unlisted companies and venture capital funds.

The taxation reform is viewed as the missing element in the ingredients for a vigorous venture capital industry, the other two components being low or no capital gains tax and legislation enabling superannuation and trustee funds to invest in venture funds (King 1988). The last two ingredients are found in New Zealand, but it is oversimplistic to assume that achieving the third will overcome other weaknesses. The experience of 1985–7 is that a shortage of skilled venture capitalists and worthwhile projects are the more critical hurdles to the growth of venture capital in New Zealand.

A more direct approach to increasing the flow of venture funds would be through a public sector agency or via tax incentives such as the UK's business expansion scheme (Mason 1987b). Neither mechanism is supported by the present Labour Government. Taxation concessions are seen to distort market signals which are regarded as more effective than subsidies in identifying growth industries. The brief history of the private venture capital industry in New Zealand does not vindicate this faith in market forces as applied to one sector of the finance market. The round of private venture capital investment during 1985–7 has to date produced no new enterprises which have achieved significant growth. There are also questions over the skills of venture capitalists in terms of their ability to select worthwhile projects or add value to their investments. The main interest of the NZVCA was to emphasize the size of the industry rather than to enhance the quality of investments and venture capital management.

CONCLUSION

The review of venture capital in New Zealand offers a different experience from that in larger economies. The distinctiveness of venture capital in the supply of business finance is difficult to sustain for New Zealand. Internationally, venture capital has attracted attention because of its image as a supporter of high-risk investment at the leading edge of technological advancement. Venture capitalists are seen to offer experience and specialized skills which add value to their investments over a long-term association. These characteristics have not been met in New Zealand. Innovative and technology-based activities accounted for a small proportion of investments. The commitment of venture capitalists proved short-lived and post-1985 largely unsuccessful in bringing forward profitable industries.

Evidence on the demand–supply balance of investment finance is fragmented, but the lack of impact from investment during 1985–7 suggests that the demise of the venture capital industry is not a notable constraint on economic growth. A level of venture capital investment equivalent to that in the United Kingdomn and United States implies fifteen to twenty annual investments, but it is doubtful that this modest demand exists. On the other hand, the cumulative impact of a small number of high-growth enterprises is significant, so that the supply of venture capital should still be of concern to policy makers. Venture capitalists argue that the main priority is to facilitate the formation of independent venture funds as this will revive the flow of funds and provide a more stable supply than an industry dominated by captive funds. These claims are justified by the distinctive role of independent venture funds overseas, but the potential impact in New Zealand needs to be tempered by three considerations. The first is the instability of captive funds in New Zealand derived, in part, from the overoptimistic investment environment engendered by the rapid deregulation of the financial market. The gradual return of captive funds may be expected to be on a more permanent basis with the benefit of earlier experience. Second, the supply and quality of venture capitalists needs consideration as well as the supply of funds. Third, the low level of innovation is a more intractable problem than the supply of finance and reflects wider issues connected with the funding of research and development, the investment strategies of large companies, and access to technical expertise.

NOTES

1 NZ$1.00 = US$0.60, August 1989.
1 Estimated by G. Norman (Venture Funding Ltd) in an unpublished report to the Market Development Board. The estimate was based on information collected from former members of the NZVCA.
2 Instability of investment company shares has also been identified in the United States by Arbel *et al.* (1988).
4 Cave (1989) provides a case study of the break from usual banking standards over this period in the country's largest bank, the Bank of New Zealand.
5 N. James (Department of Commerce), G. Todd (Department of Scientific and Industrial Research), G. Norman (Venture Funding Ltd) and O. MacShane (Restech International).
6 Unpublished report to Northland Regional Development Council by McDermott Associates Ltd. The recommendation has subsequently been progressed with proposals for a Northland Regional Development Corporation with a $1 million loan and equity fund supported by local business and public authorities.
7 See note 2.
8 G. Todd (Department of Scientific and Industrial Research), April 1989.

7 Venture capital in Canada
Rod B. McNaughton

An increasing amount of investment capital is made available by
Canada's institutional venture capital firms. The total capital
managed by Canadian venture investors is approximately $2.3
billion, a sum that is growing by about $800 million per year in new
commitments (Gittins, 1988). While the venture capital market is
small compared to investment in mature equity, venture investment
has a significant impact on the Canadian small business sector.
Venture capitalists are sophisticated investors, combining equity
participation with managerial skills. By evaluating proposals for
additions to their portfolios, venture capitalists act as filters in the
new firm formation and expansion process. This process selects
those firms that have the potential for above average financial
performance, and thus the potential for above average returns on
investment. This translates into high levels of employment creation,
exports, and research and development activity (Green *et al.* 1988).

The Canadian venture capital market has three major components:
independent firms, subsidiaries of major industrial and financial
corporations, and government programs. The historical development
of these components is discussed in the first section of this chapter.
The history of venture capital firms is not well documented in
comparison with other financial institutions, such as commercial
banks and insurance companies. In part, this is because of the
prevalence of limited partnerships with specified lifetimes. Long
corporate histories are simply not developed. Further, the history of
the industry is very much that of the efforts of people rather than
corporations. Two popular books are worth reading in this regard:
Wilson (1985) gives a journalistic account of the major players in
the American market, and Ross (1975) provides an account of the
activities of Canadian venturers. This chapter relies heavily on the
historical account provided by Fells (1988, 1989). The second part of

the chapter provides an overview of contemporary office location and investment characteristics. This section is based largely on the results of a survey of Canadian venture capitalists conducted by the author (McNaughton and Green 1989) and a survey of exits conducted by Venture Economics Canada (1986).

HISTORICAL DEVELOPMENT

The beginnings of the venture capital industry can be traced to the Middle Ages when merchants, noblemen, and clergy joined in partnerships to underwrite trading voyages. These partnerships became institutionalized in a precursor to the modern banking system. However, the amount of capital that could be raised through the partnerships was insufficient to fund increasingly expensive attempts to exploit resources in the New World.

During the 1500s the joint stock company became the common device for pooling capital resources but by 1720 had fallen into disrepute as a result of the collapse of the speculative episode known as the South Sea Bubble (La Force 1963). The South Sea Company, an English mercantilist firm with a monopoly on trade in Spanish America, underwrote the English national debt at 5 per cent. This sparked a frenzy of stock speculation that increased the value of shares tenfold. When the government attempted to halt the speculation, there was a dramatic fall in the value of the shares. The collapse resulted in a general distrust of joint stock companies as an investment vehicle. This meant that 'the entrepreneurs who created the industrial revolution, for the most part, had to provide their own capital or seek help from their suppliers or customers' (Wilson 1985: 15).

The modern idea of investment banking was spawned in Europe during the late 1800s. Private banks were especially important in Germany, where the Rothschilds, Bleichroeders, and Oppenheims played an important role in backing railroads, mining ventures, and manufacturing. In the United States, domestic and European investors were responsible for the development of several new industries including railroads, steel, petroleum, and glass (Rind 1981).

Previous to the Second World War, the norm of corporate success was represented by a coincidental matching of entrepreneurial talent with established capital. Entrepreneurs of the early 1900s depended on friends, relatives, local merchants, and other sources of what is now called informal venture capital. Characteristic of the time was the lack of a formal and disciplined process for matching innovators with the needed capital and management resources. Successes were rare and seemingly unpredictable.

After the Second World War, independent pioneering efforts in the United States resulted in organizations that provided the conceptual framework for today's institutional venture capital industry. One of the first venture organizations, J. H. Whitney and Company, founded in 1946, started with an initial capitalization of $10 million. The Rockefeller family also began their venture activities in the late 1940s by setting up the American Research and Development Corporation (ARDC). ARDC represented a landmark as the first venture organization open to public investment, and remained the only publicly held venture company in operation until 1960.

In Canada, the institutional venture capital industry formally started with the opening of Charterhouse Canada Limited in 1952. Charterhouse remained the only firm explicitly involved in venture capital until 1962 when it was joined by Canadian Enterprise Development (CED), which was modeled after the success of General Doriot's Associated Research and Development (ARD) in Boston. By the end of the 1960s, several firms were operating in the Canadian market, including TD Capital Group, Roymark, Cavendish, and Ventures West.

Venture capital is available from three primary sources: independent venture capital firms, corporate subsidiaries, and government programs. Independent firms are often interested in more glamorous ventures that will translate into a significant contribution to technology. Corporate venture activities allow major financial and industrial corporations to invest in related but noncompeting fields. They often act as an information gathering organ for the parent company, cultivating potential merger candidates, suppliers, and customers (Liles, 1974). Both independent firms and subsidiaries are highly sophisticated, preferring well-researched proposals and higher investment amounts.

Together, independent firms and corporate subsidiaries account for most of venture capital investment in both Canada and the United States. Considerable differences exist, however, in the sources of public sector venture capital between the two countries. Approximately one-third of the American venture capital market is made up of federally licensed Small Business Investment Companies (SBICs) that leverage their founding capital with the Small Business Administration (SBA). The investment patterns of these firms are considerably different from those of their private counterparts. SBICs have smaller capital bases, make smaller investments, invest in lower technology traditional business sectors, rely on debt-like financing structures, and are more parochial in their choice of investment locations (Green 1989).

In Canada, federal funds are made available through the Federal Business Development Bank (FBDB) and the Canadian Development Corporation (CDC). In contrast with the American approach, these corporations have very large capital bases and closely mimic the operation of private firms. Several provincial governments have also established venture capital programs, some based on the SBIC model and others modelled after the FBDB.

The development of the private venture capital sector in Canada can be described in three distinct periods: (1) early growth; (2) shakeout; and (3) relative maturity. The first period began with the establishment of UK based Charterhouse's Canadian subsidiary in 1952. The next entrance into the market was a decade later when CED opened. CED followed the American model, designing its operations after the successful ARD of Boston, famous for its sponsorship of Digital Equipment. In the late 1960s, several additional firms entered the market.

These early venture capital firms did well, following similar investment philosophies: (1) minority equity investment; (2) long time horizons; (3) little emphasis on liquidity; and (4) passive portfolio management (Fells 1988). However, several factors combined in the early 1970s to cause a shakeout in the industry that caused some firms to leave the market and the remaining firms to change their investment policies. First, liquidity became a major concern of venture capitalists. A drastic downturn in the stock market made it difficult to liquidate portfolio firms through initial public offerings (IPOs), and the Foreign Investment Review Act (FIRA) made a common route to liquidity more difficult. The result was that venture capital firms became concerned with their own capital flows, switching to subordinate debt instead of equity investment. This lessened the pressure for liquidation as venture capital firms had capital flows to meet overheads and to recycle into new investments.

The liquidity problems of venture capital firms, and a generally stagnant economy, discouraged new firms from entering the field from 1973 to 1978. The only major firms established during this period were SB Capital and Inco Ventures. Several firms stopped making new investments during this period, and eventually liquidated their portfolios. This is particularly true of the subsidiaries of industrial corporations that sought to redirect their investment into more profitable areas. Historically high interest rates near the end of this period provided comparable returns with significantly reduced levels of risk. Two corporate venturers, Northern Telecom and MacMillan Bloedel, left the market during this period, as did several private firms, including Varitech, Guardian Ventures, Glentech, and Venturetek (Fells 1988).

The firms that did stay in the market gradually changed their investment philosophies, learning how to make portfolios yield adequate returns under adverse conditions. The most important change was from passive involvement to active management of portfolio firms. The new emphasis became management ability – turning around potential failures before it was too late. This spawned three additional changes: (1) demand by venture capitalists for increasingly large ownership shares of portfolio firms; (2) investment projects initiated and brought together by venture capitalists; and (3) increasing technological specialization among the staff of venture capital firms.

By the late 1970s, the venture capital industry had reached a level of relative maturity, and improved market conditions caused a resurgence of interest and renewed growth in the industry. Several new venture funds were established in the early 1980s based on the American model of limited partnerships. The adoption of the limited partnership over incorporation as the preferred form of corporate organization offered distinct advantages that attracted more capital to the market. Limited partnerships allow the mingling of taxpaying investors with nontaxpayers. They also have a specified lifetime, usually 10 years, which makes it easy to assess the performance of the fund over time. The ability to assess performance is critical for attracting commitments of capital from large institutional sources such as pension funds and insurance companies.

Some of the major venture capital funds established during the early 1980s included a joint venture between SB Capital and Inco Ventures to found North American Ventures Management Ltd, general partner of North American Ventures Fund (NAVF I) capitalized with $22.5 million and NAVF II capitalized with $36 million. Others include Helix Investments ($17.5 million), Ventures West Technologies ($24 million), and VenGrowth Funds ($34 million) (Fells 1988). During the same period several industrial corporations re-entered the market, including Northern Telecom and Alberta Gas and Trunk.

The involvement of government in the provision of venture capital is motivated by the desire to fill gaps in existing capital markets. Equity gaps occur when (1) the marginal return on capital invested exceeds the marginal cost of capital, or (2) the cost of capital for small firms is higher than the cost of capital for firms in general (Dominguez 1976). Studies showing that such gaps exist in the American market were first conducted in the late 1930s by the Committee for Economic Development, US Department of Commerce. More recent studies (Kieschnick and Daniels 1978; Cohen 1979) confirm the continued existence of the problem. Similar studies in the Canadian context include those by Thorne Ridell (1981), and the Small Business Financing Review Team (1982).

The US government became interested in the venture capital market during the 1950s, creating the SBIC program to help in the stimulation and growth of small firms. The program was designed to provide more capital than was available from the few existing corporations, and to interest business professionals in the investment and supervision of high-risk capital. SBICs are licensed by the SBA under the Small Business Investment Act 1958, and are eligible for long-term loans or SBA purchased debentures with which to finance small business. SBICs may borrow at a ratio of three to one up to a maximum of $35 million. These investment companies are constrained by the requirements that not over 20 per cent of their capital may be invested in any single concern, and no more than one-third of their investments may be in the real estate sector (Waldmann and Cohn 1980).

In 1969, the program was expanded to create a new type of SBIC that specialized in funding minority enterprise. The Minority Enterprise Small Business Investment Company (MESBIC) program was modeled after Arcata Company (California) which established a venture capital firm to invest 2 per cent of their after-tax profits in minority owned businesses. MESBICs are restricted to investment in minority controlled ventures, and must be backed by a strong corporate or community sponsor. Additional historical information on the SBIC and MESBIC programs is available in Noone (1968), Rubel (1970a), Noone and Rubel (1970), Dominguez (1974; 1976), and Wilson (1985). Critical discussions of both these programs can be found in Chambers (1962), Clarke (1967), Rosenbloom and Shank (1970), Allen (1971), Karuna-Karan and Smith (1972), Osborn (1973), and Gupta (1983).

The Canadian federal government has been active in the venture capital market since 1971 when the CDC was launched through a special act of parliament. The CDC invests through its wholly owned subsidiary CDC Ventures Inc. which has an interest in several private venture capital companies: Venturetek, Innocan, Ventures West, and Alberta Ventures. In addition, the federal government provides equity capital to small firms through the FBDB (a crown corporation) that maintains close to 100 branch offices nationwide. The FBDB replaced the Industrial Development Bank (established in 1944) in 1975. The idea of a national program designed after the SBIC act, called the Venture Enterprise Investment Company (VEIC) program, received much attention in 1978, but was never operationalized.

The provincial governments have been much more active in trying to stimulate the formation of private venture funds, while committing public funds to the market. The provinces have pursued two strategies: (1) large crown-type corporations, or (2) smaller SBIC type firms that combine private and public funds. Crown-type corporations include Saskatchewan Economic Development Corporation (Saskatchewan), Société de Développement Industriel (Quebec), Provincial Holdings Ltd (New Brunswick), Industrial Enterprises Inc. (Prince Edward Island), Industrial Estate Ltd (Nova Scotia) and Idea Corporation (Ontario). Programs of the second type include Sociétés de Développement de L'Entreprise (SODEQ), Small Business Development Corporations (SBDC), Nova Scotia Venture Corporations (NSVC), Prince Edward Island Venture Corporations (PEIVC), and Manitoba Venture Capital Companies (MVCC).

While each of these programs has its own regulations, the general intent is to provide eligible venture corporations, or their shareholders, with tax incentives to channel investment into developing small businesses. The Ontario SBDC program, for example, makes an additional amount available equal to 30 per cent of the investor's start-up equity.

This is done through either a grant to individuals or corporate tax credits. The amount is recaptured by the provincial government when an SBDC either deregisters or dissolves. The longest running and most successful of these programs have been Ontario's SBDC and Quebec's SODEQ. The SBDC program replaced the unsuccessful Venture Investment Corporation (VIC) Registration Act (1977) in 1979 (Playfair 1976; Colley 1979). It had 364 participants and had raised more than $200 million by the end of 1984, while $25 million had been raised by thirteen SODEQs (Gadbois and Knight 1985). Both of these programs are small, however, when compared with

Table 7.1 Venture capital market shares

Type of venture capital firm	Canada		United States	
	% of firms	% of capital pool	% of firms	% of capital pool
Independent private	38	36	31	72
Subsidiary	25	36	7	18
Intermediary	18	–	7	–
Crown corporations	11	28	–	–
SBICs and MESBICs	–	–	49	10
Other	8	–	6	–
Firms or capital pool[a]	55	1.4	995	19.6

Source: Calculated from *Canadian Venture Capital*, August 1986: 15 and *Venture* (1985)
Note: [a] In billions of Canadian and US dollars.

more than 450 active SBICs, which had approximately $1.5 billion in assets in 1984 (Gadbois and Knight 1985).

The current market share (in terms of the number of firms) of private venture capital sources is about 84 per cent in Canada, and 51 per cent in the United States (Table 7.1). However, market share measured by capital under management provides a different picture. In the United States about 90 per cent of the venture capital is controlled by private firms, while in Canada this proportion is 72 per cent. This difference occurs because SBICs and MESBICs are numerous but have small capital bases (Table 7.2). Private sector firms are the most important market component, both in terms of their capital commitment and because they are largely responsible for determining industry trends. This core of the venture industry is represented in Canada by the Association of Canadian Venture Capital Companies (ACVCC). There are at present sixty-six firms that have met the criteria for full membership in the ACVCC. These criteria are as follows:

(1) at least $1 million invested or available for investment on an equity basis;
(2) a full-time professional commitment to venture investment;
(3) not more than 20 per cent of their funds invested in any one enterprise;
(4) willingness to reduce their equity participation as their investees mature and grow (Ernst *et al.* 1986).

Table 7.2 Venture capital firm size

Type of venture capital firm	Mean capital per firm	Median capital per firm
Independent private		
Canada[a]	21.4	19.2
United States[b]	51.7	25.0
Subsidiaries of financial corporations		
Canada	59.5	–
United States	49.1	20.5
Subsidiaries of industrial corporations		
Canada	20.0	15.0
United States	27.6	15.0
Crown corporations or SBICs		
Canada	91.8	52.5
United States	5.0	2.5
Total, all types		
Canada	30.2	20.0
United States	36.8	15.0

Source: Adapted from *Canadian Venture Capital*, August 1986: 15
Notes: [a] In millions of Canadian dollars.
[b] In millions of American dollars.

The first and second requirements serve primarily to distinguish institutional from informal or 'angel' investors. The third and fourth requirements distinguish venture capital activity from acquisition and holding companies.

The source of venture capital funds is slowly evolving away from reliance on the contributions of wealthy individuals toward corporate sources and pension funds (Table 7.3). This is particularly evident in the US market, where venture capital was originally synonymous with family names such as Rockefeller, Phipps, Doriot, and Whitney. The involvement of wealthy families in the Canadian market has never been as overt. The increase in venture funds provided by pension funds and insurance companies can be traced to the increased use of limited partnerships as an investment vehicle, combined with changes to the income tax act (Fells 1989). Before 1985, pension fund investments in limited partnerships were considered to be foreign property, and were subject to a 10 per cent maximum on foreign investment. Later modifications in the form of Small Business Investment Limited Partnerships and Qualified Limited Partnerships provide vehicles that are not classified as foreign. In addition, certain types of investments receive credit that

Table 7.3 Sources of funds added to venture capital pool

Source of venture capital	Percentage of capital added in 1985	Percentage of capital added in 1986	Total venture capital pool
Pension funds	37	67	49
Corporations	20	21	15
Individuals and families	13	3	20
Insurance companies	11	9	10
Government	19	0	2
Foreign investors	0	0	5
Endorsements and foundations	0	0	0
Total capital[a]	53	161	627

Source: Adapted from *Canadian Venture Capital*, May 1987: 18
Note: [a] In millions of Canadian dollars.

can be used to increase the allowable proportion of investment in foreign companies.

INVESTMENT CHARACTERISTICS

The historical legacy of the industry's growth has favored some regions over others in the choice of office location. Inertia has afforded Ontario more than half (54 per cent) of existing venture capital firms. More than 40 per cent of venture capital firms are headquartered in Toronto, 15 per cent of firms are headquartered in each of Montreal and Calgary, and the remainder are scattered across several regional urban centres (McNaughton and Green 1989). Toronto is also home to half of Canada's ten largest venture capital firms (Table 7.4). Ontario both originates and receives the largest number of investments, followed by Quebec, the Prairie Provinces, and British Columbia (McNaughton and Green 1989) (Map 7.1). The level of investment in Ontario was stable throughout the early 1980s, though the proportion of investment flowing into more peripheral regions, such as British Columbia and the Atlantic Provinces, varied more widely (Figure 7.1).

The venture capital market is characterized by strong regional self-bias, and investment activity decays sharply as the distance between investor and investee increases. Most investments are made

Table 7.4 Ten largest Canadian venture capital firms

Venture capital firm	Capital under management, 1987[a]
Vencap Equities Alberta Ltd (Edmonton)	244
Canadian Corporate Funding Ltd (Toronto)	142
TD Capital Group Ltd (Toronto)	122
Venture West Management Ltd (Vancouver)	85
Grayrock Shared Ventures Ltd (Rexdale)	85
Société D'Investissement Desjardins (Montreal)	82
Schroders Canadian Buyout Fund (Toronto)	60
Vengrowth Capital Funds (Toronto)	70
Noranda Enterprise Ltd (Ottawa)	70
Federal Business Development Bank (Montreal)	70

Note: [a] In millions of Canadian dollars.

within 200–300 miles of the venture capitalist's office. McNaughton and Green (1989) speculate that this is primarily the result of spatially limited informational linkages. To minimize uncertainty and risk, access to information flows must be maximized. This constrains the activity space of venture capital firms, and limits the distance over which transactions take place. Canadian venture capitalists use two mechanisms to extend the distance over which investments can be adequately monitored. The first is the syndication

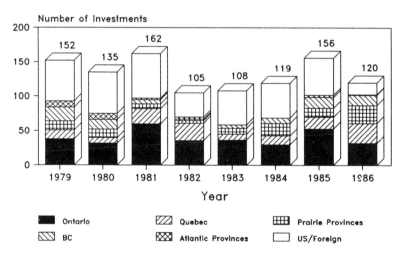

Figure 7.1 Destinations of venture capital investments
Source: Calculated from Ernst and Whinney (1979–85) and McNaughton and Green (1989)

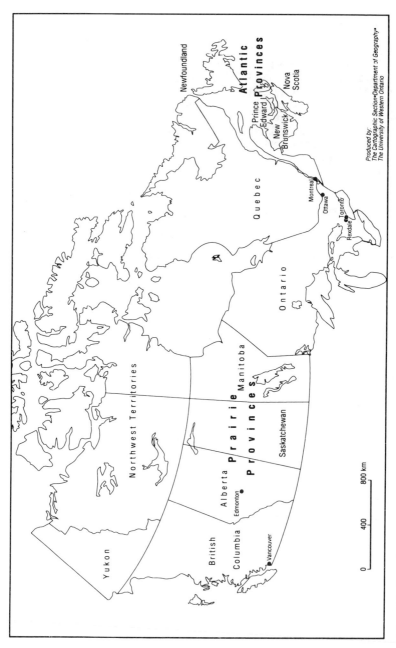

Map 7.1 Canada

Produced by:
The Cartographic Section–Department of Geography*
The University of Western Ontario

of deals with venture capital firms in other locations. Monitoring is done by the firm nearest the investment, and the risk is diversified over all firms in the syndication. This approach appears to have greater acceptance in the United States than in Canada. As one venture capitalist surveyed by McNaughton and Green (1989) explained: 'In the US venture capitalists hunt in packs of three to twelve. . . . In Canada they are lone rangers in that they feel they can do every thing themselves.' There are an average of 1.2 investors per financing in Canada, while in the United States there are an average of 3.7 investors (CVC 1986).

The second mechanism involves greater cost to the firm: the establishment of regional branch offices. Branch offices are an important part of the Canadian venture capital industry, as about one-quarter of the firms have at least one branch office (McNaughton and Green 1989). Firms with branch offices develop much more pervasive contact networks (a function of both their increased size and geographic coverage), and receive more than twice the number of investment proposals considered by their single office location counterparts. They also make fewer investments, resulting in a lower turnover ratio of investment. The turnover ratio is the proportion of proposals received that are eventually funded. This suggests that better access to information about investments allows these firms to undertake a more expansive search, and to be more selective by channelling their funds into those few investments that are most likely to be successful and provide large returns.

The regional pattern of investment is also influenced by the receipt of proposals and the turnover ratio. There is considerable regional variation in this ratio. In particular, the propensity to fund proposals generated in foreign countries and in Quebec is above average, and the propensity to fund those generated in Ontario and the Atlantic Provinces is below average (McNaughton and Green 1989). This pattern is the result of variations in the degree of competition for funds; higher levels of competition in Ontario are a function of the large number of proposals that venture capital firms have to choose from, while in the Atlantic Provinces it is a function of the paucity of capital sources.

The national turnover ratio is very low – only about 3 per cent of investment proposals receive funding. This high rejection rate is due to the very sophisticated procedures employed by venture capitalists to select their investments. The general requirements for considera-tion of a proposal by members of the ACVCC at their annual venture fair are, for example, the following:

(1) An exceptional market opportunity for products and services must have been identified.
(2) At least one product must be ready for market.
(3) The project must have a potential growth rate significantly above average for the next 5–7 years.
(4) The project must require at least $250,000 in equity within the next 12 months.
(5) An experienced management team must have been assembled that can execute a formal business plan effectively.

Venture capitalists evaluate investment proposals based on carefully prepared business plans that outline the nature of the product, process, or service, market potential, capital requirements, and the experience of the existing management. The references that accompany these proposals are very important; nearly two-thirds are referred from other venture capitalists, personal acquaintances, banks, or accountants (Tyebjee and Bruno 1984).

Canadian venture capitalists specialize in the types of investment that they will consider. This specialization may take the form of a particular geographic area, industrial sector, stage in the funding cycle, or a combination of these three. Investments within the same geographic area are usually preferred because of greater market

Table 7.5 Industrial sector of venture capital investments

Industrial sector	Percentage
Standardized technologies	39
Industrial services/products	20
Consumer services/products	19
High-tech	37
Computer related	11
Other electronics instruments	11
Communications	10
Medical/pharmaceuticals/biotech	5
Traditional sectors	21
Natural resources	11
Holding/leasing/finance	6
Transportation	4
Missing	3

Source: Adapted from *The Financial Post*, 21 July 1988: 16
Note: Adapted from McNaughton and Green (1989), $N = 84$.

Table 7.6 Funding stage of venture capital
investments

Funding stage	Percentage
Beginning firms	44
Start-up	27
Seed	17
Growing firms	35
Expansion	31
Bridge/mezzanine	4
Restructuring	20
End receivership	1
Leveraged buyout	10
Acquisition	8
Refinance	1
Missing	1

Source: Adapted from McNaughton and Green (1989)
Note: N = 84.

knowledge and ease of monitoring. Canadian venture firms most
often invest in industrial and consumer services and products
(standardized technologies), and in computers and other electronics
(high technologies) (Table 7.5). Most firms prefer to invest in the
expansion of existing firms rather than in riskier seed and start-up
situations (Table 7.6). Recently, interest has grown in the corporate
debt market because of the demand created by an ever increasing
number of acquisitions and leveraged buyouts (LBOs).

Exiting profitably is the final goal of a venture capital investment.
Exits can be made through several vehicles: repurchase by the
portfolio firm; acquisition; IPO; or writeoff. IPOs are more
common in the United States than in Canada by a ratio of almost
three to one (Table 7.7). This is primarily the result of a more
receptive public market for venture-backed companies. Within
Canada, IPOs are most common in British Columbia and Quebec,
both of which have developed significant over-the-counter markets
for the trading of smaller firms. Repurchases by the entrepreneur
are twice as common in Canada as in the United States, reflecting a
greater concern of Canadian entrepreneurs for regaining control of
their company. Writeoffs account for a similar proportion of exits in
both countries, suggesting that similar levels of risk are undertaken
in both markets.

Table 7.7 Form of exit by region

	BC	Prairie Prov.	Ont.	Quebec	Atlantic Prov.	All Canada	USA
IPO	29	6	8	25	0	12	32
Acquisition	0	11	23	14	29	18	14
Repurchase	43	28	22	25	14	25	11
Reverse	0	6	0	0	0	1	0
Writeoff	14	11	37	29	43	30	32
Other	14	39	11	7	14	14	11
N =	7	18	65	28	7	125	28

Source: Adapted from *Venture Economics Canada* (1986: 10)
Note: Values are expressed as a percentage of the column totals.

The notion that similar levels of risk exist in both markets is borne out by the mean internal rate of return on investments (IRR) which is equivalent in both countries (Table 7.8). When disaggregated by industrial sector, the mean IRR is highest in the communications, computers, and electronics sectors. It is surprisingly low (by comparison) in the biotechnology and medical related fields. The growth of interest in LBOs buyouts is easily explained by a large mean IRR, and short mean holding period. Further, as LBO investments are usually in the form of debt rather than equity, and a track record is established, the level of risk is significantly reduced. As they are often very large, LBO investments contribute to the positive relationship observed between investment size and mean IRR (VEC 1986). This relationship may also show that investors do not provide sufficient capital to support growth, or it may simply reflect the fact that follow-on financing is not provided to investments that provide inferior returns. Finally, one of the most salient observations about portfolio returns is that a small number of investments provide superior rates of return contributing to an adequate overall mean IRR (Venture Economics Canada 1986). Only 15 per cent of exits generate returns greater than 50 per cent, and these are almost exclusively IPOs. These IPOs play a significant role in producing a mean IRR of 23 per cent for all investments.

SUMMARY

This chapter provided a historical context for the development of the Canadian venture capital industry, and a discussion of the implications for current market shares, office locations, and

Table 7.8 Exit characteristics, by location, industrial sector, and funding stage

	Number	%	Mean invest.[a]	Holding period[b]	Mean IRR(%)[c]
Location					
Quebec	28	17	855	4.6	28
Canada less Quebec	100	60	588	3.9	23
Canada	128	77	684	4.0	24
United States	28	17	654	3.5	23
Industrial sector					
Communication	17	10			28
Computer related	20	12			29
Other electronic	8	5			29
Biotechnology	2	1			12
Medical/health	8	5			12
Energy	16	10			17
Consumer related	26	16			23
Industrial products	25	15			26
Other	38	23			19
Unknown	7	4			–
Funding stage					
Seed/start-up	60	36	545	4.5	16
Expansion	45	27	707	3.8	22
Leveraged buyout	14	8	1,098	2.4	55
Turnaround	11	7	879	4.0	23
Other	1	1	–	–	–
Unknown	36	22	324	4.9	15
Total	167	100	647	4.3	23

Source: Adapted from *Venture Economics Canada* (1986: 12–15)
Notes: [a] In thousands of Canadian dollars. Not available by industrial sector.
[b] In years. Not available by industrial sector.
[c] Internal rate of return in percent.

investment characteristics. The locational choice of a venture capital firm is one variable that can be manipulated to maximize access to information. As accessibility to both business services and information on potential investments is greatest in the larger urban centres; it is there that venture capital firms tend to concentrate. The early dominance of Ontario (and specifically of Toronto) has afforded it the bulk of Canadian venture capital activity.

The selection of investments is an important process because it screens potential high-growth firms, and provides them with needed capital and human resources. Despite careful and sophisticated procedures for selection, almost one-third of Canadian venture investments are written off through closure or bankruptcy. In an effort to prevent this, and to increase the value of their holdings, venture capitalists closely monitor the day-to-day activities of their investments and contribute managerial expertise. One of the results of this monitoring is a strong bias toward local investments as distance represents a cost in terms of both time and travel. The number of proposals submitted from local firms, and the increased availability of information with which to judge these proposals, translates into a bias in the absolute number of investments made within a region. However, the turnover ratio for investments is often higher for investment projects further afield. These investments offer above average returns, and the risk is significantly reduced through referral, syndication, or reconnaissance provided by a branch office.

Canadian venture capitalists specialize in the funding of particular industrial sectors. The choice of this specialization is constrained by the production function of the region, and specifically by the economic base of the center within which the venture capitalist is located. This pattern of regional bias in both investment location and industrial sector implies that there is a greater ability to support high-growth firms in some regions than others. The Canadian pattern of investment clearly favors the Toronto region.

The Canadian venture capital industry is still young. Future growth may extend significant benefits into other regions. However, because of information requirements, and the difficulties of monitoring investments over long distances, true expansion will require the physical movement of venture capital offices into these regions. The diffusion of venture capital activity within Canada is also dependent on continued growth in the amount of capital under management. The potential inflow of funds is enormous; it is estimated, for example, that only 0.6 per cent of the assets of

Canada's twenty largest pension funds are directed into venture capital (Fells 1989). The ability to tap this source, however, seems to be a constraining factor. The paucity of experienced venture managers and the emphasis of pension managers on short-run performance are slowing the movement of pension funds into this market.

The Canadian venture capital market is not well studied. Surprisingly little, for example, is known about the effects of government policies on the availability and distribution of venture capital. Research into the availability of venture capital generally points to the importance of tax incentives and of general economic conditions. However, we need to consider the effects of other types of policies as well, in particular those that affect the liquidity of investments. This includes the development of secondary and over-the-counter markets, and the legal requirements of both domestic and foreign acquisitions.

The recent Free Trade Agreement between Canada and the United States may also have significant impacts on the venture capital market. The liberalization and increased thresholds for the review of foreign acquisitions, for example, may have the effect of increasing the liquidity of some investments as sale to a foreign interest becomes easier. This is especially true since review requirements act as a perceptual barrier that is greater than the actual legal impediment. As tariff barriers are lowered and it becomes more evident in which sectors Canada has a comparative advantage, there may be a shift in the industrial sectors that are favored for venture investment. Finally, the changes in the legislation governing the financial services sector may lead to greater integration of financial functions between the two countries, and the diversification of commercial banking institutions into an increasing number of financial functions. The result may be increased cross-border capital flows, and the consideration of higher risk loans by commercial institutions because of increased competition. In any case, it is clear that the character of the Canadian venture capital industry will change significantly over the next few years as it matures and adapts to the rapidly changing business environment.

8 Venture capital, the equity gap and the 'north-south divide' in the United Kingdom

Colin M. Mason and Richard T. Harrison

INTRODUCTION

The emergence of a venture capital industry in the United Kingdom, which contained fewer than twenty firms prior to 1979 compared with over 150 firms 10 years later (Lloyd 1989), is just one aspect of the emergence, or re-emergence, of an 'enterprise culture' in the United Kingdom during the 1980s – the decade of 'Thatcherism' (Riddell 1989). The number of business start-ups has increased from 158,000 in 1980 to 230,000 in 1988 (*British Business* 1989). Self-employment has increased from 1.9 million in 1979 (8 per cent of total employment) to 3.2 million in 1988 (12 per cent of total employment) (Hakim 1989). Attitudes to enterprise have also changed. The professions and administration have traditionally been the most socially acceptable occupations in the United Kingdom. The Bolton Report commented in 1971 on 'the climate of opinion . . . [was] . . . antipathetic to . . . small business' and 'the social standing of the independent businessman . . . may now be lower than it has ever been' (HM Government 1971: 24). But only a decade later Bannock – a member of the Committee – claimed that it is now 'no longer a disgrace for a clever young person to set up in business instead of going into the civil service, teaching or a large company' (Bannock 1981). Similarly, during the 1980s many of the constraints on the formation and growth of new firms, in such areas as the availability of finance, premises, information and advice, and enterprise training, have been alleviated – partly through direct provision by local and central government and central government encouragement of the private sector to play a greater role. Thus, the clearing banks, which have traditionally been unsympathetic to small businesses, have introduced a variety of special lending schemes (NEDC 1986), in addition to participation in the government sponsored Loan Guarantee Scheme (Harrison and Mason 1986). Many large firms have also contributed to the funding and staffing of enterprise agencies, of which there are now over 300, which provide free business information, advice, and counselling to small business owner-managers and potential new firm founders (Mason 1987a). The limited supply of small premises (Coopers and Lybrand/Drivers Jonas 1980) has been enhanced by the greater willingness of property developers to build small premises and incubator units (Ambler and Kennett 1985).

Our objective in this chapter is to review the growth, evolution, and investment activity of the venture capital industry in the United Kingdom during the 1980s. The picture which emerges is of an industry which has rapidly moved away from providing start-up and early stage finance to small firms in technology related sectors in favor of making very large investments in management buyouts and which has concentrated its investments in the already more prosperous regions of southern England. Neither informal sources of venture capital nor public sector initiatives have filled these gaps in supply. The concluding section of the chapter therefore considers ways in which the equity gap can be closed and the regional imbalance in the supply of venture capital can be redressed.

THE UK VENTURE CAPITAL INDUSTRY: ORIGINS AND GROWTH

Definition

We define venture capital as an activity by which corporate investors support entrepreneurial ventures with finance and business skills to exploit market opportunities and thus obtain long-term capital gains (Shilson 1984). In practice, venture capital activity includes a variety of different types of financing: the provision of start-up finance, specialist portfolio investment in small unquoted companies, the provision of second and subsequent rounds of development capital for later stages of business expansion, and the financing of management buyouts and buyins. All of these different types of financing share a number of common features: they are equity oriented, highly selective in the choice of investee businesses to minimize risk (on a case-by-case basis, not a portfolio basis), make a medium- to long-term commitment of finance with the aim of making eventual capital gains rather than generating running income, require an identifiable exit route, and have some degree of active 'hands on' involvement in the management of the business receiving the finance in order to 'add value' to the investment. It is the latter characteristic that distinguishes venture capital from other, passive, forms of investment in business ventures (Dixon 1989).

Origins, recent growth, and current structure

The provision of equity finance for small companies is part of the British financial tradition, with the original venture capitalists being the investment trusts which spread the risk of investment through buying shares in other companies. However, by the post-war period investment trusts were no longer investing in risky, entrepreneurial companies; indeed, many invested exclusively in large quoted companies. Thus, by the 1960s few sources of equity finance for small enterprises existed (Clark 1987). Indeed, prior to the 1980s, the only sources of venture capital were the small business finance arms of the clearing banks, merchant banks which specialized in small business clients (for example, Charterhouse), some government agencies (notably the National Research and Development Corporation and the National Enterprise Board, subsequently merged and renamed the British Technology Group) and Investors in Industry (3i) (formerly named the Industrial and Commercial Financial Corporation (ICFC)) (Harrison and Mason 1989).

3i was by far the most important of these sources of small business finance. It had been established in 1945 by the Bank of England and the major clearing banks to provide long-term finance (not necessarily equity) to growing firms (Clark 1987). Only part of 3i's activities can be considered as 'pure' venture capital, that is, investment in shares in small unquoted companies with the expectation of capital gain. About two-thirds of its investments are in small businesses, mostly in the form of a package of loans and equity. Unlike 'pure' venture capital firms which gain their returns from selling their shares to a third party or when the company goes public, 3i seeks a high running return from its investments because it is funded largely by debt. Moreover, 3i does not require its investee companies to commit themselves to a public flotation: it is prepared to hold shares indefinitely, provided they pay dividends. 'Pure' venture-type investments (by 3i Ventures) account for only around one-third of 3i's total investment activity (Clark 1987).

Despite the formation of Charterhouse Industrial Development in 1934 (Baird 1988) and ICFC (3i) in 1945, the venture capital industry was slow to develop in the United Kingdom (Holborn and Edwards 1971). However, in the 1960s the venture capital industry in the United Kingdom developed through the expanded activities of 3i and other private and public sector initiatives; there was general acceptance of the view that the small firm finance gap had effectively been closed (Economists Advisory Group, 1971). In the 1970s this early development of the UK venture capital industry was not maintained as rising interest rates made high-risk investments less attractive, and the structure of the financial markets (with, for example, no junior stock market or over-the-counter market equivalent to that in the United States) limited the opportunities for realizing venture capital investments (Meade 1977).

However, during the 1980s an enormous expansion occurred in the number of private venture capital funds. Prior to 1979 there were just over twenty venture capital funds with a total investment of £20 million. Some 10 years later there were over 150 funds which invested over £1 billion in the United Kingdom in 1988, although, as Cary (1989: 7) notes, some of this expansion is simply the 'rechristening' by 'many financial institutions . . . [of] . . . their traditional financing of unquoted companies as "venture capital" because this sounds better'. In the 5 years to 1988 approximately £3 billion has been invested by UK venture capitalists, 89 per cent in the United Kingdom, 9 per cent in the United States and 2 per cent elsewhere (Pratt 1990).

These new funds are of two main types. First, many have been established by financial institutions, notably pension funds, insurance companies, merchant banks, and clearing banks. These venture capital funds, in the jargon of the industry, are termed 'captives': that is, they form part of larger financial institutions through which they are also primarily funded, although they have considerable operational autonomy from their larger affiliates (Clark 1987). Clearing bank captive funds are open ended: they have no fixed amount of capital for investment and tend to look for part of their return in the form of continuing income rather than just from capital gains upon realization. Captive institutional funds (for example, affiliates of pension funds and insurance companies), by contrast, are usually closed-end funds. They are allocated either a fixed amount of capital for investment or a fixed proportion of the institution's total portfolio (Dixon 1989). Second, various independent venture capital funds have been formed. They include UK subsidiaries of large US venture capital firms (for example, Alan Patricof Associates and TA Associates) and independent firms formed by venture capital managers who have 'spun-off' from established venture capital firms such as 3i (see Hamilton Fazey (1989a) for two case studies). Independent venture capital organizations raise capital for investment from a variety of sources, including pension funds, insurance companies, and foreign institutions (Table 8.1). Typically, independent firms set up funds of a predetermined size, duration, and investment strategy. Investors commit funds which are drawn down as investment opportunities arise. The objective is normally to liquidate the fund after a specified date, usually 7–10 years later (Pratt 1990)

Independent funds have increased in significance during the 1980s and are now the largest category of venture capital organization, accounting for just over one-half of the number of venture capital investments and two-thirds of the total amount invested in the United Kingdom in 1988 (Table 8.2). The share of total investments made by captive funds has declined from 43 per cent in 1984 to 31 per cent in 1988. The remaining sources of venture capital are funds

Table 8.1 Sources of capital for independent venture capital funds

| | Percentages of capital committed | | | | |
Source	1984	1985	1986	1987	1988
UK pension funds	40	40	41	33	37
Foreign institutions	10	21	12	36	26
UK insurers and fund managers	18	19	20	16	19
Private individuals/family trusts	19	13	15	4	11
Industrial corporations	9	4	4	3	6
UK banks	1	1	6	6	–
Other	3	2	2	2	1
Total (£million)	231	278	239	684	612

Source: Pratt (1990)

Table 8.2 UK investments, by type of investment vehicle

| | Percentages of amount invested | | | | |
	1984	1985	1986	1987	1988
Independent	34	40	49	68	66
Captive	43	43	42	25	31
BES	20	14	8	6	2
Government/local authorities	3	3	1	1	1

Source: Pratt (1990)

created by government agencies, notably the Scottish and Welsh Development Agencies and various local authorities (Mawson and Miller 1986; McKean and Coulson 1987; Lawless 1988), and Business Expansion Scheme (BES) funds. The BES allows individuals to claim tax relief on investments in new equity in unquoted companies (Harrison and Mason 1989). BES funds are specialist funds established by financial institutions which pool investors' capital to invest in a portfolio of companies. There has been a marked decline in the relative importance of BES funds as a source of venture capital: in 1988 only 2 per cent of venture capital investment was made through BES funds compared with 20 per cent in 1984. By contrast, government and local authority funds have always been a very minor source of venture capital.

A further change in the structure of the industry is that it is becoming increasingly concentrated. A Venture Economics survey (Lloyd 1989) noted that at the end of 1987 just 25 per cent of organizations controlled 70 per cent of the capital pool (if 3i is included, 26 per cent of firms control 78 per cent of the capital pool). While the majority of these large organizations are 'captives', a growing number are quasi-independent groups affiliated to a merchant bank or another financial institution with large amounts of institutional money under management. Only around one-quarter of these large organizations are truly independent firms. At the other extreme, 34 per cent of venture capital funds, each with £10 million or less under management, controlled 4 per cent of the total pool of capital. Indeed, Lloyd (1989) suggests that it is becoming increasingly hard for the unaffiliated groups, especially if new, to raise new capital: it appears that the most likely way of overcoming these high barriers to entry into the modern venture capital industry in the United Kingdom is to adopt a very specific investment focused either regionally or, more particularly, by industrial sector. Conversely, groups that have access to in-house managed funds, and can use this capital to leverage their fund raising efforts, appear to have little difficulty in raising significant sums of capital.

As the UK venture capital industry has matured, so it has quickly developed many of the characteristics of its US counterpart. For example, the British Venture Capital Association (BVCA) was created in 1982 to identify and research the issues facing the industry and to lobby the government for legislative changes (for example, in company law and tax legislation) to help the venture capital industry, and Venture Economics Inc. (which provides venture capital statistics in the United States) established a UK subsidiary, Venture Economics Ltd, to provide information and undertake research on the venture capital industry in the United Kingdom. At the same time the industry has gained a high profile; for example, since 1984 the *Financial Times* has published an annual review of the industry and there are now various guidebooks and directories of the venture capital industry (for example, Stoy Hayward 1988; Cary 1989).

The growth of venture capital in the United Kingdom is mirrored elsewhere in Europe. According to the European Venture Capital Association the size of the European venture capital pool (funds invested and available for investment) in 1988 was Ecu 18.7 billion (£13.3 billion); this compares with the comparable US pool of Ecu 26 billion. However, the European venture capital pool is increasing faster than the pool in the United States, recording an 18.5 per cent increase in 1987 compared with just 7 per cent in the United States (Batchelor 1989a). Moreover, in 1987, for the first time, more finance was raised in Europe (Ecu £3.9 billion, £2.6 billion) than in the United States (Ecu 2.8 billion) for venture capital (Batchelor 1988a). The growth of venture capital in Europe is, in part, due to UK funds forming links with their continental counterparts and raising new funds dedicated to the Continent (Batchelor 1989a). However, despite the recent development of venture capital industries in such countries as France, Italy, and The Netherlands the United Kingdom still dominates, accounting for 56 per cent of all funds raised in 1988 (Table 8.3). Furthermore by 1985 it was proportionately larger than that of the United States (measured in terms of the amount raised as a proportion of gross domestic product (GDP)) (Burns 1987). However, despite this growth there is very little evidence for the emergence of corporate venturing (venture capital funds financed by large private sector corporations) in the United Kingdom equivalent to the situation in both the United States and Continental Europe (Batchelor 1989a); only around twenty British companies (for example, Shell, BP, and BOC) are engaged in corporate venturing (Batchelor 1987; Pratt 1990).

Reasons for Growth

This growth of venture capital in the United Kingdom has occurred as a result of the combination of various environmental factors which created a climate favorable to its development as well as specific supply-side and demand-side factors. First, the general

Table 8.3 New capital raised for independent venture capital funds in Europe

Country	Number of funds	Amount raised (million Ecu)	Percentage of total
United Kingdom	43	1,000.0	55.6
France	19	314.8	17.5
West Germany	3	136.2	7.6
Netherlands	4	88.5	4.9
Spain	5	65.2	3.6
Italy	2	65.0	3.6
Ireland	2	31.2	1.7
Denmark	1	18.7	1.0
Sweden	1	15.3	0.9
Austria	1	13.7	0.8
Norway	3	10.4	0.6
Others	9	40.0	2.2
Total	93	1,799.0	100.0

Source: European Venture Capital Association, cited in the *Financial Times*, 30 November 1989
Note: Excludes finance raised and invested by venture capital subsidiaries of banks etc.

climate of the 1980s was pro-enterprise. The Conservative Government which was first elected in 1979 was an enthusiastic supporter of the small business sector. In its first term of office alone (1979–83) the government claimed to have introduced over 100 measures to assist small businesses in such areas as advice, enterprise training, premises, reduction in legislative and administrative burdens, and finance (Frank *et al.* 1984; Burns and Dewhurst 1986; Mason and Harrison, 1986). Enthusiasm for venture capital in the United Kingdom was also stimulated by the growing awareness of the US venture capital industry and the spectacular success of some of the businesses that it had financed, including Tandem Computers, Federal Express, Apple Computer, and LSI Logic (Dickson 1984).

A number of factors also stimulated an increase in the supply of venture capital. First, the government has taken specific measures to assist the venture capital industry. These include the indexing of capital gains tax and the replacement of income tax liability in respect of certain share options by a capital gains tax liability, a change that helped small, fast-growing firms to attract key employees (Shilson 1984). Developments in the UK share market (Shilson, 1984) are a second factor. The establishment by the Stock

Exchange of the Unlisted Securities Market (USM) in 1980 with less onerous admission requirements has provided an important means whereby venture capitalists can ultimately realize their gains and entrepreneurs can convert their 'paper' wealth to real wealth. The subsequent growth of the USM – at least until the October 1987 stock market crash – to the present situation where over 400 companies are quoted has also given considerable encouragement to venture capitalists. In particular, recent survey evidence suggests that for many companies seeking a flotation on the USM, realization of shareholders' stakes was as important as, if not more important than, raising finance for further growth (Binder Hamlyn 1986; Hall and Hutchinson 1988; Buckland and Davis 1989). In addition, changes in company law which have allowed companies to repurchase their shares are likely to have made entrepreneurs more willing to look for outside equity because they can regain overall control at a later date and provide investors with another 'exit route'. Third, longer-term investment became more attractive because of the prolonged bull conditions in the capital markets and the general economic optimism of the mid-1980s (Dixon 1989). Finally, the BES prompted many financial institutions with little previous experience of venture capital to set up specialist managed BES funds (Harrison and Mason 1988, 1989; Mason *et al.* 1988). On the demand side, the key factors have been the expanding financial requirements which have stemmed from the increasing number of new business start-ups, including many in technology related sectors, and management buyouts (Wright and Coyne, 1985) during the economic recovery from the 1979–81 recession, and the growing appreciation amongst small business owners of the benefits of equity finance. As a result, the increased supply of venture capital has been matched by an increase in demand. For example, Alan Patricof Associates received over 1,000 proposals in 1988 compared with 200 in 1980 (Cohen 1989).

Appraisal criteria

UK venture capital funds have a high rejection rate. Information on 111 funds (Cary 1989) indicates that almost 94 per cent of funds accepted for investment less than 10 per cent of the proposals received, and two-thirds invested in fewer than 5 per cent of proposals (see Table 8.4). The initial screening process is severe: only 11 per cent of funds invested in fewer than 5 per cent of proposals actually reviewed, while over 20 per cent invested in at least 25 per cent of proposals reviewed and almost half of funds invested in at least 15 per cent of reviewed proposals (Table 8.4). In a survey of thirty London-based firms Dixon (1989) found that three-quarters of proposals were rejected at the initial screening stage, with a further 20 per cent rejected or withdrawn during the 'due diligence' process. Only an average of 3.4 per cent of the total proposals received obtained investment. Whether such high rejection rates reflect the poor quality of proposals or excessively cautious appraisal systems is unclear (Chapman 1986). Not surprisingly, the venture capital industry believes that there is a lack of suitable investment opportunities. In Dixon's (1989) sample, almost two-thirds of venture capital funds were restricted in their investment by a lack of suitable proposals. However, only a small minority of funds stated that they were prepared to lower the terms on which they invest in order to attract more proposals.

According to Dixon's (1989) survey, the factors considered most important by venture capitalists in their evaluation of investment proposals are investee managerial experience in the sector, the market sector of the business, and the marketing skills of the management team. Other highly ranked considerations are the projected growth in turnover, the size of investees' investment in relation to means, and the financial skills of the management team. The single most important consideration of venture capitalists is therefore the quality of the management team behind the proposal. This is well illustrated by the following quotes from venture capitalists:

Table 8.4 Proportions of invested proposals reviewed and financed by venture capital funds

Proportion accepted	Investments made relative to proposals received	Investments made relative to proposals reviewed
(%)	(% of funds)	(% of funds)
0–2.4	41.1	4.5
2.5–4.9	26.1	6.3
5.0–9.9	26.1	20.1
10.0–14.9	2.7	20.1
15.0–19.9	1.8	11.7
20.0–24.9	0.9	15.3
25.0–49.9	–	14.4
Over 50.0	0.9	6.3

Source: based on data in Cary (1989)

'We're looking for a management team that has spotted a market opportunity and has the skills to exploit it'

(cited by Hill 1989)

'We look at the people first and then at the numbers. Deciding who to back is all about people. Relevant experience is the key'

(cited by Batchelor 1988c).

A good management team is thought to reduce the risk of failure and boost potential returns. Venture capitalists placed little importance on the financial analysis of proposals during the initial screening. However, various investment appraisal techniques – notably internal rate of return – were used during the due diligence process. Financial ratios are also calculated, although there is little consistency in those which are used. Thus, appraisal techniques involve a combination of subjective judgement in weighing up the individual, the product, and the market, and objective analysis in analyzing financial ratios (Batchelor 1988b).

The majority of funds derive their return from the investment through capital gains on redemption and do not normally require a dividend (Dixon 1989). Most funds therefore evaluate proposals against a maximum exit time-span of around 7 years: they are unlikely to be prepared to invest in proposals which will take a long time to develop to the stage where they can be sold to another company or floated on the Stock Exchange or USM (Dixon 1989). This in part explains the growing attraction of management buyouts and buyins to the UK venture capital industry (see next section): there is an ongoing business and a known management team which can be evaluated, and the payback period to realization of the investment is relatively short. As a result, the UK venture capital industry is coming under criticism for its increased short-termism (Pratt 1990).

However, trade sales have always been the most common – if least visible – exit route. From the venture capitalist's perspective, the buyer can be required to pay a premium for control on the grounds that there are technical or synergetic benefits. Moreover, the venture capitalist is likely to be able to sell the entire equity stake and receive a straight cash return whereas in a Stock Exchange flotation the investor may be unable to sell his entire holding immediately. From the company's perspective, a trade sale enables it to choose its partner, whereas a flotation offers the risk of an unfriendly takeover. The 1987 Stock Exchange crash had only a short-lived effect on the level of flotations, although the number of venture-backed companies going public has declined since the beginning of 1989 as a result of the impact of tightening monetary policy on business confidence and unfavorable conditions in the equity market (Pratt 1990). The latter factor has reduced the returns to the investor from flotation and has diminished the benefits of a stock market quote, such as the ability to raise future finance and to use quoted paper to fund acquisitions (Tait 1989a).

The majority of venture capital firms evaluate the risk of projects in isolation, rather than in the context of their overall portfolio of investments, and largely on the basis of the financing stage of the project. Indeed, only a minority of funds specifically diversify their portfolios, for example by industrial sector or stage of investment (Dixon 1989). To reduce the variability of their returns (as well as giving an increased incentive to investees) many venture capital firms used 'rachets', whereby the final percentage equity stake held by the venture capital fund and the investee depends upon investee performance measured against projected performance. The better the performance, the higher the stake that the investee retains.

Most funds monitor their investments by appointing a director to the board, or reserving the right to appoint a director at a later stage. Most also require monthly or quarterly accounts. Around three-quarters of the funds in Dixon's sample also had occasion to replace the management of investee companies. However, in contrast with the popular view, Dixon (1989) found that only 20 per cent of his sample provided continuing managerial help to investee companies.

The average failure rate of investments by the funds in Dixon's sample, with failure defined as written-off investments, was 5.0 per cent of the portfolio, by value. Not surprisingly, start-ups had by far the highest average failure rate by value, while management buyouts had an extremely low failure rate (Table 8.5). However,

Table 8.5 Investments written off, by financing stage

Stage of financing	Failure rate by value
	(%)
Start-ups	16.3
Development capital	5.2
Rescue capital	2.8
Management buyouts	0.9

Source: Dixon (1989)

Table 8.6 Investment activity in the United Kingdom

	1984	*1985*	*1986*	*1987*	*1988*
Total amount invested (£million)	228	279	396	795	1006
Number of companies financed	582	597	665	638	625
Average received per company (£000)	392	467	595	1246	1610

Source: Pratt (1990)

these figures do not take into account investments which have failed to yield the required rate of return, or which have not been recouped in the projected time-span (Dixon 1989).

PATTERNS OF VENTURE CAPITAL INVESTMENT

Size of Investments

The rapid growth in venture capital activity during the 1980s (Table 8.6) has been accompanied by a number of significant shifts in the pattern of investments. The most significant change has been the striking increase in the size of investments. The average venture capital investment has increased from less than £400,000 in 1984 to £1.6 million in 1988 (Table 8.6). The venture capital industry is now dominated by large investments. Deals of over £2 million accounted for two-thirds of the total amount invested in 1988 compared with under one-third in 1985. By contrast, financings of under £200,000 have fallen from 10 per cent of the total in 1985 to just under 5 per cent in 1988 (Pratt 1990). In the case of 3i, one of the largest venture capital providers, only 7.5 per cent of loan and equity investments were for sums of £150,000 or less (3i Group plc 1989). Nevertheless, investments of under £500,000 continue to be the most numerous, accounting for 66 per cent of all investments made in 1987 compared with 76 per cent in 1983 (Dixon 1989). One consequence of the increase in the size of investments is that a growing number are now syndicated among several firms.

Management buyouts

The increasing size of investments reflects the growing dominance of management buyouts in UK venture capital activity. There were less than fifty management buyouts in 1980 compared with 373 in 1988. More significantly, the value of management buyouts has increased from £28 million in 1980 to £3.7 billion in 1988 (Table 8.7) and there has been a marked increase in the average size of buyouts. The early management buyouts often involved either the rescue of troubled or bankrupt companies or the sale of loss-making subsidiaries, but in recent years the majority of buyouts have involved sales by large diversified companies of businesses which were deemed to be peripheral to their 'core' activities. Some buyouts, for example shipbuilding and bus companies, have also resulted from privatizations and denationalization. The Stock Exchange crash has given a further boost to management buyouts. Finding the share prices of their companies depressed and the advantages of a stock market quote in terms of fund-raising or acquisition finance at least temporarily absent, the directors of some publicly listed companies (for example, Virgin Group) have also staged management buy-outs with the intention of taking the company private (Tait 1989b).

In the typical management buyout deal the managers put up a relatively small sum to finance the deal and the financial institutions finance the bulk of the deal by a combination of equity and loan finance. The financial structure therefore comprises layers of different kinds of finance: ordinary shares, which usually account for a relatively small proportion of the total financing, preferential

Table 8.7 UK management buyouts

	Number	Value	Average size
		(£million)	(£million)
1979	18	14	0.8
1980	36	28	0.8
1981	145	193	1.3
1982	238	348	1.5
1983	234	364	1.6
1984	238	403	1.7
1985	261	1,141	4.4
1986	313	1,188	3.8
1987	344	3,220	9.4
1988	373	3,717	10.0
1989[a]	182	1,838	10.1

Source: Centre for Management Buy-out Research, University of Nottingham
Note: [a]Second quarter.

shares, subordinated loans or debentures; and ordinary term loans and bank overdraft facilities. As Table 8.8 indicates, between 1985 and 1988 management buyout activity was achieved by the equal expansion of equity and debt financing, with the introduction of a limited amount of mezzanine finance. This contrasts with the situation in the United States where the buyout business is dominated by large, highly leveraged deals often involving taking public companies private and then selling off assets to repay the massive debt incurred, and more usually motivated by the high level of fees earned than potential capital gains (Lloyd 1989). However, the sharp increase in the use of mezzanine finance and, more significantly, the major reduction in the share of equity finance in management buyouts in 1989, which has resulted in a rise in the debt-to-equity ratio of around five to one, suggests that management buyout activity in the UK may be moving closer to the American model of highly leveraged, junk bond financed financial engineering (although the average UK gearing ratio is still much lower than that in the United States where management buyouts typically involve equity to borrowing ratios of nine or ten to one), and are thus becoming even less like the conventional understanding of pure venture capital (Batchelor 1989c; also see Table 8.8). Gearing ratios have been rising for two principal reasons. First, as noted above, the nature of the businesses that are being bought out has changed: whereas in the early 1980s they tended to be loss-making companies which their parent companies were glad to sell off, often at a discount to net asset value, now most buyouts are profitable businesses which are being sold because they do not fit into the parent company's 'core' activities and are valued on a multiple of past and projected cash flow. Second, the profitability of management buyouts has encouraged banks to be more generous in their lending (Batchelor 1989d). Even though management buyouts have not been excessively geared, the combination of high interest rates and high prices paid for some buyouts in the pre-crash bull stock market, which inflated vendors expectations of what a buyout company is worth, have made it harder for some management buy-outs to pay their debts, and some – notably in depressed sectors such as retailing and home furnishings – have been forced to defer loan repayments and seek re-financing in 1989 (Batchelor 1989c).

Management buyouts have been very attractive to UK venture capitalists for four main reasons. First, they have a lower risk than other types of investments, notably start-ups and early stage investments (see Table 8.5). Management buyouts involve

Table 8.8 Gearing ratios of management buyouts

Year	Total value	Equity	Mezzanine	debt	gearing
	(£million)	(£million)	(£million)	(£million)	(%)
1981	46	31	–	15	48
1982	469	194	–	275	142
1983	161	46	–	115	250
1984	171	85	–	86	101
1985	855	233	123	499	267
1986	960	297	96	567	223
1987	2,772	813	213	1,746	241
1988	4,471	1,214	282	2,975	268
1989[a]	4,989	795	778	3,416	528
Total	14,894	3,708	1,492	9,694	302

Source: Peat Marwick, McLintock, cited in *Financial Times*, Management Buy-out Survey, 11 September 1989
Note: [a] To 15 September.

businesses that are established and profitable (or potentially profitable), the products are developed, the market is known, long-established links exist with customers, and a management team which is familiar with all aspects of the business, is in place. Second, for the same reasons, venture capitalists need to devote less time and effort to research management buyouts prior to investment and to support of them afterwards. Third, because management buyouts usually involve well-established businesses in mature industries generating a comfortable and regular cash flow they have produced the highest returns. Fourth, management buyouts offer a quicker exit route than most other types of investment. The Centre for Management Buyout Research at the University of Nottingham (Wright 1989) notes that the average period between buyout and flotation was only 3 years and 5 months in 1989 (compared with just over 4 years in 1986 and 1988). Trade sales offer an alternative exit route; indeed they exceed the number of flotations (161 compared with 141 between 1985 and 1989) and have outstripped flotations to an increasing extent since 1987. New ways are emerging in which investors can realize their equity stake in management buyouts, including management buy-back of shares, financial restructuring (for example, re-leverage, re-financing), and a management buyin. The larger management buyouts offer the quickest exit: by 1989 36 per cent of management buyouts of £25 million or more had been floated or sold compared with 14 per cent of all management buyouts (Wright 1989).

The impact of this increase in management buyout activity on the venture capital industry has been significant: the proportion of finance invested in management buyouts by venture capital companies has increased between 1984 and 1988 from 28 per cent to 62 per cent. Reflecting the increasing size of management buyouts, they comprised 17 per cent of all venture capital investments in 1984 and 24 per cent in 1988 (Table 8.9). In contrast, although the amount invested in start-ups and early stage finance has increased, the proportion of total funds accounted for by such investments declined between 1984 and 1988 from 27 per cent to 7 per cent by value and from 32 per cent to 26 per cent by volume (Table 8.9). Management buyouts and buyins by BVCA members in 1988 had an average size of £2.6 million in 1988 compared with an overall average investment of £957,000. However, as this figure is distorted by several very large buyout financings the median value of £570,000 is a better indicator (BVCA 1988).

Many venture-backed management buyouts have been extremely successful. Subsidiaries or divisions freed from central office overheads and supervision by the parent company have been able to grow faster than before, in spite of the burden of increased bank lending. Those which have achieved a stock market flotation (almost

Table 8.9 Investments, by financing stage

Stage	1984	1985	1986	1987	1988
	(%)	(%)	(%)	(%)	(%)
A Amount invested					
Start-up	17	13	16	8	5
Other early stage	10	6	7	4	2
Expansion	39	36	27	22	27
Buyout/buyin/acquisition	28	38	44	63	62
Secondary purchase	5	6	5	3	4
Other	1	1	1	–	–
Total (£million)	228	279	396	795	1,006
B Number of investments					
Start-up	19	19	21	19	18
Other early stage	13	11	11	9	8
Expansion	46	48	44	47	43
Buyout/buyin/acquisition	17	16	19	21	24
Secondary purchase	4	5	4	4	7
Other	1	1	1	–	–

Source: Pratt (1990)

Table 8.10 Management buyins

	Number	Value	Average size
		(£million)	(£million)
1979	1	0.5	0.5
1980	–	–	–
1981	5	11	2.1
1982	8	316	39.5
1983	8	8	1.1
1984	5	3	0.7
1985	29	39	1.3
1986	49	297	6.1
1987	89	307	3.5
1988	105	1,226	11.7
1989	63	390	6.2

Source: Centre for Management Buy-out Research, University of Nottingham

100 in the period 1986–88: Lloyd 1989) and others which have been sold to other companies have provided investors with an early exit from their investments, thereby providing an important source of current income for venture capital firms (Clark 1987), and often generated considerable capital gains for their investors. In financing management buyouts, venture capital funds would therefore appear to have made a valuable contribution to the UK economy by helping to regenerate companies. However, recent research appears to qualify this conclusion. According to a Warwick Business School study, while buyout companies perform better than other companies in their sector for the first 3 years, from year four it is worse than average. This feature may reflect the fact that opportunities to cut costs and improve margins have been exhausted by this time (Batchelor 1989d).

Venture capital firms have also begun to finance buyins. This is where one or more managers from outside the company will purchase and seek to revitalize a business with finance raised from venture capital and other financial backers. Prior to 1985 there were fewer than ten buyins in any year; however, there has been a rapid increase in the number of buyins since 1985, with more than 100 occurring in 1988. Both the amount invested and the average value of buyins also significantly increased in 1988 (Table 8.10). Many of the buyins that have occurred to date have been promoted by venture capital firms. Buyins do carry greater risks than management buyouts: the buyin team do not have the same detailed knowledge of the company and its problems as the incumbent

Table 8.11 Investments, by industry sector

Industry	Percentage of companies financed					Percentage of amount invested				
	1984	1985	1986	1987	1988	1984	1985	1986	1987	1988
Consumer related	19.3	22.6	24.7	22.0	23.0	23.0	19.6	20.4	27.8	35.2
Computer related	16.7	16.7	14.1	10.0	9.6	20.2	19.1	11.3	4.9	4.3
Electronics	10.2	9.2	7.7	6.2	5.1	9.6	12.3	7.8	4.2	1.5
Medical/ biotechnology	8.2	3.8	7.1	4.9	3.9	5.9	3.9	9.2	4.9	1.8
Industrial products	7.9	10.4	7.7	10.6	11.7	5.2	6.9	6.9	10.8	7.9
Communications	6.6	8.0	6.2	4.5	2.8	5.9	7.6	7.6	1.9	1.4
Transportation	3.3	4.7	5.1	4.5	4.7	2.5	3.4	8.2	3.9	3.1
Energy/mining	6.2	1.7	0.7	1.2	1.4	4.3	1.2	0.3	0.9	0.5
Construction	2.6	4.5	2.0	4.7	4.4	2.0	3.7	1.9	4.9	6.5
Other manuf.	7.5	7.3	5.3	12.0	15.7	5.7	8.0	3.2	7.5	19.6
Financial svs	[a]	3.3	5.3	3.1	9.5	[a]	5.7	9.8	4.9	12.8
Other services	11.5[a]	7.8	14.1	16.3	8.2	15.7[a]	8.6	13.4	23.4	5.5
Total	100	100	100	100	100	100	100	100	100	100

Source: BVCA (1988)
Note: [a] In 1984 financial services were included within the other services category.

management; they will not have worked together as a team and may have difficulty in working together. For these reasons buyins have higher failure rates than buyouts. However, they also offer greater returns than management buyouts (40–50 per cent compared with 30–40 per cent) where competition for suitable investment opportunities has significantly increased (Batchelor 1989b).

Investments by sector

Unfortunately, data on the sectoral distribution of investments (BVCA annual reports) have not been compiled on a consistent basis over time: prior to 1987 management buyouts were excluded (Dixon, 1989; Martin, 1989) but have been included since then. Statistics on temporal trends in the sectoral pattern of investments should therefore be interpreted cautiously. However, it would appear that there have been significant shifts in the sectoral distribution of venture capital investments (Table 8.11). The initial preference for computer related and electronics companies in the early years of the venture capital industry was quickly replaced by a shift towards consumer related, financial services and other service sector companies. Although the amount of venture capital invested in these sectors increased from £34 million in 1984 to £75 million in 1988, its share declined from 30 to 9 per cent. In contrast, consumer related activities increased their share of total venture capital financing from 23 to 35 per cent between 1984 and 1988. The financial services sector also attracted an increasing amount of venture capital investments, rising from £9.8 million (6 per cent) in 1985 to £166 million (13 per cent) in 1988 (it was not identified as a separate sector in the 1984 statistics). The proportion of venture capital invested in the other services sector also increased from 16 to 23 per cent between 1984 and 1987, but its share fell back to 6 per cent in 1988. The US venture capital industry has also shifted from computer and electronics industries towards consumer and service sectors. Nevertheless, the financing of technology related companies is a much more prominent feature of the US venture capital industry (Zagor 1989). This may reflect the difficulty of establishing a large high-technology company in the UK because of the smallness of the domestic market. Alternatively, it may stem from a 'lack of appetite amongst [British] venture capital houses for higher risks associated with investing in new technologies' (*Financial Times* 1985b).

Summary

Thus, there has been a distinct trend amongst venture capitalists to invest in larger, less risky investments – notably management buyouts. However, there is a widespread view that the financing of management buyouts cannot be regarded as venture investment. Indeed, Cary (1989: 7) states that 'the capital invested [in management buyouts] simply enables a change in ownership and should more properly be labelled "traditional corporate finance" rather than "venture capital"' while Batchelor (1989c: 1) has argued that 'a number of recent buyouts have depended more on the mergers and acquisitions expertise of City corporate finance teams than on the more traditional skills of venture capitalists and the specialist buy-out funds'. The converse of this concentration on management buyouts is that the venture capital industry has been reluctant to finance companies requiring smaller amounts of capital, especially those at the start-up and early stages of business development. Of course, an economic case can be made for not investing small amounts in new and small businesses: such investments require as much, if not more, time to investigate than larger proposals, demand considerable time and attention, have a payback period of at least 5–7 years, and have the highest risk. Venture capitalists made just twenty-four seed capital investments in 1987 amounting to £1.9 million – just 0.2 per cent of total investment activity – with such funding largely restricted to a small group of about five dedicated seed capital funds: the 1988 figure was even lower. The situation in Europe is no better. Members of the European Venture Capital Association invested only 0.3 per cent in seed funds in 1988 (Pratt 1990). This compares with the United States where seed investments accounted for 2 per cent of venture spending (Batchelor 1989e). The concern expressed in a National Economic Development Office report in 1986 (Chapman 1986) that venture capital was failing to bridge the long-standing equity gap therefore remains valid.

LOCATIONAL DISTRIBUTION OF VENTURE CAPITAL INVESTMENTS

Spatial patterns of investment activity

The regional pattern of venture capital investments shows a consistent pattern. Throughout the 1984–88 period the southeast

Table 8.12 Regional distribution of venture capital investment, 1984–1988

| Region | Percentages of amounts invested | | | | | Location quotient[a] |
	1984	1985	1986	1987	1988	
Southeast	55	60	63	62	55	1.71
East Anglia	5	6	5	3	3	1.07
Southwest	4	7	5	7	3	0.54
Midlands[b]	9	10	6	10	16	0.66
North[c]	10	6	11	9	14	0.48
Wales	6	4	3	4	1	0.68
Scotland	11	7	7	5	7	1.04
Northern Ireland	–	–	–	–	1	0.06

Sources: Pratt (1990), *British Business* (1989)
Notes: [a] The location quotient is calculated as follows:

$$LQ_i = \frac{VC_i}{S_i}$$

where LQ_i is the location quotient in region i, VC_i is the percentage of total capital investment in region i, 1984–8, and S_i is the average stock of VAT-registered businesses in each region, 1984–8.
[b] East and West Midlands.
[c] Northwest, Yorkshire–Humberside and the Northern region.

region has accounted for well over one-half of the amount invested (Table 8.12). When compared with its share of the total stock of VAT-registered businesses in this period (34.6 per cent), it is clear that venture capital investments have been disproportionately concentrated in the southeast and also, but to a much lesser extent, in East Anglia. In the remainder of the country only Scotland has attracted more shares of venture capital investments than its share of the stock of businesses. In all other regions the proportion of venture capital investment has been well below the proportion of the stock of UK businesses. Year-on-year figures suggest that the southeast region has maintained – and even increased slightly – its share of venture capital investments while Scotland's relative share has fallen (Martin 1989).

The regional distribution of investments by BVCA members (including 3i) exhibits a broadly similar spatial pattern (Map 8.1). The southeast accounted for 38 per cent of companies financed and 50 per cent of the amount invested in 1988, well above the proportion of the stock of UK businesses in the region (34.7 per cent). East Anglia also contained more than its 'fair share' of

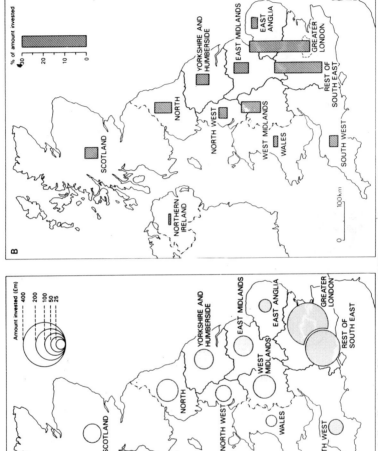

Map 8.1 Regional distribution of investments by BVCA members 1988
Source: BVCA

companies raising venture capital. It is apparent from a comparison of location quotients that the over-concentration of venture capital investments in the southeast region is largely a function of investment activity in Greater London. The proportion of investments in the rest of the southeast was largely in line with its proportion of the national stock of businesses. Scotland and Wales also contained more than their 'fair share' of companies raising venture capital, although on account of the small average size of investments in these regions they both contained less than their 'fair share' of venture capital investments by value. However, both the north and the West Midlands also attracted more than their 'fair shares' of venture capital activity, in terms of both the proportion of companies financed and the amount invested. Martin (1989) has suggested, on the basis of 1986 data, that the West Midlands, the north, Scotland, and Wales were least likely to receive investment from London-based venture capital funds and were more reliant on regionally based sources of funding. Given that it is unlikely that the geographical investment preferences of London-based fund managers have changed significantly since then, these seem to be the first signs that venture capital activity is becoming established in at least some of the UK regions.

Explaining the uneven geography of venture capital investments

In seeking to explain the over-concentration of venture capital investments in the southeast region it is conceptually helpful to distinguish between demand-related and supply-related factors (Harrison and Mason 1986). Demand-related explanations include such factors as the inherent dynamism of the regional stock of small businesses, the potential for new firm formation, and the availability of alternative or substitutional forms of finance which might 'crowd out' the use of venture capital (for example, government loans and grants in assisted areas). The major supply-related explanation concerns the availability of venture capital in different regions of the country (Mason and Harrison 1989). As the following discussion makes clear, regional variations in venture capital activity in the United Kingdom are associated with both demand- and supply-side factors.

The most significant demand-side factor is that suitable investment opportunities are largely concentrated in the southeast region. New firm formation rates are highest in the southeast region and parts of adjacent regions and lowest in the older urban-industrial areas of northern and western Britain (*British Business* 1989; Mason and Harrison 1990a). The small business stock in southern regions is also qualitatively superior to that in the remainder of the country. Successful small enterprises are overwhelmingly concentrated in the southeast region (Mason 1985, 1989). O'Farrell and Hitchens (1989) and Hitchens and O'Farrell (1987) suggest that small firms in the southeast are more competitive than their counterparts in northern regions. Independent firms in the southeast are more innovative than their counterparts in northern regions (Thwaites 1982). High-technology industry (Keeble 1988) and new technology-based enterprises (Keeble and Kelly 1986) are both disproportionately concentrated in southern England. Martin (1989) notes that the three southern regions of the southeast, East Anglia and the southwest captured a disproportionate share – 73 per cent – of high-technology financings in the period 1984–86. Anecdotal evidence of the difficulty that some venture capitalists have had in finding suitable investment opportunities in the north of England and Wales (Mason 1987b; Mason and Harrison 1989) further confirms the importance of demand-side factors in contributing to the relative lack of venture capital investment outside the southeast region.

The high proportion of venture capital investments which have financed management buyouts and buyins has also been a major

Table 8.13 Regional distribution of management buyins and buyouts to June 1989

Region	Buyins	Buyouts		Larger buyouts (over £25 million)	
	Number	Number	Value	Number	Value
	(%)	(%)	(%)	(%)	(%)
Southeast	39.8	36.4	62.2	54.7	71.1
East Anglia	1.7	3.6	1.4	1.9	0.8
Southwest	6.4	7.3	3.0	3.8	1.4
West Midlands	12.8	11.7	5.2	4.7	2.6
East Midlands	8.4	5.7	4.2	5.7	3.5
Yorkshire–Humberside	5.2	9.5	9.7	13.2	10.0
Northwest	10.8	8.2	5.6	8.5	4.6
North	3.2	2.8	1.1	–	–
Wales	4.6	3.7	3.0	2.8	3.2
Scotland	7.0	10.6	4.2	3.8	2.5
Northern Ireland	–	0.5	0.4	0.9	0.3
Total	100.0	100.0	100.0	100.0	100.0

Source: Centre for Management Buy-out Research, University of Nottingham

contributory factor to the over-concentration of investments in the southeast region. The spatial division of labor within large enterprises has resulted in the greatest opportunities for management buyouts and buyins being concentrated in southern England (Table 8.13). Branch plants in the southeast are likely to be complete divisions or subsidiaries – the most frequent target for management buyouts – with a full complement of management functions. Conversely, in northern regions externally owned branch plants of multi-locational enterprises are oriented towards production and assembly operations and have little or no marketing and research and development (R&D) functions (Hood and Young 1983; Storey 1983; also see Wright *et al.* 1984). The limited range of management expertise is therefore likely to be too narrow to attract the interest of venture capital firms. The vast majority of management buyouts in the north of England and Scotland are therefore small private, often family, businesses where the managing members of the family buy out the non managing ones (Buxton 1989; Hamilton Fazey 1989b). As a consequence, the average size of management buyouts in such regions is much lower than in the southeast (Table 8.13).

A recent study to examine why the northwest has attracted less than its 'fair share' of venture capital investments has suggested a further demand-side factor to explain the lack of venture capital investments in peripheral UK regions. It noted that businesses and their professional advisors in northwest England had only a patchy understanding of the availability, advantages, and sources of venture capital and the factors which venture capitalists take into account in assessing funding proposals. As a consequence, proposals from firms were often outside the investment criteria of the funds to which they were sent and tended to emphasize figures rather than business strategy (Invest North West Working Party 1989).

The key supply-side factor which contributes to the over-concentration of venture capital investments in the southeast is that the vast majority of firms are based in London and they account for the bulk of the funds invested. The concentration of venture capital activity in London is the result of historical and institutional forces rather than directly associated with demand factors (Martin 1989). London has long been the pre-eminent financial centre in the UK, containing various financial and related institutions and a diverse range of investment expertise and business consultancy services. Hence, as Martin (1989) notes, for these reasons it was inevitable that the development of the venture capital industry, a further specialist division of the finance industry, should be focused there.

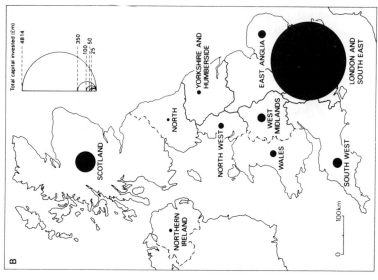

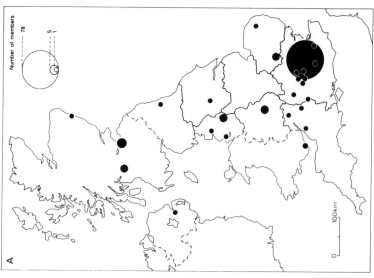

A

Number of members
78
5
1

B

Total capital invested (£m)
4814
350
100
50
25

SCOTLAND

NORTHERN
IRELAND

NORTH

NORTH WEST

WALES

WEST
MIDLANDS

YORKSHIRE AND
HUMBERSIDE

EAST ANGLIA

LONDON AND
SOUTH EAST

SOUTH WEST

0 100km

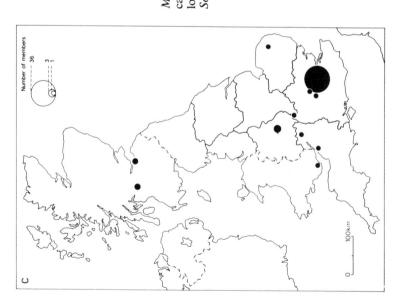

Map 8.2 (a) Location of BVCA members, 1989; (b) total capital invested by BVCA members (excluding 3i); (c) location of BVCA members, 1985
Source: BVCA

Most of the 'captive' funds have been established by companies which are located in London and many of the independent funds have been established in London for reasons connected with the pool of professional labor and existence of agglomeration economies.

Of the 120 full members of the BVCA at the end of 1989, almost two-thirds (seventy-eight) were located or headquartered in London and a further 8 per cent (ten funds) were based elsewhere in the southeast region (Map 8.2(a)). The main provincial clusters of venture capital funds – Edinburgh (five), Birmingham (four), Cambridge (three) and Glasgow (three) – are all very small in comparison. The largest regional concentrations outside the southeast are Scotland (nine), the northwest (six) and the West Midlands (four). If venture capital funds that are linked to the public sector in some way (for example, central government agency, responsible to local authorities, managing local authority funds) are excluded then the presence of venture capital funds in the midlands and north becomes even more limited, with just seventeen private sector firms, eight of which are based in Scotland. The dominance of London as the main source of venture capital in the United Kingdom is even greater when the amount of capital invested is considered: London-based venture capital organizations account for 88 per cent of the total capital invested by BVCA members (Map 8.2(b)). Comparison with the location of BVCA full members in 1985 indicates that there has been only a marginal decrease in the southeast domination of venture capital companies (from 78 to 73 per cent). Nevertheless, there has been a noticeable increase in venture capital firms in the north of England since 1985. There were no BVCA members in the north, northwest and Yorkshire–Humberside in 1985 but eleven in 1989 (six of which were in the northwest). Scotland maintained its share of venture capital companies (8 per cent) between 1985 and 1989 (Map 8.2(c)).

There are a number of ways in which the concentration of venture capital suppliers in London and the southeast is likely to diminish the supply of venture capital in the peripheral regions. First, the 'hands on' style of investment activity adopted by most venture capital organizations – involving close contact with the investee companies, representation on the board as a non-executive director and provision of management assistance in some cases – makes geographical proximity between investor and investee highly desirable. This consideration may therefore have encouraged southeast-based venture capital organizations to concentrate their investments in areas within easy travelling distance for ease of monitoring. Conversely, such organizations may be reluctant to invest in businesses located in northern regions because of the additional monitoring costs (Mason 1987b; Martin 1989). Second, London-based venture capital organizations may be less aware of investment opportunities in northern regions. It is widely accepted within the venture capital industry that 'good local knowledge [is required] to succeed in any region' (Hamilton Fazey 1986). Third, London-based venture capitalists have little need to look for investment opportunities in northern regions because there is a wide range of suitable businesses in which to invest in the southeast and adjacent counties (Hamilton Fazey 1986). Fourth, because of their high managerial unit costs, London-based venture capital firms find it uneconomic to make smaller investments. For example, it is reported that one fund considers it uneconomic to make investments of less than £500,000 from its London base (West Midlands Enterprise Board 1988). As a consequence, the flow of investments to northern regions – where the main type of demand is for amounts of capital below the minimum threshold of London-based venture capital organizations – is likely to have been constrained. Indeed, another fund considered that it was uneconomic for any London-based fund to consider investment proposals from any companies located over 100 miles away from London (West Midlands Enterprise Board 1988). Finally, it has been suggested that the lack of venture capital investments by London-based funds in the peripheral regions may reflect their prejudices. A former Secretary of State for Wales accused City of London financial institutions of 'derisively dismissing any venture in Wales . . . on the general assumption that Wales is a bad place, that there are no capable businesses there, and that in any case there is nothing to be seen but decaying coal mines, rundown steelworks and slag heaps' (*Financial Times* 1985a).

A review of management buyout activity in the West Midlands provides further support for the importance of the supply-side explanation (Lovejoy 1988). The evidence indicates that despite a high level of management buyouts in the West Midlands, there are difficulties in raising suitable buyout finance in the region, especially for smaller buyouts. This is related to the failure of financial institutions in the region to develop and refine their financial provision to meet the particular need of West Midlands buyouts. The consequence is that a number of potential buyouts have not occurred, while many of those which have taken place have relied on debt rather than equity finance. Furthermore, this bank finance has been made available on a shorter term than the national average for buyouts.

The fact that Scotland and, to a lesser extent, the West Midlands, which contain a number of suppliers of venture capital, have also attracted more than their 'fair share' of venture capital investments provides confirmation of the plausibility of the supply-side explanation. Furthermore, the increase in the number of venture capital organizations in provincial centres, and the establishment of northern branch offices by some London-based organizations (Hamilton Fazey 1988) are both consistent with evidence (Table 8.12) from the BVCA data examined above of a slight reduction in the over-concentration of venture capital investments in the southeast between 1987 and 1988. Nevertheless, despite its network of twenty-four regional offices in the United Kingdom, over half of 3i's loan and share investments in 1988–89 were in the southeast region (3i Group plc 1989). Thus, the concentration of venture capital suppliers in London is not a total explanation for the southeast's disproportionate share of venture capital investments.

The regional structure of the venture capital industry

Using data from the UK Venture Capital Report (VCR) (Cary 1989) it is possible to develop a more detailed impression of regional variations in the structure and orientation of the venture capital industry in the United Kingdom. Confirming the discussion above, of the funds for which information is available from the VCR database, the majority (64 percent) are based in Greater London. A further 15 per cent are based elsewhere in the south of England, with a minor concentration in the Cambridge area, while only 20 per cent of funds are based in the Midlands and northern regions of the United Kingdom (Table 8.14). However, in terms of the value of venture capital funds under management (either invested or available for investment) the dominance of Greater London is even more pronounced, with almost 90 per cent of funds under management compared with 4 per cent in the south and 6 per cent in the north. This is reflected in the average size of funds under management, which, if two exceptionally large cases in the northern group are omitted, are of similar magnitude in the two non-London groups but are dwarfed by the very much larger London-based funds. If there is a spatial bias in the investment preferences and decision-making criteria of London-based venture capitalists (see above), this discrepancy in the availability of funds under manage-

Table 8.14 Regional structure of the venture capital industry

	Greater London	South[a]	North–Midlands[b]
Number of funds	75	18	25
Average venture capital	89.7	10.8	30.7
Funds under management[c] (£million)	(61.9)[d]		(12.9)[e]
Smallest investment (£'000)	225	75	54
Largest investment (£'000)	3,408	1,120	1,367
Average investment (£'000)	721	242	299
Minimum investment (£'000)	231	79	103
Minimum equity stake (%)	4	6	4
Maximum equity stake (%)	53	63	49
Investments made (% of porfolio)			
Sole investor	35	53	51
Lead investor	27	21	12
Consortium leader	38	26	37
Investment phase (% of portfolio)			
Start-up	21	31	27
Development	40	56	47
Buyout	32	8	23
Others (rescue etc.)	6	6	3

Source: Based on data in Cary (1989)
Notes: [a] Southeast (excluding Greater London), East Anglia, Southwest.
   [b] Rest of United Kingdom.
   [c] Includes funds already invested and available for investment.
   [d] Average size excluding 3i portfolio.
   [e] Average size excluding two exceptionally large institutional funds which did not separate out their specifically venture capital funds.

ment will continue to reinforce the north–south divide in the availability of venture capital.

These differences in the number and size of venture capital funds among the three groups are reinforced when the size, mode, and stage of investments already made by these funds is examined. Whether measured in terms of the smallest, largest, or average investments made, it is clear that London venture capital funds make investments in significantly larger tranches than do funds elsewhere (Table 8.14). This partly reflects differences in the stage of company development funded relative to non-London funds (see below) and in the mode of investment. It also strongly implies that London funds are operating at a larger scale of funding than is required to close the equity gap for many small firms outside the

London region, which has been estimated to be particularly acute for tranches of funding of less than £100,000 (NEDC 1986). By contrast, funds in the Midlands and northern regions of the United Kingdom have been prepared to make significantly smaller investments than funds in the south, although with a slightly higher average investment. The VCR data also suggest that there is a slow upward drift in the minimum investment threshold which will be considered for funding in the future relative to past experience. This gap between the average portfolio minimum investment (£52,000) and the fund managers' preferred minimum future investment (£103,000) is most pronounced for northern funds, and suggests that firms in this part of the country seeking venture capital may be placed at a further disadvantage in the future.

Funds in the south on average will expect a larger equity stake in investee companies (which may reflect their tendency to invest in start-ups and high-technology situations where risks are higher), while venture capital funds in the north have the lowest average maximum equity target, and are thus likely to impose less onerous conditions, in terms of the dilution of the entrepreneur's control and ownership, than are funds elsewhere. In this sense, the venture capital available in the north at present has come in smaller tranches and with more flexible control obligations, making it relatively more attractive to recipient businesses. This may in part explain the recent rise in the proportion of venture capital being invested in the north of England in particular. However, as our previous discussion has made clear, the funds available have not been sufficiently large scale to change significantly the north–south inequality in the distribution of venture capital.

Partly reflecting the significant difference in the size of investment considered, funds in London are much less likely than those elsewhere to act as sole investor in a project (35 per cent of investments by London-based funds are as sole investors compared with just over 50 per cent in the other regions). Conversely, London-based funds were more likely to syndicate their investment and in particular, were more likely to act as lead investor in a syndicate than were funds in other parts of the United Kingdom (Table 8.14). Funds in the north were least likely to act as lead investor in a syndicate, although they were marginally more inclined to syndicate than were funds in the south. However, the VCR data do not provide sufficient detail on the syndication process. In particular, from the perspective of closing the regional equity gap in venture capital provision and thereby contributing to the regional development process it is important to identify the extent to which syndication of venture capital investment in the north is intra-regional, linking funds within the region to invest in projects also within the region, or inter-regional. In the latter case, it then becomes important to know whether the syndication process acts as a mechanism for bringing in funds from outside the region to invest within the region, thus deepening the regional capital base, or operates as a means of channelling venture capital funds into investments outside the region in which the lead investor is a London-based or southern-based fund.

The inter-regional differences in venture capital investment size and mode are reflected in, and in part caused by, significant inter-regional differences in the stage of investment of the investee business (Table 8.14). In particular, funds in the south and, to a lesser extent, the north have been more inclined to invest in the start-up and development stages. More significantly, however, almost one-third of the portfolio of investments made by London-based venture capital funds has been in management buyouts and buyins: in absolute terms the London-based venture capital industry has been the dominant force in this most rapidly growing area of venture capital activity in recent years, with the result that less capital, in relative terms, has been available for investment in those start-up and early stage ventures which face the greatest difficulties in raising external finance (Walker 1989). However, almost one-quarter of venture capital investments by northern funds have been management buyouts. Unfortunately, the data do not permit identification of the location of buyouts, but this may reflect an underlying inter-regional difference in the motivations and context of management buyouts in the United Kingdom which parallels the inter-temporal variation suggested for the United Kingdom as a whole (see above). In particular, this concentration of northern venture capital on management buyouts may reflect regional support for divisional buyouts in response to threatened closure or withdrawal by the parent company rather than the buyout, often increasingly highly leveraged, of entire companies as in other parts of the country. If so, and only further more detailed research will provide an answer, this carries the implication that the more economically precarious context of such enforced management buyouts may be reflected ultimately in lower rates of return for the venture capital funds involved, which may not therefore share in the expected high returns from such activity (Lloyd 1989).

One aspect of the operation of the venture capital industry which

Table 8.15 Regional venture capital industry characteristics

	Greater London	South[a]	North–Midlands[b]
Take-up rates			
(a) Projects reviewed as % of those received	26	34	46
(b) Investments made as % of projects reviewed	4	3	11
Industry preferences (% of funds)			
High tech	24	50	4
General manufacturing/services	11	11	28
None specified	65	39	68
Geographical preferences[c] (% of funds)			
Local area (subregional)	1	17	12
Region	1	17	44
Macro-region[d]	5	22	16
United Kingdom	63	47	36
Overseas	43	11	4
None specified	20	0	8

Source: Based on data in Cary (1989)
Notes: [a] Southeast (excluding Greater London), East Anglia, Southwest.
[b] Rest of United Kingdom.
[c] Figure sum to more than 100% due to multiple responses.
[d] Investment preferences limited to two or three (usually adjacent) specified regions.

has not received attention in the regional context, despite its importance in understanding regional variations in the supply and demand for such finance (Mason *et al.* 1988), is the possible existence of inter-regional differences in rejection rates. Using VCR data it is possible to begin to address this issue. From Table 8.15 it is clear that the likelihood of an investment proposal being reviewed by the venture capitalist increases steadily with distance from London. Only 26 per cent of proposals received by venture capitalists in London are reviewed, compared with almost half in the north. Furthermore, and more significantly, there is a clear north–south divide in acceptance rates. Venture capitalists in London and the south invest in only 3–4 per cent of proposals received, confirming the generally accepted conclusion that venture capitalists are less willing to make risky investments in small firms than entrepreneurs often expect (Maier and Walker 1987). However, venture capitalists in the north on average invest in 11 per cent of proposals received. This may reflect the more extensive reviewing process, which lets fewer potentially viable investment projects slip through the net (although this does not appear to apply in the case of southern venture capitalists). It may also reflect, of course, a lower level of demand for venture capital in the north compared with either London or the south, and hence a less severe rationing process. This pattern may also be affected by two other aspects of fund managers' investment preference functions (Table 8.15).

First, in terms of the industrial sectors in which fund managers will consider investing, there is a very clear inter-regional difference in attitudes to high-technology investment. Around one-quarter of London-based funds specify a restriction to high-technology investments, where the returns are potentially realized in a relatively short time horizon (Florida and Kenney 1988d), and only 11 per cent specify a general non-high-technology emphasis. However, funds in the south are heavily oriented to high-technology investment, with 50 per cent of the funds specifying investment in particular technologies (biotechnology, medical science technology, information technologies). This emphasis largely reflects the influence of the particular form in which industrial development has taken place in the Cambridge area (Segal, Quince, and Wicksteed 1985; Keeble 1989) and along the M4 corridor (Hall *et al.* 1987). In the north, however, only 4 per cent of funds expressed an interest in high-technology investment, and 28 per cent specified other non-high-technology activities, often describing their interests as 'traditional manufacturing' or 'any low-technology activity'. While these sectors may have lower potential returns, they also involve lower risks and, because the technologies and product ranges are more likely to be familiar to, and understood by, the venture capitalist, may therefore have a higher chance of receiving venture capital investments.

Second, there are also clear regional differences in the preferred geographical location of fund investments. London-based funds describe themselves as having a predominantly UK or overseas orientation (the latter usually attained through other, overseas located, venture capital funds within the parent corporate organization). Funds in the south are more likely to express an interest in investing within the locality or region (34 per cent) or in restricting their interests to the sub-national scale. However, almost half nevertheless claim to be prepared to consider any UK investment. Funds in the north, by contrast, are much more locally oriented. Over half are prepared to consider investments only within the locality or region, and 16 per cent to consider investment in a limited number of regions. Conversely, just over one-third are prepared to consider investments in the UK as a whole and only 4 per cent would consider overseas investments. The degree of local orientation of northern funds is undoubtedly swollen by the inclusion of a number of public sector venture capital providers (such as regional development agencies). Nevertheless, this much stronger local/regional orientation in investment preferences implies that investment decisions are more likely to be taken in the context of more highly developed networks of information, business contacts, and trust (Lorenz 1988) than in other regions. As such, the venture capital investment decision-making process takes on some elements of the informal investment process (Mason and Harrison 1990b) in which it is estimated that up to 30 per cent of the proposals received by informal investors will receive investment (Gaston and Bell 1988).

Summary

From this review it is clear that, despite the emergence of some elements of a regional venture capital industry in the United Kingdom which is more likely to make investments locally, in smaller tranches, and in a wider range of industrial sectors than London-based organizations, there is still a significant north–south divide in the provision of venture capitalism in the United Kingdom. This reinforces the apparent widening of the equity gap generally as the venture capital industry nationally has provided increasingly large tranches of finance to late stage developments and management buyouts. This spatial pattern of venture capital activity in the United Kingdom has a number of important implications for regional economic development. First, promising small firms in peripheral regions of the United Kingdom are likely to encounter a lack of risk capital which will constrain their development and slow down the process of indigenously generated regional economic development. Second, many of the southeast-based venture capital firms are likely to utilize nation-wide pension funds and other savings, a high proportion of which are re-invested in the southeast region. Thus, the venture capital industry is contributing to a flow of investment finance from economically-depressed regions in the north and west to the prosperous south.

The general move of the UK venture capital industry away from the small scale financing of early stage businesses has prompted increased attention to the provision of informal risk capital in the United Kingdom, which according to a recent review (Walker 1989) is more appropriate than venture capital as a source of early stage finance. In the United States informal investors – or 'business angels' – are a major source of venture capital. Informal investors are private investors who provide risk capital directly to new and growing businesses. It is now agreed that informal investment is the largest single source of risk capital in the United States (Wetzel 1986a; Gaston 1989a, 1989b). Wetzel (1986b: 88) suggests that they 'finance as many as twenty times the number of firms financed by institutional venture capitalists', while 'the aggregate amount they invest is perhaps twice as big' (Wetzel 1986b: 88). Gaston (1989a, 1989b) suggests that informal investors provide capital to over forty times the number of firms receiving investments from professional venture capital funds, and the amount of their investments almost exceeds all other sources of external equity capital for new and growing small businesses combined. Informal investors are particularly important in providing seed and start-up finance (Freear and Wetzel 1988).

In the United Kingdom, by contrast, there was a consensus of opinion that the informal investor – or 'Aunt Agatha' figure – became extinct sometime during the 1960s or 1970s. However, there is a variety of anecdotal and circumstantial evidence (reviewed in Mason and Harrison (1990b)), including the establishment of financial match-making services and investor syndicates and case studies in the financial press (Batchelor 1988b, 1989f, g) to conclude that 'private individuals are starting to [re-]emerge as an alternative source of finance in Britain for the small company which is unable to raise money from more conventional sources' (Batchelor 1988b: 9).

Only fragmentary evidence exists to indicate the size of the informal risk capital pool in the United Kingdom or its significance as a source of equity capital. Cary (1989) reports that about one-third of the thousand or so businesses featured in VCR were successful in raising some or all of the finance that they sought (based on a 90 per cent response rate to the survey): the single most important sources of finance were private individuals, who backed eighty-four projects. A study of businesses on United Kingdom science parks noted that 2 per cent of firms used private equity capital at start-up and 3 per cent had private investors as a current source of finance. This compares with 3 per cent of firms which had raised start-up finance from venture capital funds and 8 per cent of firms whose current sources of finance included venture capital sources (Monck *et al.* 1988). A national stratified random sample of businesses with less than fifty full-time employees found that 2 per cent of firms raised equity from private investors; only family and friends (4 per cent) and banks (9 per cent) were more significant as sources of equity finance. Informal investors were the source of finance for about one in seven of the firms which raised equity capital (Mason and Harrison 1990b).

Informal investors therefore do play a role in the provision of venture capital in the United Kingdom, especially in the provision of seed capital. However, until research evidence is forthcoming it is impossible to assess the size and operation of the informal risk capital market. Nevertheless, frequent complaints by businesses which have sought private investors about the difficulty of finding them, criticisms of existing approaches to link businesses seeking finance with potential investors, and the lack of sophisticated computer matching services of the kind found in the United States and Canada (Wetzel 1984; Foss 1985; Gaston 1989a) lead us to believe that informal risk capital is probably not a particularly significant source of venture capital in the United Kingdom. Moreover, the supply of informal risk capital seems likely to be just as concentrated in the south of England as formal sources. The national survey of a stratified sample of businesses with less than fifty employees referred to above found that 3 per cent of firms in the south of England cited informal investors as a source of finance compared with less than 0.5 per cent in the Midlands and north of England (Mason and Harrison 1990b). The businesses which seek to raise finance from subscribers to the VCR are also disproportionately concentrated in the south of England (Mason 1985).

CONCLUSION

There has been a remarkable growth of venture capital activity in the United Kingdom during the 1980s. By the mid-1980s the volume of capital raised and invested by United Kingdom venture capital funds was larger than anywhere else in Europe and was higher, proportionately, than in the United States. However, aggregate statistics on the growth of venture capital presents a very misleading picture of the availability or the extent to which this type of finance is available to all types of businesses and in all parts of the country. The supply of venture capital is limited in two key respects. First, a large and increasing proportion of capital has been invested in management buyouts and buyins and there has been very little investment in start-ups and early stage investments, especially in technology-based sectors, and in amounts of under £250,000. Cary

(1989: 9) has stated the problem as follows: 'as the size of the individual funds has increased so the size of the minimum investment has also risen in proportion. Thus, the "equity gap", which had begun to close in the early 1980s, has again widened.' Second, investments have been disproportionately concentrated in the southeast and East Anglia. Both are long-standing features of the industry, having been identified in the mid-1980s as giving grounds for concern (for example, Chapman 1986) and criticized by government ministers as well as by some within the industry itself, and are the subject of debate about how they can be corrected.

There are at least three perspectives on how the industry can reduce its attachment to management buyouts and devote a higher proportion of finance to smaller, earlier stage, and start-up investments. These are first, the self-correction argument, second the stimulation of demand for this type of venture capital financing, and third, an expansion of the supply of seed, start-up, and early stage capital.

The first perspective reflects a view within the venture capital industry itself that the emphasis on management buyouts and later stage investments will correct itself. It has been claimed by venture capitalists that the industry 'moves in cycles'. 'Early stage deals will become popular again' (cited by Batchelor 1988a). Other venture capitalists have argued in similar vein: 'buyouts have been a bull market phenomenon. Over the next few years venture capitalists will have to focus on being more hands-on, backing start-ups and early stage companies at the start of the spectrum and buyins and restructuring at the other' (cited by Batchelor 1989d). However, the issue does not appear as clear cut as this. First, flotation is only one exit route for investors: trade sales exceed flotations as a means whereby investors can realize their equity stakes in management buyouts and new options on realization are emerging. Second, the fall in the stock market since October 1987 has resulted in an increase in the number of listed companies staging management buyouts. Any reduction in the attractiveness of management buyouts will mean that deals become more attractively priced. Third, should the UK economy move into recession in the early 1990s, as is widely predicted, this will maintain the pressure on companies to dispose of marginally profitable and noncore businesses (Batchelor 1989d). Thus, the view that the venture capital industry will significantly reduce the proportion of finance that is devoted to management buyouts through 'self-correcting' mechanisms seems suspect. Specific strategies are therefore required to stimulate the supply of seed, start-up, and early stage capital.

Alternative views on how the venture capital industry can make a more positive contribution towards filling the equity gap advocate both demand-side and supply-side strategies. The BVCA diagnoses the lack of investment in new and recently established technology related companies as a demand-side problem. They argue that the United Kingdom lacks sufficient numbers of good young companies with proficient management. Whereas the venture capital industry has been successful in attracting experienced and professional managers to run management buyouts and buyins they have failed to attract such managers to establish their own companies. The BVCA are therefore lobbying the government for various changes to the tax system, notably the introduction of BES-style tax-breaks for investment by entrepreneurs in their own businesses (the BES gives passive investors exemption from income and capital gains tax but not owner-managers) to increase the risk-taking incentive as a means of encouraging more managers to set up their own businesses (Pratt 1990). However, the Treasury is likely to be concerned about the possible abuses of such changes.

On the supply side, at least four solutions have been advocated. First, the BVCA, government ministers and even Prince Charles (BVCA, 1989) have each proposed that more venture capital organizations should establish funds specializing in seed, start-up, and early stage investments. The BVCA is actively encouraging the establishment of seed capital funds (Batchelor 1989a; Pratt 1990). However, Batchelor (1989h) suggests that is 'little chance of persuading established venture capital groups . . . to move way from more lucrative later stage deals'. The recent European Community (EC) initiative to provide financial support to enable the establishment of seed funds may provide some stimulus; however, as only three funds will be established in the United Kingdom under this initiative (twenty-four across the EC) any significant impact on the supply of seed capital will depend upon a large demonstration effect (Batchelor 1989h). The key constraint on the establishment of funds specializing in the provision of seed, start-up, and early stage capital is their high cost: the need to assess and monitor large numbers of small investments and to provide a high level of 'hands-on' investment requires a large input of professional time. Such funds cannot therefore be justified under conventional commercial criteria. Indeed, existing seed funds in the United Kingdom either rely on being subsidized by the parent organization's other activities (for example, consultancy) or have been established by noncommercial organizations such as local enterprise agencies (Batchelor 1989h). This suggests that without some kind of government support or public agency involvement (as occurs in the United States) venture capital funds specializing in seed, start-up, and early stage investments are unlikely to be established in sufficient numbers to increase the supply of such finance significantly.

Some observers advocate corporate venturing as another means of increasing the supply of seed, start-up, and early stage capital in the United Kingdom. Corporate venturing involves large companies making minority equity investments in small businesses. The investment process can take various forms, including via an independent venture capital fund to which the large company subscribes, via an internally managed venture capital fund, and direct investments in new businesses and in 'sponsored spin-offs'. The benefits of corporate venturing for the large firm include diversification, providing a window on new technology, commercialization of internally developed technology which for various reasons (for example, lack of specific expertise, insufficient market potential) it does not wish to exploit, and spreading the financial burden of R&D. Small firms gain access to the marketing expertise and distribution networks of the sponsoring company, production and R&D support, more sophisticated financial control and advice, and increased credibility with customers, suppliers, and financial institutions (Oakley 1987; Ormerod and Burns 19878). However, corporate venturing by large companies in the United Kingdom has been on a very limited scale compared with the United States and the rest of Europe. The National Economic Development Office (NEDC) has recently set up a Corporate Venturing Centre to provide advice and consultancy and established a corporate venturing register in an effort to promote corporate venturing in the United Kingdom (NEDC 1987), but it seems improbable that this will be sufficient to stimulate a large increase in the availability of such finance.

A third supply-side approach would be to revitalize the BES as a source of risk capital for trading companies. Since 1988, when the scheme was widened to include rented housing let under assured tenancies, it has become almost exclusively an instrument of housing policy. Admittedly, prior to this change the scheme had failed to meet the government's declared aims of increasing the flow of equity capital to small firms, particularly new firms and those engaged in high-risk activities, not least because it was increasingly used as a means of tax avoidance. Nevertheless, unlike the venture capital industry, it did channel investment predominantly into start-ups rather than established businesses and made a more substantial contribution, in relative terms, to reducing the equity gap at the lower end of the scale (Harrison and Mason 1989). Changes along the lines of those suggested by Mason *et al.* (1988), notably setting a maximum company funding limit of around £1 million, excluding heavily asset-backed businesses and allowing 'hands-on' investors to qualify for tax relief and capital gains tax exemption, would eliminate many of the distortions to the scheme which emerged prior to 1988 and so enhance its ability to close the equity gap.

A final supply-side solution – originally suggested by the Wilson Committee (HM Government 1979) and more recently advocated by the Confederation of British Industry (CBI 1983; Peters 1987) – is for the establishment of Local Investment Companies (LICs) (alternatively known as Small Firms Investment Companies). An LIC would pool monies raised from both individual and corporate investors who would qualify for tax relief up to a pre-set limit (in the way that currently operates under the BES for individuals) in order to take equity in, and make long-term loans to, a portfolio of new and established smaller companies. Investors would hold shares in the LIC – which could be quoted – rather than in the investee companies. LICs would be locally based and linked to existing sources of local and regional support for smaller firms, such as local enterprise agencies. This approach is claimed to have a number of advantages over alternative strategies such as corporate venturing and the BES (Peters 1987). In particular, LICs could provide 'packages' of loan and equity finance, can link the provision of finance to a comprehensive after-care service, reduce the administrative burdens for investee companies which need only deal with one shareholder (the LIC) rather than a number of individual shareholders (as under the BES), overcome the burden for larger companies in monitoring a number of small investments, and encourage both individuals and larger companies to invest in their local economies. A further advantage is that shares of an LIC will be more marketable than those of small unquoted companies; the LIC may even be listed. This will enable investors more easily to realize their holdings than is the case with the BES.

It is probably unrealistic either to expect that the UK venture capital industry will dramatically re-orient itself towards providing small amounts of capital, making seed, start-up, and early stage investments, and investing in technology related ventures or that a large number of seed capital funds will be established by new entrants to the venture capital industry. Even in the United States such investments account for a small proportion of venture capital activity, with such financing largely provided by informal investors (Walker 1989). As Freear and Wetzel (1988: 353) note: 'private individuals and venture capital funds appear to play complementary . . . roles in the financing of new technology-based firms. Private individuals are most prominent at the early stages of a firm's development, when relatively small amounts are involved, and in those later stage financings involving under $1 million.' Thus, a further strategy in the United Kingdom would be to promote informal risk capital investment. Until more is known about the characteristics and motivations of informal investors (Mason and Harrison 1990b) it is difficult to be precise on how this can be achieved, but enhancing the mechanisms whereby potential investors can be put in touch with businesses requiring venture capital would seem to be a logical starting point.

Strategies to increase the proportion of the venture capital pool that is invested in the Midlands and northern regions of the United Kingdom can also be considered in terms of demand-side and supply-side actions. To the extent that the lack of venture capital investments in the regions reflects their lower rate of new firm formation and lack of dynamism in their small business population, which can in turn be largely related to the spatial division of labor within the United Kingdom (Massey 1984), the scope for demand-side action is very limited. However, steps to 'educate' owner-managers of small and medium sized firms and professional intermediaries in the regions about the availability, advantages and sources of venture capital – which has been identified as a demand-side constraint – would be a positive step to overcoming deficiencies in the quality and quantity of investment proposals from firms in these regions. However, to the extent that this requires a change of culture rather than merely improved communications it must inevitably be regarded as a long-term task (Invest North West Working Party 1989).

The supply side is the key to achieving a more equitable geographical distribution of venture capital investments, particularly in the short to medium term. Indeed, should the venture capital industry radically re-orient itself towards funding start-ups and early stage investments this may further disadvantage regions outside the southeast because the need for a much greater hands-on role limits the geographical area over which such funds are likely to operate. It is largely accepted that the concentration of venture capital funds in

London is the major – although not exclusive – explanation for the lack of venture capital investment in the United Kingdom regions. It is therefore essential that the number of regionally based venture capital funds is increased.

To some extent the sources of supply in the regions is occurring 'naturally' as a result of increasing competition for good investments in the south of England. In turn, this has encouraged London- and southeast-based funds to look further afield for more attractively priced investment opportunities. Some London-based funds have either established regional funds or enhanced their regional operations through the establishment of branch offices (Hamilton Fazey 1988). In addition, some regional funds have been established. However, the presence of a branch office in a region does not necessarily result in all investment decisions being made locally: the London head office may still make the major investment decisions in the regions. There are some indications that this activity may have slightly reduced the southeast region's share of venture capital investments in 1988 compared with previous years. For example, as a result of the upgrading by County Nat West of its Midlands and northern offices, the proportion of total investment accounted for by its Birmingham, Manchester, and Leeds offices increased from 14 per cent in 1986 to 39 per cent in 1988 (Hamilton Fazey 1988).

However, from the evidence on the regional structure of the venture capital industry and the analysis of the public sector provision in this chapter, it is clear that much of the emerging regional venture capital industry is locally oriented and biased towards the provision of relatively small tranches of investment. This partly reflects the much smaller average size of these funds in terms of total funds under management or available for investment, and the corresponding need to avoid the concentration of the portfolio in one or two large investments. While this emphasis represents a major strength of the regional venture capital industry, it does raise the possibility, which will require further more detailed research, that there may be a 'reverse' regional equity gap in which companies outside the southeast of England seeking to raise relatively large sums find themselves compromised by the small scale of the regional venture capital industry on the one hand and by the spatially restricted decision-making and evaluation procedures of London-based venture capitalists on the other.

Nevertheless, it is unrealistic to expect that these 'natural' mechanisms can achieve a significant reduction in the geographical inequality of venture capital activity in the United Kingdom without specific complementary strategies. Although the establishment of seed capital funds and a commitment to the development of a network of LICs could have some impact on the regional venture capital gap, any significant reduction in the over-concentration of venture capital investments in southeast England is likely to depend largely on the willingness of private sector venture capitalists to establish regional funds and of public (for example, local authorities, public utilities, universities) and private sector organizations to review their pension funds policies to ensure that some employee savings are channeled into venture capital funds located in the regions in which their employees are based (Aysz 1986). However, with the exception of Edinburgh, United Kingdom provincial cities do not appear to have developed sufficiently as financial centres to be confident that such developments will occur on a sufficiently large scale to support a marked reduction in the geographical inequality in venture capital investment activity.

9 Asian venture capital: financing risk opportunities in the Pacific Rim

Thomas R. Leinbach

As is evident from the central theme of this volume, venture capital is no longer an American monopoly. Today the concept is truly a mechanism for the flow of capital and ideas on a global basis. As one might expect some of the fastest growth over the past 5 years has occurred in Europe where in 1987, according to the European Venture Capital Association, $5.1 billion was raised for venture capital. To mark the importance of that figure in the industry we need only to compare it with funds generated within the United States in the same year – $4.9 billion. This development is all the more striking given the lack of a recent tradition of entrepreneurial risk taking throughout Western Europe (Patricof 1989; Thompson 1989a).

Quite apart from the European developments, however, are those in Asia where the venture capital concept has taken hold and grown rapidly over the last several years (Table 9.1). This venture capital thrust, moreover, has been applied in several forms. For example, beginning in the mid-1980's a move toward cross-border partnerships between United States venture capitalists and other independent venture capital pools in Asia or overseas industrial companies or financial institutions with venture capital arms was begun. Termed 'strategic alliances' these link-ups have been aimed at raising money from pension funds, banks, insurance companies, corporations, and even wealthy individuals to create large pools of funds. The funds can then be invested in the United States or other regions where opportunities exist. An important advantage of such an arrangement is that along with the acquisition of funds comes an exchange of advice on new product development and cooperation in licensing, marketing, and sales. The technique of using a partner as an intermediary to reach investors and prospective companies is perhaps a 'next logical step' in the evolution of the venture capital

Table 9.1 Venture capital in Asia, 1989

	Firms	Funds
		(US$)
Japan	90	6 billion
Hong Kong	25	1 billion
Korea	33	900 million
Singapore	10	300 million
Taiwan	12	250 million
Thailand	5	50 million

Source: Burt (1989: 3)

concept. This trend has been encouraged by a number of political and economic changes in both Europe and Asia. First and foremost has been the deregulation of overseas capital markets which now encourage the inquiries of US-backed venture capital companies. In addition less confiscatory tax policies have also encouraged entrepreneurship (Goldenberg 1988).

The variety of partnerships comprising these strategic alliances is quite diverse. But within Asia the current view is that the Japanese are proving to be ideal partners. While the money, advanced technology, and the Asian market are all attractive reasons for engaging in a relationship with the Japanese, it is their willingness to take a long-term view of the investment proposition which is most satisfying. Above all every firm hopes that the expertise of managing partners from different geographical spheres will add a special synergy where a global information exchange mechanism has been established (Marton 1986: 157–8).

In addition, and closely related to these developments, is the US entrepreneurial search for Asian partners in an attempt to gain capital or new markets for infant technology start-ups. Corporate investors from Japan and the Asian Newly industrializing countries (NICs) have seized upon US technologies as a way to enter into a long-term strategy to diversify and survive. The partnerships take on various forms which extend from outright acquisition and simple licensing of a product or technology to agreements that link licensing, manufacturing, and distribution. There is some disagreement among entrepreneurs, however, on the benefits to be derived. The gains which include access to competitive markets, the opportunity to spread the costs, and risks of new product development, as well as the stream of licensing fees and royalties, may not outweigh the potential negative impact of sharing proprietary information. Yet in the last analysis many entrepreneurs must assume this risk for opportunities in the United States are much more limited (Juilland 1986).

In light of these rapid developments, this chapter has several limited yet important objectives. First an attempt is made to assess the economic and development environment of the east and southeast Asian countries in order to document conditions which have spawned the growth of venture capital, partnership–joint venture activities, and foreign investment. Second, the variation in venture capital activity across the region is examined and an explanation of the distribution and levels of activity is provided. Finally the real objectives and current obstacles to the development of venture capital in Asia are of some interest. These are assessed with some speculation on future prospects.

REGIONAL GROWTH AND THE DEVELOPMENT ENVIRONMENT

It is now all too obvious that Japan has staked out a role as a major economic power in the world and in so doing has amassed trade surpluses which have alarmed many of its trading partners. Japan's gross domestic product grew at an average of 10.5 per cent between 1950 and 1973 compared with a worldwide rate of 4.7 per cent over the same period. More recently protectionist tendencies in the West and a slowdown in Japan's own appetite for consumer goods have produced a more modest rate of growth – 3 per cent per year (Smith 1985).

The development of the Japanese economy through the early 1960s however, was brought about without intensive research. Since new technologies essentially were adopted from external sources, commercial and industrial risks were limited. In more recent years there has been a tendency towards innovation in place of replication. An adapted research policy gradually came about and this was fed by debt financing. In the boom environment of the early 1970s, a number of quasi-venture capital firms emerged and provided loans to small enterprises (SMEs). But these operations were only partly successful. However, in the early 1980s successful growth from SMEs again created a new interest in venture capital. This new vigor was in part stimulated by direct policies of the Nakasone government. Two elements stand out. One of these was the creation of a secondary market in November 1983: the Osaka

Stock Exchange. The second was the exemption of taxes on capital gains of individual investors (Ooghe *et al.* 1989: 41). While these policies have served to stimulate somewhat the growth of venture capital, a number of barriers continue to exist which have resulted in much lower than expected developments. These will be discussed at some length later in the chapter. Along with Japan, the four dragons of Asia – Taiwan, Singapore, Korea, and Hong Kong – have also enjoyed strong growth in gross national product (GNP) and trade surpluses in recent years. The result in essence has been the development of a supply of capital which is a critical ingredient for high-risk investment.

A similar comment on economic vitality may be extended to a number of the other Asian economies. This is especially true of the Association of Southeast Asian Nations (ASEAN) (Indonesia, Malaysia, Philippines, Thailand, Brunei, and Singapore). Despite some variation in the level and growth of economic development, for example between Singapore and Indonesia, overall the countries are relatively prosperous *vis à vis* other developing countries, especially those in Africa. While an international recession, a tin crisis, depressed oil prices, and economic mismanagement have in the recent past affected the countries to varying degrees, nowhere in the region is there reference to a 'lifeboat' thesis or futility in any effort to improve economic predicaments (Wong 1979). Although primary commodities have been major sources of growth in GNP since the mid-1970s, there has also been a gradual restructuring of economies away from agriculture. The shift toward industrialization is perhaps most dramatic in Indonesia where agriculture in 1965 accounted for nearly 60 per cent of GNP and now accounts for less than 25 per cent (Leinbach and Chia 1989).

In a number of the Asian countries, efforts have for sometime focused upon moving from a labor-intensive manufacturing environment to technology oriented value-added processes. Clearly governments have had to create a favorable infrastructure base in this transition and it is precisely such a development which is conducive to venture capital formation. The Taiwan government, for example, has established a favorable tax structure for venture capital investment and technology oriented firms. But, in addition, the establishment of a Science Park in Taipei provides not only a standard factory and on-site dormitories but research and development (R&D) assistance, including low cost loans, as a way of encouraging the growth of venture capital. Indeed in many Asian countries government funds have been allocated to venture activities in an effort to spur employment creation, market development, and the importation of technology (Hou 1988).

The dynamism currently exhibited in the Pacific Rim countries is a product of a variety of influences. But clearly one major factor is the recognition of the importance of human capital. While low cost, unskilled labor has attracted some investments, it is the traditional Asian appreciation of an emphasis on education which is of critical importance in the development of venture capital opportunities. The result of the expansion of both local education opportunities and the training of students abroad has meant that there has been an accumulation of talent available to step into new opportunities. The recent economic growth trend has certainly stimulated venture activities. This in turn will attract local talent which may otherwise have been drained abroad.

In the same social vein, however, there are impediments to the development of venture capital activities. A major influence is the traditional Asian reliance on relatives or trusted friends to manage investments. In borrowing 'local' too often, ideal management skills are not an accompaniment to the acquisition of funding for new investments. Mistrust of outsiders and reliance on family is not uncommon, particularly in smaller enterprises. Moreover often this 'closed' business mentality can hamper the growth of companies since any firm's size will be constrained by the lack of management resources – hence the preponderance of smaller enterprises rather than medium sized or large firms (Hou 1988).

The growth of venture activity is clearly not unrelated to the private foreign investment boom which has developed over the last few years. In 1986 and 1987 it is estimated that such investment in the more developed Pacific Basin economies grew 50 per cent. For the NICs, as well as the ASEAN economies, foreign investment growth was much higher. This growth is also remarkable for its new, multi-directional flow patterns. Basically East Asian and ASEAN economies are no longer simply the recipients of foreign funds but have engaged in foreign investment themselves. Moreover such investment is also much more diversified.

Foreign investment has been drawn to the Asian Rim countries because of the rich growth environment and accompanying opportunities. China, South Korea, Taiwan, and Hong Kong all reported near double digit expansion in the late 1980s. A second related reason for the investment has been the emergence of substantial trade balances among countries in the region. Very large surpluses in Japan and Taiwan, for example, generated foreign exchange reserves that were best recycled through investment in foreign assets.

It is important to recognize that the rapid growth in foreign investment may also be attributed to currency realignments such as the rise in value of the Japanese yen, the Taiwan NT dollar, and the Korean won. These changes have forced firms to establish production facilities in other countries as a way of remaining competitive internationally (Akrasanee 1988). The consumer electrronics boom in Malaysia has in fact been fueled in this manner. Here an undervalued ringgit, political stability, and a cheap labor force has drawn considerable investment from Japan in particular (Goldstein 1989). Finally new production technology and improvements in telecommunications and transport systems have also encouraged foreign investment. These advances essentially have allowed firms to assemble parts manufactured in many different countries and thus produce goods that are truly international in origin.

The impact of the surge of foreign investment is having significant impacts on the Asian economies so that economic and technological integration is occurring at an accelerated rate. Trade has increased among the various countries and consequently economies are much more open and influenced by international trade and finance. A profound effect also is seen in the development of securities markets and improved access to international capital markets. A host of other influences are noticeable. These include specialized stage production in certain industries, the faster diffusion of process and product technologies, and the intensified competition for local resources including labor which in turn has led to rising land prices and wages (Akrasanee 1988). With this backcloth of a rich and dynamic environment, we now turn attention to the emergence of venture capital efforts in various countries.

EAST ASIA

In 1982 total venture capital investment in Japan totaled only ¥17 billion. By late 1989 this amount had grown to over ¥860 billion. (US$6 billion) with ninety firms involved (Burt, 1989). While this growth was encouraging for the venture capital industry it also meant that there has frequently been an excess of funds in search of too few viable projects. The result in the mid-1980s was a series of spectacular bankruptcies. Hasty assessment of the opportunities and an adverse exchange rate produced these disappointing results. The failures have also resulted, however, from management problems and these stem from the fact that entrepreneurs have traditionally been absorbed by Japan's industrial giants. The rule has been that technicians with an innovative product normally seek funding from a large company in exchange for a fixed financial return. Too often venture managers have been individuals who have been left out of this traditional system (Sullivan 1987).

From the early 1970s until the late 1980s the number of firms grew from sixty to roughly ninety venture capital companies in Japan. Approximately half of these operated as specialized investment firms for banks and securities houses and thus could offer comprehensive services. In addition these firms enjoyed greater flexibility since venture capital is less rigorously controlled by government regulation, including financial, than is true with other companies.

The excessive liquidity in the domestic venture capital market however, has pushed firms to look at developing countries. In addition to setting up investment operations in these areas, the Japanese venture capital firms stress presence abroad as a way of identifying new trends in technology. Clearly this is most applicable to operations in the United States and Europe. One important trend, however, that has brought new growth in Japan has been a recent focus by venture capitalists on low-technology service businesses at home and high-technology operations overseas (*The Economist* 1988).

While clearly venture capitalism is thriving in Japan, several real obstacles remain. First there is a mentality that slows down individual initiative and does not lead young entrepreneurs to develop their own businesses (Ooghe *et al.* 1989). Innate conservatism and also the prestige of working for a large firm discourages entrepreneurship in Japan. When small firms do start up there is difficulty in luring competent managers and researchers away from large corporations. Moreover Japanese fund managers are quite conservative and thus are reluctant to back start-up ventures. Still the emphasis on service industries is encouraging local growth. In addition the profit expectations from long-term Japanese investors is considerably lower than those of their counterparts in the United States. While some high-technology ventures, such as bio-technology and health care firms, are being pursued in Japan, most Japanese venture capital moves abroad when it wishes to invest in high-technology concepts (*The Economist* 1988; Hayashi 1988).

The dynamism of venture capital activity is clearly illustrated by developments in Hong Kong. Within a space of 5 years, from 1984 to 1989, venture funding in the colony multiplied tenfold. It is estimated that a total of US$1 billion is now available through twenty-five management firms (Montagu Pollack 1988; *AVCJ* 1989d: 28). Most of the projects are low-technology and emphasize low risk and fast return. The reasons for this emphasis relate to several factors: an absence of government encouragement and control, the pending return to Chinese rule; and Hong Kong's role as a major financial center (*AVCJ* 1989d: 29). In the latter case Hong Kong is widely regarded as a good location for basing regional funds given its legal, tax, and communication structures. Funds are often set up to reflect the short-term interests of money managers in the region. These payback expectations rule out high-risk ventures. Finally the research concentrations which spawn these ideas and are needed for innovation do not exist. Consequently investment is in proven systems imported from elsewhere. High-risk ventures are also discouraged by the lack of an over-the-counter market. Hong Kong's stock market requires that firms show a profit for at least 3 years in order to be listed (Keating 1987). Thus the need to move up the technology frontier is not being met largely for these reasons. A final consideration here is that there has been some capital flight as a result of a perceived political risk associated with the reversion to Chinese rule in 1997 (WuDunn 1990).

The role of venture capital in China is much more difficult to assess. It appears, at the current time, that there is only one firm which could be termed a venture capital firm and this is the Beijing based China Venturetech. Along with this single firm, however, there have been some other activities which relate to venture capital. One of these is the development of a high-technology district in Beijing. The Zhongguancun area may be likened to Silicon Valley where science is being commercialized. Still another development surrounds the efforts to develop a Stock Exchange in Beijing. However, given the 1989 incidents in Beijing it is now likely that much of this activity has at least slowed and perhaps even ceased. While rumors suggest some activity associated with at least one Zhongguancun company, it is likely that with the decline from power of the advocates of change, venture capital activities in general will slow down dramatically. In part this hinges on the ability of firms to draw talent from major Beijing universities, especially Qinghua (*AVCJ* 1989b).

The events in China have clearly had an effect on venture capital developments in Hong Kong. Hong Kong companies have led the world investment in China especially in Guangdong and Fujian provinces. These projects have tended to be small, export oriented, and labor intensive. As a result of the military action in Beijing no Hong Kong company is expanding its investments in China although some production activities in the Pearl River Delta area are being maintained. As an alternative, opportunities are being explored in ASEAN states and especially Indonesia, Malaysia, and Thailand.

Venture capital operations in Taiwan began in 1984. As a result of a visit to the United States, the Taiwanese finance minister, Hsu Le Teh, began to promote venture capital activity as a means of spurring Taiwan's economic restructuring from traditional labor-intensive to high-technology industries (Shapiro 1987). There are now four firms offering venture capital and a new momentum has been set in place as a result of more favorable tax incentives as well as the liberalization of restrictions on investment. A major plus factor is the mature nature of the island's technological infrastructure. Despite this apparently favorable environment, venture financing is still seen as risky and less preferred compared with family financing.

Korea's venture capital industry is one of the most successful in Asia. The first fund was started up in 1974. The Korean venture capital community now has thirty-three venture firms and nineteen partnerships. With paid-in capital and borrowings totaling over 600 billion won (US$898 million), the industry is the second largest in Asia (behind Japan) and equivalent to that of Hong Kong and Australia. The growth has come about as a result of changes in legislation and also liberalization of the stock market. In May 1986 the small and medium sized Venture Business Creation Act gave increased financial incentives to fund development. This coupled with a Venture Capital Industry Law exempts firms from capital gains taxes, allows investment losses to be offset against taxes, permits venture firms to do leasing and factoring business (which is very attractive in Korea), and grants preferred treatment to dividends. The traditional pattern of Korean venture firms has been to focus on helping small companies adapt foreign technology rather than investing in riskier ventures. The Korea Development Investment Corporation is a major player in these efforts and is trying to serve as a broker in establishing joint manufacturing ventures between foreign and domestic firms (Clifford 1988; *AVCJ* 1989c).

Despite the size and rapid growth, Korean venture capital is now largely a domestic industry where government is highly visible. To date venture capital firms have been concerned with a close control

and nurturing of small businesses within South Korea. Howeve.,
recently the Korean venture capital community has developed an
international outlook. In part this has occurred because labor costs
have increased by 75 per cent in the last 3 years. As a consequence
plant relocation to nations with lower labor costs, in Southeast Asia
especially, has been necessary. Firms are now searching for overseas
projects with technology transfer potential. Although there remains
a government restriction which limits the extent of foreign
participation, many venture partnerships are looking for foreign
investors with the purpose of networking rather than the need for
funds. Yet it is clear as the government moves toward the opening
of capital markets in 1992, that foreign participation will increase
substantially (*AVCJ* 1989c: 15).

SOUTHEAST ASIA

A minor venture capital industry existed in Singapore in 1983. But
in 1986 the Economic Committee Report called for the establishment
of more funds to help develop indigenous entrepreneurship and
technological innovations. Subsequent to this recommendation the
government set up the Venture Capital Club and a S$100 million
(US$50 million) Venture Capital Fund as well as a tax incentive
scheme. The industry has expanded considerably since 1983 with
several more major funds and over thirty corporate venture
investors. About S$600 million (US$300 million) is available for
investment.

Basically venture capital is viewed as completely consistent with
the means of achieving the country's economic growth goals and a
key part of this is the globalizing of Singapore's businesses.
Generally the investments of the venture capital funds have been
aimed towards the development of small and medium sized
enterprises which account for 90 per cent of the total establishments
and 44 per cent of employment. The major thrust has clearly been
in biotechnology, computer hardware, robotics, microelectronics,
medical equipment and health care products. The SMEs have in the
past not performed well and the government wishes to develop them
into a strong supporting industry and service base for multi-national
corporations. In this regard the Economic Development Bank
(EDB) is helping venture capital firms to provide seed capital and
early stage financing for promising SMEs. Tax incentives and
'pioneer status' are offered as part of the EDB strategy.

Despite these rapid and positive developments, the industry still faces a number of constraints. Most important is the relative dearth of worthwhile opportunities in Singapore. This situation has resulted from a short supply of entrepreneurs who have a proper mix of risk attitude and technical–managerial competence. Because of this some funding has in fact been dedicated to Thailand. As entrepreneurs graduate from Singapore's educational institutions, deal-flow prospects may increase.

In response to this situation the government has adopted a variety of plans to upgrade the productivity and management of existing SMEs as well as to promote innovative and entrepreneurial start-ups. In this respect, along with the activities of the EDB, a multi-agency approach between the National Computer Board, National Productivity Board, and other statutory bodies has been effected. To encourage more R&D activities the government has granted an extended period of pioneer status for firms embarking on this development path as well as a generous investment allowance of up to 50 per cent to R&D equipment. The general belief is that the strong emphasis on technology and science and a superb infrastructure to support this effort will gradually boost the level of venture activities in Singapore (Development Bank of Singapore 1988; Hock 1988).

Within Thailand venture capital firms are appearing in response to a manufacturing investment boom. Both international and local institutions have assembled nearly US$40 million for Thai based entrepreneurs, primarily those involved in the electronics and agroindustry sectors. The Business Venture Promotion (BVP) was formed in 1987 by six Thai banks and the US Agency for International Development. Since then a Singapore based fund and three other funds have emerged on the scene. Projects financed by BVP include printed circuit boards, integrated circuit assembly, and two agricultural ventures (Sharp 1987; Handley 1988).

Although the dynamic economic environment has encouraged venture growth there are several constraints. One problem is the restricted number of exit points or ways to reorganize an operation or restructure its finances if a project should fail. In addition it is felt that an over-the-counter market must be created to make venture capital really succeed in Thailand.

In Malaysia too there is considerable potential for venture capital development since here also there is a strong investment surge especially in consumer electronics as a result of an undervalued currency, quality infrastructure, and a stable political environment with a cheap labor force (Goldstein 1989). There are currently three venture firms in Malaysia. Malaysian Ventures Management (MVM) was established in late 1984 and is the Malaysian arm of the Southeast Asian Venture Investment Program. Over 60 per cent of the supplied capital of US$6 million came from local investors while the remainder has come from the World Bank through the International Finance Corporation which supports private sector projects (Todd 1987: 45). Investments of MVM have been in technological aspects of palm oil refining, microcomputers, electrical transformers, and an engineering, concern. As in Singapore there is a dearth of innovative proposals with a high-technology emphasis and this may force investment in other fields. In addition Pica and the recently established Southern Bank Venture Capital Corporation are in operation. The measures taken by the government to encourage private investment will also be of benefit to venture capital practitioners. These measures include pioneer status incentives, reinvestment allowances, investment tax allowances, and double deduction for export promotion.

A number of barriers and disincentives have existed for some time in Indonesia to discourage venture capital activities. These include a small and inactive Stock Exchange, fear of loss of company control, high fixed returns from bonds and bank time deposits, and the lack of acceptable accounting standards. Coupled with this Indonesia has long been notorious for her onerous government regulations and a high withholding tax on remittances.

At the same time the government has recognized the need for new technology and an improvement in capital deficiency. Since 1986, there has been a gradual deregulation effort which is aimed at encouraging private sector growth and foreign investment. As part of this changing posture, the government established a venture capital company, Bahana. This firm uses equity and bridge financing as well as technical and management assistance to develop small and medium sized firms. Equity financing for these purposes is also provided by the Islamic Development Bank. The Asian Development Bank has provided technical and consulting services to Bahana to assist its activities. A positive note for future developments is that venture capital is felt to be the most appropriate form of financing for the Muslim business community for it embodies the principle of *musharakah* which is essentially joint venture profit sharing (*AVCJ* 1989a: 13).

PROBLEMS AND THE FUTURE

There appears to be a growing awareness that venture capital, while clearly not a panacea for industrial development, is an important tool in furthering three objectives of development. These are to transfer technology, to promote entrepreneurship and to broaden the industrial base. It is fair to say that there is considerable potential in many of Asia's developing countries for venture capital. Although high technology might be a target for investment, so too should be enterprises in agroindustry and the services sector.

Despite the potential, a number of impediments must be overcome before venture capital financing will take hold and truly flourish in Asia. Initially it is important to persuade the market that low technology and 'appropriate' technology areas, not just high-technology projects, are worthy of investment. Frequently venture capital activity is discouraged in Asia because business culture and practices are inward looking and conservative. Entrepreneurs may be reluctant to share management control and strategies with outsiders. In addition seed capital is often difficult to find and in another vein there is too much emphasis on fast paybacks.

The financial system operating in Asia also serves, to a certain extent, to deter venture capital activity. For example, local banking systems tend to concentrate only on collateral-based financing. Thus if an entrepreneur does not have collateral he often will not be able to secure financing. While government owned development institutions can be a source of funding they may not approve applications quickly. The final, and in some ways the most serious, obstacle, as has been mentioned previously, is the lack of a mechanism by which the venture capitalist can 'exit' from his investments. Too often securities markets in the Asian countries are immature and merchant banking is not particularly well developed. This combined with government restrictions on share placement and price offerings can produce serious handicaps (*Asian Finance* 1988).

There is little doubt that, with the exception of Japan, venture capital in Asia is still in an immature state. As we have noted in all of the countries surveyed, there is an abundance of capital, infrastructure, and in many cases qualified managers. As has been true in other situations there is here, however, an example where Asia should not necessarily follow the Western model. Within a development context, venture capital opportunities must do more than maximize profit gains (Hou 1988). The mechanism of venture capital can and should follow the individual national economic policy objectives. Used wisely venture capital can also be aimed at satisfying local needs on a priority basis rather than achieving breakthroughs which may be unsupported by the local market. Given the recent privatization efforts in the developing world, local entrepreneurship needs to be further stimulated. Venture capital may be a fine source of funds to assist new entrepreneurs once an encouraging economic environment for entrepreneurial developments has been established (Ibanez 1989).

References

Akrasanee, N. (1988) 'Foreign investment in the Pacific Basin', *Federal Reserve Bank of San Francisco Weekly Letter*, 1 July.

Allen, L. (1971) 'How an SBIC Supplies Venture Capital to small business concerns', *Business Lawyer*, 26: 727–34.

Allen, T., Hyman D., and Pinckney, D. (1983) 'Transfering technology to the small manufacturing firms: a study of technology transfer in three countries', *Research Policy*, 12: 199–211.

Ambler, M. and Kennett, S. (1985) *The Small Workshops Scheme: A Review of the Impact of the Scheme and an Assessment of the Current Market Position for Small Workshops*. London: HMSO.

Anderson, G. and McElveen, I. (1982) *Proceedings of the First Conference on Innovation, Enterprise and Venture Capital*, National Institute for Higher Education, Limerick, Ireland, 29–30 November.

Arbel, A., Arvell, C., and Postnieks, E. (1988) 'The smart crash of October 19th', *Harvard Business Review*, (May–June): 114–36.

Asian Finance (1988) 'Six problems that need to be overcome', 14 (5) (15 May): 56–63.

Associated Press (1988), 'High-tech companies, towns thrive on military funds', *Pittsburgh Press*, 27 June: B7.

AVCJ (Asian Venture Capital Journal) (1989a) 'Venture capital takes shape in Indonesia', 2: (4): 13.

——(1989b) 'Where is venture capital in China now?', 2 (4): 24–5.

——(1989c) 'Korea: a venture capital dragon in Asia', 2 (5): 15–21.

——(1989d) 'Growth despite uncertainty brings Hong Kong unique opportunities', 2 (6): 28–32.

Aydalot, P. and Keeble, D. (1988) *High Technology Industry and Innovative Environments: the European Experience*, London: Routledge.

Aysz, B. (1986) 'Venture capital' *Financial Times*, 26 June: 25.

Baird, R.G. (1988) 'The Charterhouse Group', *Royal Bank of Scotland Review*, (157): 51–4.

Bannock, G. (1981) *The Economics of Small Firms: Return From the Wilderness*, London: Basil Blackwell.

——(1987) *Britain in the 1980s: Enterprise Reborn?*, London: Investors in Industry.

Barff, R. (1987) 'Industrial clustering and the organization of production: a point pattern analysis of manufacturing in Cincinnati, Ohio', *Annals of the Association of American Geographers*, 77 (1): 89–103.

Batchelor, C. (1987) 'Corporate venturing: success rate proves patchy', *Financial Times*, Small Businesses Survey, 29 April: X.

——(1988a) 'Venture capital: diversions in the maze', *Financial Times*, Venture Capital Survey, 30 November: I.

——(1988b) 'Private financing: money and time to offer', *Financial Times*, 19 July: 9.

——(1989a) 'Venture capital: poised for a radical shift', *Financial Times*, Venture Capital Survey, 30 November: I.

——(1989b) 'Buy-ins: popular alternative to the buy-out', *Financial Times*, Management Buy-out Survey, 11 October: IV.

——(1989c) 'Management buy-outs: caution tempers the euphoria', *Financial Times*, Management Buy-out Survey, 11 October: I.

——(1989d) 'Management buy-outs: interest rate doubts', *Financial Times*, Venture Capital Survey, 30 November: VI.

——(1989e) 'Seed capital grows on support from EC', *Financial Times*, Venture Capital Survey, 30 November: II.

——(1989f) 'Private investors: not just a wing and a prayer', *Financial Times*, 24 January: 17.

——(1989g) 'Business angels: an investment of time and money', *Financial Times*, 21 November: 21.

——(1989h) 'Seed capital: EC to plug the gap for early stages', *Financial Times*, 5 December: 13.

Batler, E. (1973) 'The growth and development of venture capital', *Cost and Management* (January–February): 17–26.

Baumol, W. (1968) 'Entrepreneurship in economic theory', *American Economic Review* 58: 64–71.

Bean, A., Schiffel, D., and Mongee, M. (1975) 'The venture capital market and technological innovation', *Research Policy* 4: 380–408.

Binder Hamlyn (1986) *Going to the Market: A Survey of Businessmen's Experience of the USM*, London: Binder Hamlyn.

Bollard, A. and Buckle, B. (1987) *Economic Liberalization in New Zealand*, Wellington: Allen & Unwin.

Bollinger, L., Hope, K. and Utterback, J. (1983) 'A review of literature and hypothesis on new technology-based firms', *Research Policy* 12: 1–14.

British Business (1989) 'Vat registrations and deregistrations of UK businesses: 1980–88', 25 August: 10–12.

Britton, S. and Le Heron, R. (1987) 'Regions and restructuring in New Zealand: issues and questions in the 1980s', *New Zealand Geographer* 43: 129–39.

Brophy, D. (1981) 'Venture capital investment, 1981', in *Proceedings: Babson Research Conference*, Wellesley, MA: Center for Entrepreneurial Studies, Babson College, pp. 246–80.

——(1982) 'Venture capital research' in C. Kent, D. Sexton, and K. Vesper (eds) *Encyclopaedia of Entrepreneurship*, Englewood Cliffs, NJ: Prentice-Hall, pp. 165–92.

Browne, L. (1989) 'Shifting regional fortunes: the wheel turns', *New England Economic Review, Federal Reserve Bank of Boston* (May–June): 27–40.

Brunning, S. (1988) 'Venture capital and how to use it', *Accountant* (August): 6–9.

Buckland, R. and Davis, E.W. (1989) *The Unlisted Securities Market*, Oxford: Clarendon Press.

Burgan, J. (1985) 'Cyclical behavior of high tech industries', *BLS Monthly Labor Review* (May): 9–15.

Burns, P. (1987) *Financing the Growing Firm*, Proceedings of the 10th National Small Firms Policy and Research Conference, Cranfield School of Management, Cranfield Institute of Technology, Cranfield, Beds.

——and Dewhurst, J. (1986) 'Great Britain and Northern Ireland', in P. Burns and J. Dewhurst (eds) *Small Business in Europe*, Basingstoke, Hants: Macmillan, pp. 51–98.

Burt, L. (1989) 'Growth burgeons in Asia's venture capital communities', *Asian Venture Capital Journal* 2 (6): 3.

Buttle Wilson (1987) *Investment Yearbook 1987*, Auckland: Buttle Wilson.

Buxton, J. (1989) 'Scotland: buy-out mood positive', *Financial Times*, Management Buy-outs Survey, 11 October: XI.

BVCA (British Venture Capital Association) (1985) *Report on Investment Activity*, London: British Venture Capital Association.

——(1988) Report on Investment Activity, British Venture Capital Association, London.

——(1989) Speech given by HRH The Price of Wales at the BVCA Annual Dinner at the Plaisterers Hall on Wednesday, 14 June 1989. British Venture Capital Association, London.

Bygrave, W. (1987) 'Syndicated investments by venture capital firms: a networking perspective', *Journal of Business Venturing* 2: 139–54.

——(1988) 'The structure of the investment networks of venture capital firms', *Journal of Business Venturing* 3: 137–57.

——and Timmons, J. (1985) 'An empirical model for the flows of venture capital', in *Proceedings: Babson Research Conference*, Wellesley, MA: Center for Entrepreneurial Studies, Babson College, pp. 105–25.

——Timmons, J. and Fast, N. (1984) 'Seed and startup venture capital investing in technological companies', in *Frontiers of Entrepreneurship Research: Proceedings of the Entrepreneurship Research Conference*, Wellesley, MA: Center for Entrepreneurial Studies, Babson College, pp. 1–17.

Calvo, G. and Wellisz, S. (1980) 'Technology, entrepreneurs, and firm size', *Quarterly Journal of Economics* 4: 663–78.

Cary, L. (1989) *The Venture Capital Report Guide to Venture Capital in the UK*, London: Pitman, 4th edn.

Cave, S. (1989) 'Your bank: the loss lender' *Listener*, 22 April: 14-17.

Chambers, F. (1962) 'Small business investment companies', *Financial Analysts Journal* 18: 75-8.

Chapman, J. (1986) *Venture Capital in the UK and Its Impact on the Small Business Sector*, Staff Working Paper, National Economic Development Office.

Charles River Associates (1976) *An Analysis of Venture Capital Market Imperfections*, Cambridge, MA: Charles River Associates for the National Bureau of Standards, Experimental Technology Improvement Program.

Churchill, N. and Hornaday, J. (1987) 'Frontiers of entrepreneurship research: topical index 1981–1987', *Frontiers of Entrepreneurship Research*, Wellesley, MA: Center for Entrepreneurial Studies, Babson College.

Clark, R. (1987) *Venture Capital in Britain, America and Japan*, London: Croom Helm.

Clarke, M. (1967) 'Small business investment companies', *Mergers and Acquisitions* 2 (2): 81–95.

Clifford, M. (1988) 'Stake in the future: South Korea's venture capital firms blossom', *Far Eastern Economic Review* 139 (13): 52.

Coburn, C. and Patton, W. (1989) *State of Ohio Public Pension Funds: Investment in Venture Capital*, unpublished draft, Ohio's Thomas Edison Program, 77 South High Street, 26th Floor, Columbus, OH 43266–0330, February.

Cohen, D. (1979) *Small Business Capital Formation*, prepared for the Federal Reserve Study on Capital Formation, Washington, DC, July.

Cohen, R. (1989) 'Invitation to a careful dance', *Weekend Financial Times*, 18 March: IX.

Cohen, Y. and Berry, B. (1975) *Spatial Components of Manufacturing Activity*, New York: Wiley & Sons.

Colley, G. (1979) 'New Ontario incentive – SBDCs', *CAmagazine*, (December): 56–61.

Confederation of British Industry (1983) *Smaller Firms in the Economy*, London: CBI.

Conlin, E. (1989) 'Adventure capital', *INC Magazine* (September): 32–48.

Cook, N. R. 1985, 'Three-way analyses', in D. Haoglin, F. Mosteller and J. Tukey (eds) *Exploring Data Tables, Trends, and Shapes*, New York: Wiley, 125–88.

Cooper, A. (1985) 'The role of incubator organizations in the funding of growth oriented firms', *Journal of Business Venturing* 1 (1): 75–86.

Cooper, I. (1977) 'A model of venture capital investment', PhD dissertation, University of North Carolina.

Coopers and Lybrand/Drivers Jonas (1980) *Provision of Small Industrial Premises*, London: Department of Industry.

Corporate Technology Information Service Directory (1987)

Coutarelli, S. (1977) *Venture Capital in Europe*, New York: Praeger Special Studies in International Economics and Development.

Crane, P. (1972) *Venture Capital in Canada: A Profile*, Toronto: Faculty of Management Studies, University of Toronto.

Canadian Venture Capital (CVC) (1986) 'Venture Capital Industry Resources', vol. 1, no. 4, August, pp. 14-20.

Davis, B. (1986) 'Role of venture capital in the economic renaissance of an area' in R. Hisrich (ed) *Entrepreneurship, Intrapreneurship, and Venture Capital*, Lexington, MA: Lexington Books, pp. 107–118.

Deane, R. (1985) 'Reflections on the New Zealand financial sector', *Reserve Bank Bulletin*, 48 (8): 441–5.

De Geus, H. (1988), founder of Synopsis, a Silicon Valley company, April, personal interview.

DeHudy, T., Fast, N., and Pratt, S. (1981) *The Venture Capital Industry: Opportunities and Considerations for Investors*, Wellesley Hills, MA: Capital Publishing Corporation.

Department of Labour (1987) *Supplementary Tables to the Labour and Employment Gazette*, Wellington: Department of Labour.

Department of Trade and Industry (1988) 'The New Zealand venture capital market – a business perspective', Discussion Paper, DTI, Wellington.

Derven, R. (1987) 'What plan sponsors say about venture capital today', *Pension World* 23 (8) (August): 26–8.

Development Bank of Singapore (1988) 'Venture capital business in Singapore', *Economic Report No. 6*, Research Department.

DFC (Development Finance Corporation) (1985) *Annual Report*, Wellington: DFC.

——(1986) *Annual Report*, Wellington: DFC.

Dickson, T. (1984) 'Venture capital: lending that helping hand', *Financial Times*, Venture Capital Survey, 28 November: I–II

Dixon, R. (1985) 'In search of the silicon tundra', *Alaska Business Monthly* (November): 29.

——(1989) 'Venture capitalists and investment appraisal', *National Westminster Bank Quarterly Review* (November): 2–21.

DMS (1989) *Million Dollar Directory: America's Leading Public & Private Companies*, Series 1989, Parsippany, NJ: Dun's Marketing Services, Dun and Bradstreet Corporation.

Doerflinger, T. and Rivkin, J. (1987) *Risk and Reward: Venture Capital and the Making of America's Great Industries*, New York: Random House.

Dolan, C. (1983) 'Land of plenty: how high tech ideas often become reality in the Silicon Valley', *Wall Street Journal*, 2 August, 1: 16.

——(1974) *Venture Capital*, Lexington, MA: Lexington Books.

Dominguez, J. (1976) *Capital Flows in Minority Areas*, D.C. Heath.

Dow Jones and Irwin (1986, 1988) *Dow Jones – Irwin Business and Investment Almanac*, New York: Dow Jones.

Dun and Bradstreet Corporation (1988), *Business Starts Record, 1986/87*, Economic Analysis Department, Parsipanny, NJ: Dun and Bradstreet Corporation, p. 4.

Easton, B. (1988) 'Agriculture in New Zealand's economy', in L. Wallace and R. Lattimore (eds) 'Rural New Zealand – what next?', *Agribusiness and Economics Research Unit Discussion Paper 19*, Lincoln College, Canterbury.

The Economist (1988) 'Japanese venture capitalism: low minded', 13 August (7563): 68,70.

Economists Advisory Group (1971) *Problems of the Small Firm in Raising External Finance: The Results of a Sample Survey*, London: Committee of Inquiry on Small Firms, Research Report No 5, HMSO.

The Enterprise Corporation of Pittsburgh (1987) *A Survey of Venture Capital in Pittsburgh*, Pittsburgh, PA.

Ernst and Whinney (various years to 1986) *Unaudited Information regarding the Investment Activities of the Association Members*, studies conducted for the Association of Canadian Venture Capital Companies, Toronto.

——(1981) *Capital Formation Survey of Companies Financed by Canadian Sources*, study conducted for the Association of Canadian Venture Capital Companies, Toronto, April.

Farrell, K. (1985), 'The States enter the venture capital game', *New York Times*, 27 January: 12F.

Fast, N. (1982) 'Venture capital investment and technology development', in *Frontiers of Entrepreneurship Research: Proceedings of the Conference on Entrepreneurship at Babson College*, Wellesley, MA: Babson College, pp. 288–93.

Faucett, R. (1971) 'The management of venture capital investment companies', unpublished MSc Thesis, Sloan School of Management, MIT.

Fells, G. (1974) 'Venture capital and the small business', *Business Quarterly* 39: 21–31.

——(1975) 'Venture capital – can a Canadian entrepreneur find it here?', *Cost and Management* (January–February): 29–32.

——(1988) 'Venture capital in Canada – a ten year review', *Business Quarterly* 52 (4): 57–63.

——(1989) 'Venture capital and the new entrepreneurial society', *Business Quarterly* 53 (3): 22–7.

Financial Times (1985a) 'Minister attacks the city', 9 March: 1.

——(1985b) 'Venture capitalists invest £190m', 21 May: 7.

- — (1985c) 'International companies and finance; boost for South Korean venture capital industry', 11 November: 26.

Flanigan, J. (1988) 'Venture capital heads to Mexico', *Columbus Dispatch*, 7 February: H3, reprinted from the *Los Angeles Times*.

Florida, R. and Kenney, M. (1988a) 'Venture capital's geography: a comment on Leinbach and Amrhein', *Professional Geographer* 40 (2): 214-217.

——(1988b) 'Venture capital, high technology and regional development' *Regional Studies* 22 (1): 33-48.

——(1988c) 'Venture capital and high technology entrepreneurship', *Journal of Business Venturing*, 3: 301-19.

——(1988d) 'Venture capital-financed innovation and technological change in the U.S', *Research Policy* 17: 119-37.

Fortune (1987) 'Foreign affairs of a venture capitalist', 7 February.

Foss, D. C. (1985) 'Venture capital network: the first six months of an experiment', in J. Hornaday, E. Shils, J. Timmons, and K. H. Vesper (eds) *Frontiers of Entrepreneurship Research 1985*, Wellesley, MA: Babson College, pp. 314-24.

Frank, C. E. J., Miall, R. H. C. and Rees, R. D. (1984) 'Issues in small firms research of relevance to policy-making', *Regional Studies* 18: 257-66.

Franson, P. (1979) 'Silicon Valley: entrepreneurs' paradise', *Venture* 1: 39-46.

Freear, J. and Wetzel, W. (1988) 'Equity financing for new technology-based firms', in B.A. Kirchhoff, W.A. Long, W.E. McMullen, K.H. Vesper and W.E. Wetzel (eds) *Frontiers of Entrepreneurship Research 1988*, Wellesley, MA: Babson College, pp. 347-67.

Fried, V. and Hisrich. R. (1988) 'Venture capital research: past, present, and future', *Entrepreneurship, Theory and Practice* 13 (1) (Fall): 15-28.

Gadbois, A. and Knight, R. (1985) 'The 1980's – ascending years for venture capital', *Journal of Small Business – Canada* 1 (4): 21-5.

Gaston, R. J. (1989a) *Finding Private Venture Capital For Your Firm: A Complete Guide*, New York: Wiley.

——(1989b) 'The scale of informal capital markets', *Small Business Economics* 1: 223-30.

——and Bell, S. E. (1988) *The Informal Supply of Capital*, Oak Ridge, TN:

Applied Economics Group, or the US Small Business Administration under contract SBA–2024–AER–87.

Gilmour, J. (1974) 'External economies of scale, inter-industrial linkages, and decision-making', in F. Hamilton (ed.) *Spatial Perspectives on Industrial Organization and Decision-Making*, New York: Wiley, pp. 335–62.

Gittins, S. (1988) 'Venture capital is growing, but in "Safe Fields"', *Financial Post*, 21 July: 16-17.

Gladstone, D. (1983) *Venture Capital Handbook*, Reston, VA: Reston Publishing.

Glazer, S. (1987) 'Research parks plug into the electronics industry', *Electronic Business* 15: 100-101.

Goldenberg, S. (1988) *Hands Across the Ocean: Managing Joint Ventures With a Spotlight on China and Japan*, Cambridge, MA: Harvard University Press.

Goldstein, C. (1989) 'Chips of change: electronics transforms the face of Malaysia's industry', *Far Eastern Economic Review* 7 (September): 98-9.

Grant, W. (1982) *The Political Economy of Industrial Policy*, London: Butterworths.

Green, M. (1989) 'Patterns of preference for venture capital investment in the United States 1970–1985', *Environment and Planning C* 7: 205-22.

——and McNaughton, R. (1988) 'Interurban variation in venture capital investment characteristics', *Urban Studies*, 26: 199-213.

——McNaughton, R. and Venture Economics Canada (1988) *Economic Benefits of Venture Capital Investments in Canada*, Toronto: Association of Canadian Venture Capital Companies.

Grieve, A. (1972) 'Venture capital sources and the Canadian entrepreneur', *Business Quarterly*, 37 (1): 54-9.

Gupta, U. (1983) 'SBICs', *Venture*, 5: 66-8.

Hakim, C. (1989) 'New recruits to self-employment in the 1980s', *Employment Gazette* (June): 286-97.

Hall, G. and Hutchinson, P. J. (1988) 'Changes in the financial characteristics of newly quoted small firms 1970–73 and 1980–83', mimeo, Manchester Business School.

Hall, P., Breheny, M., McQuaid, R., and Hart, D. (1987) *Western Sunrise: The Genesis and Growth of Britain's Major High Tech Corridor*, Hemel Hempstead, Herts: Allen and Unwin.

Hambrecht, W. (1984) 'Venture capital and the growth of Silicon Valley', *California Management Review* 26 (2): 74-84.

Hamilton Fazey, I. (1986) 'The regions: pioneer funds may herald expansion', *Financial Times*, Venture Capital Survey, 8 December: IX.

——(1988) 'Local knowledge an asset for the North's players', *Financial Times*, Venture Capital Survey, 30 November: III.

——(1989a) 'Dispensers join the supplicants', *Weekend Financial Times*, 20 May: VI.

——(1989b) 'Market remains strong', *Financial Times*, Management Buy-out Survey, 11 October: XI.

Handley, P. (1988) 'Venturing into a boom', *Far Eastern Economic Review* 142 (45): 86.

Harper, D. (1986) 'The financial services industry: effects of regulatory reform', *New Zealand Institute of Economic Research: Research Paper 35*, Wellington.

——and Bollard, A. (1985) 'Employment dynamics project: the generation of jobs and businesses in New Zealand manufacturing 1980–84', *New Zealand Institute of Economic Research: Working Paper*, Wellington

Harrison, B. (1982) 'The tendency towards instability and inequality underlying the "revival" of New England', *Papers of the Regional Science Association* 50: 41-65.

Harrison, R.T. and Mason, C. M. (1986) 'The regional impact of the Loan Guarantee Scheme in the UK', *Regional Studies* 20: 535-50.

——(1988) 'Risk finance, the equity gap and new venture formation in the United Kingdom: the impact of the Business Expansion Scheme' in B.A. Kirchhoff, W.A. Long, W.E. McMullen, K.H. Vesper, and W.W.Wetzel (eds) *Frontiers of Entrepreneurship Research 1988*, Wellesley, MA: Babson College, pp. 595–609.

——(1989) 'The Role of the Business Expansion Scheme in the United Kingdom', *Omega* 17: 147–57.

Haslett, B. (1984) 'Venture capital and regional high technology development', in *Technology, Innovation, and Regional Economic Development*, Office of Technology Assessment Report OTA–STI–238, Washington, DC: US GPO, pp. 41–50.

Hatras, D. (1984) 'Silicon Valley: the story of an original', *High Tech Facilities*, (May): H12–H17.

Hayashi, A. M. (1988) 'Putting Japanese venture capital to work in America', *Electronic Business* 14 (9): 92–5.

Hebert, R. and Link, A. (1982) *The Entrepreneur*, New York: Praeger.

Henderson, Y. (1989a) 'The emergence of the venture capital industry', *New England Economic Review, Federal Reserve Bank of Boston* (July–August): 64–79.

——(1989b) 'Venture capital and economic development', paper to the New England Advisory Council, Federal Reserve Bank of Boston, MA, 11 July.

Hill, A. (1989) 'Teaming up with the experts', *Financial Times*, Venture Capital Survey, 30 November: IV.

Hisrich, R. (1986) *Entrepreneurship, Intrapreneurship, and Venture Capital*, Lexington, MA: Lexington Books.

Hitchens, D. N. W. M. and O'Farrell, P. N. (1987) 'Inter-regional comparisons of small firm performance: the case of Northern Ireland and South East England', *Regional Studies* 21: 543–55.

H.M. Government (1971) *Report of the Committee of Inquiry on Small Firms* (Bolton Report), London: HMSO, Cmnd 4811.

——(1979) *Interim Report on the Financing of Small Firms* (Wilson Report), London: HMSO, Cmnd 7503.

Hoban, J. (1976) 'Characteristics of venture capital investments', PhD Dissertation. School of Business Administration, University of Utah.

——(1981) 'Characteristics of venture capital investments', *American Journal of Small Business* 6 (2): 3–12.

Hock, T. L. (1988), 'Singapore: high tech vision turns industry wheels', *Asian Finance (Hong Kong)* 14 (9): 92-5.

Hogue, P. (1983) 'Trends affect the American workplace', *Community*

Economics (86), University of Wisconsin-Extension.

Holborn, P. R. M. and Edwards, E. C. N. (1971) 'Development of the UK venture capital market', *Banker* 121: 488-92.

Hood, N. and Young, S. (1983) *Multinational Investment Strategies in the British Isles: A Study of MNEs in the UK Assisted Areas and Republic of Ireland*, London: HMSO.

Hooper, D. and Walker, D. (1983), 'Innovative and cooperative entrepreneurship: towards a new thrust in industrial development policy', in F.E.I. Hamilton and G.J.R. Linge (eds) *Spatial Analysis, Industry and the Industrial Environment*, vol. 3, New York: Wiley, pp. 217–32.

Horvitz, P. and Pettit, R. (1984) *Small Business Finance: Sources of Financing for Small Business*, Greenwich, CT: JAI Press.

Hou, S. (1988) 'Venture capital opportunities in the Pacific Rim', *Review of Business* 10 (1): 16–18.

Howse, E. (1988) 'Investments of interest to venture capitalists', in J. Morris (ed.) *Pratt's Guide to Venture Capital Sources*, 12th edn, Wellesley Hills, MA: Venture Economics, pp. 38–40.

Huntsman, B. and Hoban, J. (1980) 'Investment in new enterprise: some empirical observations on risk, return, and market structure', *Financial Management* (Summer): 44–51.

Hussayni, H. (1959) 'Corporate profits and venture capital in the postwar period', PhD dissertation, University of Michigan, Ann Arbor, MI.

Hutt, R. and Thomas, B. (1985) 'Venture capital in Arizona', in *Proceedings: Babson Research Conference*, Wellesley, MA: Center for Entrepreneurial Studies, Babson College, pp. 155–69.

Ibanez, F. (1989) 'Venture capital and entrepreneurial development', *Working Papers*, WPS 53, World Bank, Washington, DC.

Invest North West Working Party (1989) Report, Regional Executive Director, National Westminster Bank, Liverpool.

ITT (1986) 'Downer for high tech', *In These Times*, 11 March.

Janeway, W. (1986) 'Doing capitalism: notes on the practice of venture capitalism', *Journal of Economic Issues* 20 (2): 431–41.

JEC (1982) *Role of the Venture Capital Industry in the American Economy*, Hearing, 97th Congress, 2d session, US GPO, 30 September, Washington, DC.

——(1984) *Venture Capital and Innovation, A Study Prepared for the Use of the Joint Economic Committee*, Congress of the US, 98th Congress, 2d Session, S. Prt 98–288, 28 December, US GPO, Washington, DC.

——(1986) *The Bi-Coastal Economy: Regional Patterns of Economic Growth During the Reagan Administration*, Staff Study by the Democratic Staff of the Joint Economic Committee, Congress of the United States, 14 July.

Jepsen, R. (1984) 'Letter of transmittal', in *Venture Capital and Innovation, A Study Prepared for the Use of the Joint Economic Committee*, Congress of the US, 98th Congress, 2d Session, S. Prt 98–288, 28 December, US GPO, Washington, DC.

Johnson, J. (1976) *Johnson's Directory of Risk Capital for Small Business*, Kalamazoo, MI: Business Research and Service Institute, College of Business, Western Michigan University.

Johnston, M. (1985) 'Venture capital: who's got it; how entrepreneurs can get it', *Phoenix Business Journal*, 1 July: 1.

Juilland, M. (1986) 'Asian money and more', *Venture*: 34–8.

Kaiser, M. (1986) 'The New Zealand software industry', *Department of Scientific and Industrial Research: Discussion Paper 11*, Wellington.

Kanbar, S. (1980) 'A note on risk-taking entrepreneurship and Schumpeter', *Historical Political Economy* 12: 489–98.

Karuna-Karan, A. and Smith, E., II (1972) 'A constructive look at MESBICs', *California Management Review* 14 (3) (Spring): 82–7.

Kasten, R. (1989) 'Capital gains tax cuts in past created more American jobs', *Capital Times*, 6 March: 11.

Keating, J. (1987). 'Venturing into profitable new fields', *Asian Business* 23 (5): 36–7.

Keeble, D.E. (1988) 'High technology industry and local environments in the United Kingdom', in P. Aydalot and D. Keeble (eds) *High Technology Industry and Innovative Environments: The European Experience*, London: Routledge, pp. 65–98.

——(1989) 'High-technology industry and regional development in Britain: the case of the Cambridge phenomenon', *Environment and Planning C Government and Policy* 7: 153–72.

——and Kelly, T. (1986) 'New firms and high technology industry in the United Kingdom: the case of computer electronics', in D. Keeble and E. Wever (eds) *New Firms and Regional Development in Europe*, Beckenham: Croom Helm, pp. 75–104.

Kenney, M. (1986) *Biotechnology: The University–Industrial Complex*, New Haven, CT: Yale University Press.

Kierulff, H. (1986) 'Additional directions for research in venture capital', in D. Sexton and R. Smilor (eds) *The Art and Science of Entrepreneurship*, Cambridge, MA: Ballinger Publishing, pp. 145–9.

Kieschnick, M. (1979) *Venture Capital and Urban Development*, Washington, DC: Council of State Planning Agencies.

——and Daniels, B. (1978) *Preliminary Research on Capital Markets and Economic Development*, Washington, DC: National Rural Centre and Opportunity Funding Corporation.

Kilby, P. (1971) *Entrepreneurship and Economic Development*, New York: Free Press.

King, P. (1988) 'Venture capital industry faces policy obstacles', *National Business Review*, 12 April: 5.

Knight, R. (1973) *A Study of Venture Capital Financing in Canada*, London, Ontario: School of Business Administration, The University of Western Ontario.

——(1985) 'An evaluation of venture capital rejections and their subsequent performance', *Journal of Small Business and Entrepreneurship* 3 (2): 18–34.

——(1986) 'Criteria used by venture capitalists', *Journal of Small Business and Entrepreneurship* 3 (4) 3–9.

——and Ferguson, W. (1984) 'The success of Ontario's SBDC program', *Journal of Small Business-Canada* 2 (1): 37–46.

Kotkin, J. (1984) 'Why smart companies are saying no to venture capital', *Inc.* (August): 65–75.

Kozmetsky, G., Gill, M. and Smilor, R. (1985) *Financing and Managing Fast-Growth Companies: The Venture Capital Process*, Lexington, MA: Lexington Books.

Krasner, O. and Tymes, E. (1983) 'Informal risk capital in California', in J. Hornaday, J. Timmons, and K. Vesker (eds) *Frontiers of Entre-*

preneurship Research, Wellesley, MA: Babson College.

Kryanowski, L. and Giraldeau, R. (1977), 'Venture capital management: a survey of attitudes toward selection criteria', *American Journal of Small Business* 2 (1): 29–37.

Kuhn, S. (1983) 'Evaluating high tech development', *Community Economics* (80): University of Wisconsin-Extension.

La Force, J. (1963) 'Royal joint stock companies in Spain 1700–1800', *Explorations in Entrepreneurial History* 1: 232–49.

Lampe, D. (1988) *The Massachusetts Miracle*, Cambridge, MA: MIT Press.

Lardner, J. (1986) 'Unlimited opportunities in the Rust Bowl', *Research Management* 29 (2): 20–22.

Lawless, P. (1988) 'Enterprise boards: evolution and evaluation', *Planning Outlook*, 31: 13–18.

Le Heron, R. (1979) 'R&D in New Zealand manufacturing firms and the goal of the efficient and flexible economy', *Pacific Viewpoint* 20: 149–71.

——(1988) 'State economy and crisis in New Zealand in the 1980s: implications for land based production of a new mode of regulation', *Applied Geography*: 273–90.

Leinbach, T. and Amrhein, C. (1987) 'A geography of the venture capital industry', *Professional Geographer* 39: 146-58.

——(1988) 'Response to Florida and Kenney's comment on "A geography of the venture capital industry in the U.S."', *Professional Geographer* 40 (2): 217-18.

——and Chia L. S. (1989) *Southeast Asian Transport Issues in Development*, Singapore: Oxford University Press.

Levine, J. (1983) '3000 Sand Hill Rd', *Venture* 5 (December): 74-8.

Libecap, G. (1986) 'Research bibliography on entrepreneurship, innovation and venture capital', in *Advances in The Study of Entrepreneurship, Innovation, and Economic Growth* vol. 1, Greenwich, CT.: JAI Press, pp. 191-213.

Liles, P. (1974), *New Business Ventures and the Entrepreneur*, Homewood, IL: Richard D. Irwin, pp. 461-94.

Lloyd, S. (1989) 'Still breaking records', *Banking World*, (January): 30-31.

Lorenz, E. (1988) 'Neither friends nor strangers: informal networks of subcontracting in French industry', in E. Gambretta (ed.) *Trust: The Making and Breaking of Cooperative Relations*, Oxford: Basil Blackwell.

Lovejoy, B. (1988) 'Management buy-outs and policy responses in the West Midlands', *Regional Studies* 22: 344-7.

Lueck, T. (1987) 'Venture capitalists shifting focus from high technology', *New York Times*, 6 February: 1, 31.

Luger, M. (1984) 'Does North Carolina's high-tech development program work?', *Journal of the American Planning Association* (Summer): 280-9.

Lungren, D. (1984) 'Foreword', *Venture Capital and Innovation, A Study Prepared for the Use of the Joint Economic Committee*, Congress of the US, 98th Congress, 2d Session, S. Prt 98-288, 28 December, US GPO, Washington, DC.

Macmillan, I., Zemann, L. and SubbaNarasimha, P. (1987) 'Criteria distinguishing successful from unsuccessful ventures in the venture screening process', *Journal of Business Venturing* 2: 122-37.

Maier, J.B. and Walker, D. A. (1987) 'The role of venture capital in financing small business', *Journal of Business Venturing* 2: 207-14.

Malecki, E. (1985), 'The geography of high technology', *Focus* 35 (4): 3.

——(1987a) 'Hope or hyperbole? High tech and economic development', *Technology Review* (October): 49.

Mao, J. (1974) *Venture Capital Financing for Technology-Oriented Firms*, Vancouver, BC: Department of Finance, The University of British Columbia (December).

Marshall, A. (1961) *Principles of Economics*, 9th edn. London: Macmillan.

Martin, R. (1989) 'The growth and geographical anatomy of venture capitalism in the United Kingdom', *Regional Studies* 23: 389-403.

Marton, A. (1986) 'Venture capital's new foreign accent', *Pension Management* (December): 157-8.

Mason, C.M. (1985) 'The geography of successful small firms in the United Kingdom', *Environment and Planning A* 17: 1499–513.

——(1987a) 'Job creation initiatives in the UK: the large company role', *Industrial Relations Journal* 18: 298–311.

——(1987b) 'Venture capital in the UK: a geographical perspective', *National Westminster Bank Review* (May): 47–59

——(1989) 'Where are the succesful small businesses? A geographical perspective', in P. Foley and H. Green (eds) *The Secrets of Small Business Success*, London: Paul Chapman Publishing, pp. 11–26.

——and Harrison, R. T. (1986) 'The regional impact of public policy towards small firms in the United Kingdom', in D. Keeble and E. Wever (eds) *New Firms and Regional Development in Europe*, Beckenham: Croom Helm, pp. 224–55.

——(1989) 'Small firms policy and the "North–South divide" in the United Kingdom: the case of the Business Expansion Scheme', *Transactions, Institute of British Geographers* 14: 37–58.

——(1990a) 'Small firms: a phoenix from the ashes?' in D.A. Pinder (ed.) *Challenge and Change in Western Europe*, London: Bellhaven Press, pp. 72–90.

——(1990b) 'Informal risk capital: a review of US and UK evidence', Venture Finance Research Working Paper 1, University of Southampton (Urban Policy Research Unit) and University of Ulster (Department of Applied Economics).

——Harrison, J. and Harrison, R. (1988) *Closing the Equity Gap? An Assessment of the Business Expansion Scheme*, London: Small Business Research Trust.

Massey, D. (1984) *Spatial Divisions of Labour: Social Structures and the Geography of Production*, London: Macmillan.

Mawson, J. and Miller, D. (1986) 'Interventionist approaches in local employment and economic development: the experience of Labour local authorities', in V.A. Hausner (ed.) *Critical Issues in Urban Economic Development*, vol. 1, Oxford: Clarendon Press, pp.145–99.

McArthur, A. (1988) 'Innovation, information and communication', in L. Wallace and R. Lattimore (eds) 'Rural New Zealand – What Next?' *Agribusiness and Economics Research Unit: Discussion Paper 19*, Lincoln College, Canterbury.

McKean, B. and Coulson, A. (1987) 'Enterprise boards and some issues raised by taking equity and loan stock in major companies', *Regional Studies* 21: 373–84.

McLean, I. (1978) *The Future for New Zealand Agriculture: Economic Strategies for the 1980s*, Wellington: New Zealand Planning Council.

McNaughton, R. (1989) 'Access to information and specialization in urban venture capital markets', *Economic Development Journal* (June): 9–17.

——(1990) 'The performance of venture-backed Canadian firms 1980–1987', *Regional Studies*, 24 (2): 105–21.

——and Green, M. (1989) 'Spatial patterns of Canadian venture capital investment', *Regional Studies* 23 (1): 9–18.

——(1987a), 'Partitioning U.S. venture capital flows: a weighted graphic theoretic blocking analysis', *East Lakes Geographer* 22: 21–32.

——(1987b) 'An exploratory examination of the spatial behavior of Canadian venture capital firms', *Operational Geographer* 14: 19–24.

Meade, N. (1977) 'The decline of venture capital', *Omega* 5: 663–72.

Menger, C. (1981) *Principles of economics*, New York: New York University Press.

Mises, L. (1966) *Human Action*, Chicago: Henry Regnery.

Moberg, D. (1988), 'Can Chicago be saved?', *Inc.* (March): 84–9.

Monck, C.P.S., Porter, R. B., Quintas, P. R., Storey, D. J. and Wynarczyk, P. (1988) *Science Parks and the Growth of High Technology Firms*, Beckenham: Croom Helm.

Montagu–Pollack, M. (1988) 'Venture capitalism: dangerous adventure?', *Asian Business* 24 (3): 53–7.

Morris, J. (1986, 1988) *Pratt's Guide to Venture Capital Sources*, 10th and 12th edns, Wellesey Hills, MA: Capital.

——and Isenstein. S. (1989) *Pratt's Guide to Venture Capital Sources*, 13th edn, Needham, MA: Venture Economics.

Morse, R. (1976) *The Role of New Technical Enterprises in the U.S. Economy*, Report of the Commerce Technical Advisory Board to the Secretary of Commerce, Washington, DC: US Government Printing Office.

NEDC (1986) *External Capital For Small Firms: A Review of Recent Developments*, London: National Economic Development Office.

——(1987) *Corporate Venturing: A Strategy for Innovation and Growth*, London: National Economic Development Office.

New York Times (1987) 'Prospects: venture capital', 27 March.

——(1989) 'Computer changes jolt Route 128', 11 August: 28.

New Zealand Reserve Bank Bulletin (1986), Wellington.

New Zealand Venture Capital Association (1987) Chairman's statement NZVCA AGM, NZVCA, June

Noone, C. (1968) 'The 1968 Model SBIC', *Business Lawyer* 23: 1214-20.

——and Rubel, S. (1970) *SBICs: Pioneers in Organized Venture Capital*, Chicago IL: Capital Publishing.

Oakey, R. (1984b) 'Innovation and regional growth in small high technology firms: evidence from Britain and the U.S.A.', *Regional Studies* 18 (3): 237-51.

Oakley, P.G. (1987) 'External corporate venturing: the experience to date', in R. Rothwell and J. Bessant (eds) *Innovation: Adaptation and Growth*, Amsterdam: Elsevier, pp. 287-96.

Obermayer, J. (1983) 'The capital crunch for small high technology companies', in A. Eskesen (ed.) *Conference Proceedings: Examining the Process of Innovation*, Waltham, MA: Bentley College Small Business

Resource Center, pp. 30–48.

O'Connor, M. (1988), 'Increase in high-tech locations influenced by university/corporate R&D link', *Site Selection Handbook* (June): 600.

OECD (1986) *Venture Capital: Context, Development, and Policies*, Paris: Organization for Economic Cooperation and Development.

O'Farrell, P. N. and Hitchens, D. M. W. N. (1989) 'The competitiveness and performance of small manufacturing firms: an analysis of matched pairs in Scotland and England', *Environment and Planning A* 21: 1241-63.

OMB (various years) *Standard Industrial Classification Manual*, Office of Management and Budget, 1972 Revision, 1977 Supplement, and 1987 Revision, Washington, DC: US GPO.

Ooghe, H., Bekaert, A. and Bossche, P. V. D. (1989) 'Venture capital in the U.S.A., Europe and Japan', *Management International Review* 29 (1): pp. 29-45.

Ormerod, J. and Burns, I. (1988) *Raising Venture Capital in the UK*, London: Butterworths.

Osborn, R. (1973) 'The supply of equity capital by the SBICs', *Quarterly Review of Economics and Business* 13: 69-86.

OTA (1984) *Technology, Innovation, and Regional Economic Development*, Washington, DC: US Congress Office of Technology Assessment.

Patricof, A. (1989) 'The internationalization of venture capital', *Journal of Business Venturing* 4 (4): 227-30.

Pence, C. (1982) *How Venture Capitalists Make Investment Decisions*, Ann Arbor, MI: UMI Research Press.

Perry, M. (1987) 'A regional analysis of local entrepreneurial activity in New Zealand 1980-1986', *New Zealand Journal of Business* 9: 37-42.

——(1988a) 'Venture capital in New Zealand', *New Zealand Geographer* 44 (1): 2–7.

——(1988b) 'The supply and demand of small business finance in a rural region', *Tijdschrift voor Economische en Sociale Geografie* 79 (3): 188-98.

——(1989) *The Demand and Supply of Business Services in the Auckland Region*, Occasional Paper 25, Department of Geography, University of Auckland.

Peters, I. (1987) *Finance for Smaller Firms – Local Investment Companies*, London: CBI.

Peterson, R. (1977) *Small Business Building and Balanced Economy*, Toronto: Porcepic Press.

Pettit, R. (1984) *Small Business Finance: Sources of Financing for Small Business*, Greenwich, CT: JAI Press.

Playfair, J. (1976) 'New solutions to the venture capital problem', *CAmagazine* (September): 26-31.

Poindexter, J. (1976) 'The efficiency of financial markets: the venture capital case', unpublished PhD Dissertation, Graduate School of Business Administration, New York University.

Poterba, J. (1988) 'Venture capital and capital gains taxation', Working Paper 508, Department of Economics, MIT, November.

Pratt, G. (1990) 'Venture capital in the United Kingdom', *Bank of England Quarterly Review* 30: 78-83.

Pratt, S. (1977, 1981, 1983) *Guide to Venture Capital*, 4th, 5th and 6th edns, Wellesley Hills, MA: Capital Publishing.

——(1988) 'Overview and introduction to the venture capital industry', in

J. Morris (ed.) *Pratt's Guide to Venture Capital Sources*, 12th edn, Wellesley Hills, MA: Venture Economics, pp. 7–10.

Pred, A. (1977) *City Systems in Advanced Economies*, New York: Halsted Press.

Pryde, J. (1988) 'Capital and agriculture', in L. Wallace and R. Lattimore (eds) 'Rural New Zealand – what Next?', *Agribusiness and Economics Research Unit Discussion Paper 19*, Lincoln College, Canterbury.

Pulver, G. and Hustedde, R. (1988) 'Regional variables that influence the allocation of venture capital: the role of banks', *Review of Regional Studies* 18 (2) (Spring): 1-9.

Rees, J. (1986) *Technology, Regions, and Policy*, Totowa, NJ: Rowman & Littlefield.

Riddell, P. (1989) *The Thatcher Decade*, Oxford: Basil Blackwell.

Rind, K. (1981) 'The role of venture capital in corporate development', *Strategic Management Journal* 2 (2): 168-79.

——and Delong, J. (1986) 'Venture investment market stabilizes after wild early years', *Pension World* 22 (9): 53-88.

Roberts, E. (1970) 'How to succeed in a new technology enterprise', *Technology Review* 73: 22–7.

——and Hauptman, O. (1985) 'The process of technology transfer to the new biomedical and pharmaceutical firm', Working Paper Series, MIT Sloan School of Management, Cambridge, MA.

Robinson, R. (1980) 'The financing of small business in the United States', in S. Bruchey (ed.) *Small Business in American Life*, New York: Columbia University Press, pp. 280–304.

Rock, A. (1987) 'Strategy versus tactics from a venture capitalist', *Harvard Business Review* (November–December): 63-7.

Ronen, J. (1983) 'Some insights into the entrepreneurial process', in J. Ronen (ed.) *Entrepreneurship*, Lexington, MA: Lexington Books, pp. 137–73.

Rosenbloom, R. and Shank, J. (1970) 'Let's write-off MESBICs', *Harvard Business Review* (September-October): 90-97.

Ross, A. (1975) *The Risk Takers*, Toronto: MacLean-Hunter.

Rothwell, R. (1985) 'Venture finance, small firms, and public policy in the UK', *Research Policy* 14: 253-66.

——and Zegveld, W. (1982) *Innovation in Small and Medium Sized Firms*, London: Frances Pinter.

Rubel, S. (1970a) 'The first decade of the SBIC industry', *California Business* 4 (12 October): 14.

——(1970b, 1972, 1974) *Guide to Venture Capital*, 1st, 2nd and 3rd edns, Wellesley Hills, MA: Capital Publishing.

——(1972) quoted in J. Timmons and W. Bygrave (1986), 'Venture capital's role in financing innovation for economic growth', *Journal of Business Venturing* 1: 161-76.

Rubel, S. M. and Company (1975) *Analysis of Venture Capital Industry Investing, 1968-1975*, Chicago, IL: Rubel and Company.

Rundle, R. (1989) 'Biovest disbanding shows venture capitalism's pitfalls: partners found themselves raising money instead of growing companies', *Wall Street Journal*, 27 September: b2, b3.

S&P (1989) *Standard & Poor's Corporation Records*, New York, March.

Sahlman, W. and Stevenson, H. (1985) 'Capital market myopia', *Journal of*

Business Venturing 1 (1): 2-30.

Savage, J. (1986) *Economic Liberalization and the Outlook for Manufacturing*, Wellington: New Zealand Institute of Economic Research.

Saxenian, A. (1985) 'Silicon Valley and Route 128: regional prototypes or historic exceptions?', in M. Castells (ed.) *High Technology, Space, and Society*, Beverly Hills, CA: Sage, pp. 81–105.

Schatz, W. (1987) 'Making a mark as a high-tech hub', *Datamation*, 1 January: 26, 27.

Schumpeter, J. (1934) *The Theory of Economic Development*, Cambridge, MA: Harvard University Press.

——(1939) *Business Cycles*, New York: McGraw-Hill.

——(1950) *Capitalism, Socialism and Democracy*, London: Allen and Unwin.

Scott, A. (1983) 'Industrial organisation and the logic of intrametropolitan location, 2: a case study of the printed circuits industry in the Greater Los Angeles region', *Economic Geography* 59: 343-67.

——(1984) 'Industrial organisation and the logic of intrametropolitan location, 3: a case study of the women's dress industry in the Greater Los Angeles region', *Economic Geography* 60: 3-27.

——(1988) *New Industrial Spaces: Flexible Production and Regional Development in North America and Western Europe*, Studies in Society and Space, London: Pion.

——(1989) 'The technopoles of southern California', UCLA Research Papers in Economic and Urban Geography No. 1, Department of Geography, University of California–Los Angeles.

Segal, Quince, and Wicksteed (1985), *The Cambridge Phenomenon: the Growth of High Technology Industry in a University Town*, Cambridge: Segal Quince.

Seymour, C., and Wetzel, W. (1981) *Informal Risk Capital in New England*, Durham, NH: University of New Hampshire.

Shapiro, D. (1987) 'Taiwan's hi-tech plans aided by venture capital' *Asian Business* 27 (3): 37-8.

Sharp, T. (1987), 'Observing the foreign risk takers', *Asian Business* 23 (5): 47.

Shilson, D. (1984) 'Venture capital in the United Kingdom', *Bank of England Quarterly Bulletin* 24: 207-211.

Silver, A. (1984) *Who's Who In Venture Capital*, New York: Wiley.

——(1985) *Venture Capital: The Complete Guide for Investors*, New York: Wiley.

Sinclair, L. (1971) *Venture Capital*, New York: Technimetrics.

Small Business Financing Review Team (1982) *An Overview of Small Business Financing*, The Small Business Financing Review, Ottawa: Department of Industry, Trade and Commerce, 18 May.

Smith, M. (1985) *'Japan'* in *Asia's New Industrial World*, London: Methuen, pp. 5-38.

Sommerfield, F. (1986) 'Few funds venture into New York companies', *Crain's New York Business* 24: 15.

Stevenson, H., Muzyka, D. and Timmons, D. (1987) 'Venture capital in transition: a Monte-Carlo simulation of changes in investment patterns', *Journal of Business Venturing* 2: 103-21.

Storey, D. (1980) *Job Generation and Small Firms Policy in Britain*,

London: Centre of Environmental Studies.

——(1983) 'Indigenising a regional economy: the importance of management buy-outs, *Regional Studies* 17: 471-75.

Stoy Hayward (1988) *Sources of Venture and Development Capital in the United Kingdom*, London: Stoy Hayward.

Sullivan, K. (1987) 'Watching out for bright stars', *Asian Business* 23 (5): 38-42.

Suran, L., Maidique, M. and Smith, P. (1986) 'The venture capital industry in Florida and the southeast: in search of the seeds', Working Paper 86–105, University of Miami.

Swales, J. (1979) 'Entrepreneurship and regional development: implications for regional policy', in D. MacLennan and J. Parr (eds), *Regional Policy: Past experience and New Directions*, Oxford: Martin Robertson, pp. 225-41.

Sylla, R. (1980), 'Small-business banking in the United States', in S. Bruckey (ed.) *Small Business in American Life*, New York: Columbia University Press, pp. 240–62.

Tait, N. (1989a) 'Economic climate freezes options', *Financial Times*, Venture Capital Survey, 30 November: II.

——(1989b) 'Trend beginning to ease off', *Financial Times*, Management Buy-out Survey, 11 October: III.

Tatsuno, S. (1986) *The Technopolis Strategy: Japan, High Technology and the Control of the 21st Century*, Englewood Cliffs, NJ: Prentice Hall.

Taylor, C. (1969) *Starting Up High Technology Industries in California*, San Francisco, CA: Wells Fargo Investment.

Taylor, M. (1977) 'Spatial dimensions of inventiveness in New Zealand: the role of individuals and institutions', *Tijdschrift voor Economische en Sociale Geografie* 68 (6): 330–40.

Thompson, C. (1987) 'Defining high technology industry: a consensus approach', *Prometheus* 5 (2) (December): 237–62.

——(1988a) *The Geography of High Technology Development in the USA*, Final Report for the US Department of Commerce, Economic Development Administration, Technical Assistance and Research Division, Washington, DC, Grant #RED–865–G–86–10.

——(1988b) 'High technology development & recession: the local experience in the United States, 1980–82', *Economic Development Quarterly* 2 (2): 153–67.

——(1989a) 'The geography of venture capital', *Progress in Human Geography* 13 (1): 62–98.

——(1989b) 'Federal expenditure to revenue ratios in the United States, 1971–85: an exploration of spatial equity under the "new federalism"', *Environment and Planning C*, 7: 445–70.

——and Bayer, K. (1989a) *Venture Capital Recipients and Economic Development*, First Progress Report, to the Prochnow Educational Foundation Inc. of the Graduate School of Banking Inc., Madison, WI, August, 50 pp.

——and——(1989b) *Venture Capital Recipients and Economic Development*, Second Progress Report, to the Prochnow Educational Foundation Inc. of the Graduate School of Banking Inc., Madison, WI, August, 50 pp.

——and——(1990) *Venture Capital Recipients and Economic Development*, Final Report, to the Prochnow Educational Foundation Inc. of the

Graduate School of Banking Inc., Madison, WI, forthcoming.

Thorne Ridell (1981) *Small Business Venture Capital Supply and Demand Analysis*, Small Business Financing Review, Ottawa: Department of Industry, Trade and Commerce, 1 May.

3i Group plc (1989) *Annual Review*, London: Investors in Industry.

Thwaites, A.T. (1982) 'Some evidence on regional variations in the introduction and diffusion of industrial products and processes within British manufacturing industry', *Regional Studies* 16: 371–81.

Time (1984) 'Sad tales of Silicon Valley', 3 September: 58–9.

Timmons, J. and Bygrave, W. (1986) 'Venture capital's role in financing innovation for economic growth', *Journal of Business Venturing* 1: 161–76.

——Fast, N. and Bygrave, W. (1983) 'The flow of venture capital to highly innovative technical ventures', pp. 316–34 in J. Hornaday, J. Timmons, and K. Vesper (eds) *Frontiers of Entrepreneurship Research*, Wellesley, MA: Center for Entrepreneurial Studies, Babson College.

——(1984) *Venture Capital Investment and the Development of High Technology Companies*, Washington, DC: National Science Foundation.

Todd, H. (1987) 'Seed money needs time to grow in Malaysia', *Asian Business* 23 (5): 45–6.

Tribus, M. (1970) 'Panel on government and new business proceedings', *Venture Capital and Management*, Management Seminar, Boston College, Boston, Ma, 28–29 May.

Tukey, J. (1977) *Exploratory Data Analysis*, Reading, MA: Addison-Wesley.

Tyebjee, T. and Bruno, A. (1981) 'Venture capital decisions making: preliminary results of three empirical studies', *Frontiers of Entrepreneurship Research*, Wellesley, MA: Centre for Entrepreneurial Studies, Babson College.

——and——(1984) 'A model of venture capitalist investment activity', *Management Science* 30 (9): 1051–66.

US DoC (1984 and subsequent years) *County Business Patterns, 1982: United States*, US Department of Commerce, Bureau of the Census, CBP–82–1, Washington, DC: US GPO.

——(1988) *County-City Databook, 1988*, Department of Commerce, Bureau of the Census, Washington, DC: US GPO.

US GAO (1982) *Government–Industry Cooperation Can Enhance the Venture Capital Process*, Washington, DC: US General Accounting Office, 12 August.

Venture, Venture's Guide to International Venture Capital (1985), New York: Simon & Schuster.

Venture Capital Journal (1983) 'SBICs after 25 Years' (October): 6.

Venture Economics (1983) *Regional Patterns of Venture Capital Investment*, Report to the Office of the Chief Counsel for Advocacy, US Small Business Administration, 1441 L Street, NW, Washington DC 20416, 27pp.

——(1985) *The Venture Capital Industry: Opportunities and Considerations for Investors*, Wellesley Hills, MA: Venture Economics.

——(1989a) 'The capital gains war – still being waged', *Venture Capital Journal* (January): 3.

——(1989b) 'A kinder, gentler capital gains proposal', *Venture Capital*

Journal (February): 3.

——(1989c) '1988 venture industry growth brings capital pool to $31 billion', *Venture Capital Journal* (March): 9.

——(1989d) 'Capital gains bills inundate congress', *Venture Capital Journal* (June): 4-6.

Venture Economics Canada (1986) *Exiting from Venture Investments: The Canadian Experience*, study prepared for the Association of Canadian Venture Capital Companies, Toronto, November.

Waldmann, D. and Cohn, R. (1980) *Business investment in the United States*, Washington, DC: Bureau of National Affairs.

Walker, D.A. (1989) 'Financing the small firm', *Small Business Economics* 1: 285–96.

Watts, D. (1987) *Industrial Geography*, New York: Longman Scientific & Technical.

Wells, W. (1974) 'Venture capital decision making', unpublished PhD Dissertation. Carnegie Institute of Technology, Carnegie–Mellon University.

West Midlands Enterprise Board (Consultancy Services) (1988) *The Nature, Implications and Mitigation of the 'Equity Gap' in Leicestershire*, Birmingham: West Midlands Enterprise Board.

Wetzel, W. (1983) 'Angels and informal risk capital', *Sloan Management Review* 24: 23–34.

——(1984) 'Venture Capital Network Inc.: an experiment in capital formation', in J.A. Hornaday, F. Tarpley, J.A. Timmons, and K.H. Vesper (eds) *Frontiers of Entrepreneurship Research 1984*, Wellesley, MA: Babson College, pp. 111–125.

——(1986a) 'Entrepreneurs, angels and economic renaissance', in R.D. Hisrich (ed.) *Entrepreneurship, Intrapreneurship and Venture Capital*, Lexington, MA: Lexington Books, pp. 119–39.

——(1986) 'Informal risk capital: knowns and unknowns', in D. Sexton and R. Smilor (eds) *The Art and Science of Entrepreneurship*, Cambridge, MA: Ballinger Publishing.

——and Seymour, C. (1981) *Informal Risk Capital in New England*, Durham, NH: University of New Hampshire Whittlemore School of Business and Economics.

Wheeler, B. and Nash, M. (1989) *An Examination of the Sharemarket Crash and its Aftermath in New Zealand*, Wellington: Economic Development Commission.

Wilson, L. (1985) *The New Venturers*, Reading, MA: Addison–Wesley.

Wisconsin State Journal (1989a) 'Some no longer love LA; more people are leaving', article by Paul Nussbaum, Knight–Ridder Newspapers, 13 August: 2.

——(1989b) 'Surf's up, but we're moving to Wisconsin: LA's exodus isn't letting up', article by Paul Nussbaum, Knight–Ridder Newspapers, 13 August: 1.

Wong, J. (1979) *ASEAN Economics in Perspective*, London: Macmillan.

Wright, M. (1989) 'Not so many little piggies are coming to market', *Daily Telegraph*, Management Buy-out Survey, 30 October: V.

Wright, M. and Coyne, J. (1985) *Management Buyouts*, Beckenham: Croom Helm.

——and Lockley, H. (1984) 'Regional aspects of management buy-outs: some evidence', *Regional Studies* 18: 428–31.

WuDunn, C. (1990) 'Hong Kong extending its reach', *New York Times*, 15 January: 34.

Yardeni, E. (1989) 'Bi-coastal recession?', *Strategy Weekly*, Prudential–Bache Securities, 10 May: 6.

Zagor, K. (1989) 'Lower returns ends quick-buck party', *Financial Times*, Venture Capital Survey, 30 November: V.

Zock, R. (1984) 'Small business access to capital markets through pension funds', in P. Horvitz and R. Pettit (eds) *In Small Business Finance: Sources of Financing for Small Business*, Greenwich, CT: JAI Press: pp. 137–52.

Zschau, E. (1978) 'Capital formation taskforce of the American Electronics Association', Statement before the Senate Select Committee on Small Business, Washington, DC, 8 February.

Index